✿✿✿✿✿✿✿✿✿✿✿✿✿✿✿✿✿✿✿✿✿✿✿

On Man
in His
Environment

Social Scientific
Foundations for
Research and Policy

samuel z. klausner

✿✿✿✿✿✿✿✿✿✿✿✿✿✿✿✿✿✿✿✿✿✿✿✿

on man
in his
environment

Jossey-Bass Inc., Publishers
615 Montgomery Street · San Francisco · 1971

ON MAN IN HIS ENVIRONMENT
Social Scientific Foundations for Research and Policy
Samuel Z. Klausner

Jossey-Bass, Inc., Publishers
615 Montgomery Street
San Francisco, California 94111

Library of Congress Catalog Card Number 77-146736

International Standard Book Number ISBN 0-87589-086-5

Manufactured in the United States of America
  Composed and printed by York Composition Company, Inc.
  Bound by Chas. H. Bohn & Co., Inc.
  Jacket design by Susan Drucker

A publication of the program of
research on society and its physical
environment of the Center for Research
on the Acts of Man, University of Pennsylvania.

FIRST EDITION

Code 7101

✡✡✡✡✡✡✡✡✡✡✡✡✡✡✡✡✡✡✡✡✡

THE JOSSEY-BASS BEHAVIORAL SCIENCE SERIES

General Editors

WILLIAM E. HENRY, *University of Chicago*

NEVITT SANFORD, *Wright Institute, Berkeley*

☆☆☆☆☆☆☆☆☆☆☆☆☆☆☆☆☆☆☆☆☆☆

Preface

Man coaxes support from the natural environment, impedes damage from its ravages, and aggressively shapes it with the instruments of engineering. Recently economists have begun to compute costs attached to various engineering options. These economists have been social science frontiersmen in the study of the natural environment. Wrestling to solve such cost problems has led some economists to examine the noneconomic aspects of social life. The sociologists' questions dovetail with those of the economist. The economist asks how the free use of the atmosphere as a dump for automobile exhaust can be balanced against the costs of respiratory ailments and cleaning bills. The sociologist wonders whether the sense of power and privacy enjoyed in the private automobile erases sensitivity to atmospheric stench, ambiguous illness, and soiled clothes.

Whether cloud seeding will moisten farmers' fields while reducing snowfall on a ski slope is a technical question asked prior to an economic analysis. The policy oriented sociologist might ask whether the community of skiing recreationists could be or become as powerful an interest group as the farmers who encourage cloud seeding.

How much increase in the cost of water purification is incurred by a downstream community when its upstream neighbors use the river as a sewer? The sociologist might wonder whether the socioethnic and economic interests of the elites of the upstream and downstream communities can be meshed in the development of a regional water plan. How can the costs of a tsunami warning system be weighed against the number of potential victims who might be saved? Would an environmental warning system operated by local government, the police, the fire department, and the mayor's office enjoy greater public legitimation and attention—and thus have greater effectiveness—than one developed around a specialized federally monitored civil defense function?

This book discusses the relation of man and nature—the theme underlying the above questions—and could begin, with equal legitimacy, with the study of either of the two partners to that relation. The approach is that of the discipline of sociology rather than of physical environmental analysis. Rather than beginning with the characteristics of the physical environment—with the concentrations of particulate matter or sulfur dioxide in the air or the rates of thermal change in certain lakes—I begin with the characteristics of human society, taking a sociological look at the environment instead of an environmentalist look at sociology. This perspective enhances the probability of contributing to sociological theory itself and thereby to the attraction of a body of serious sociologists to the field.

Chapter One explains the current neglect of man-environment studies. Chapter Two weighs the advantages of theoretical models implicit in current man-environment research of demographers, human ecologists, and location theorists. Chapters Three and Four present a voluntaristic model for thinking social scientifically about human action oriented to the physical environment. Chapter Five uses this frame of reference to analyze social influences on the systematically developed concepts of the environment in the natural sciences and technology. The final two chapters illustrate reconceptualizations useful for research in three areas publicly defined as posing environmental problems: air pollution, noise pollution, and outdoor recreation. The Epilogue shifts abruptly from theory and research to some comments on policy for environmental research, education, and management.

The sociologist is asked to contribute to the solution of problems of water pollution, of weather hazard, or of the provision of recreational facilities. As stated, these are social rather than sociological problems. Further, water, weather, and camp stoves are common-sense physical concepts, not sociological concepts. The major contributions to understanding, and ultimately control, of the natural environment are likely to come from sociologists who reformulate environmental problems in theoretical terms. The principal thrust of this book is toward such a theoretical reformulation.

Action, however, need not wait for new theoretical formulations. The sociologist can make immediate contributions to the resolution of some program and planning problems—even while those problems are conceptualized in common-sense or physical terms. The questions posed in the opening paragraphs are of this character. Applications of well known sociological knowledge may go far toward answering such questions. Studies of communication of natural hazard warning or sociographic descriptions of participation in various types of recreation would in their raw state be useful to planners. Studies of consumer tastes and preferences, using traditional attitude and value scaling procedures, would help economists interpret the slopes and positions of demand curves. Such studies of communication, buying behavior, or attitudes are appropriate sociological service functions. Service functions are both socially and sociologically useful. The theoretical development and application of knowledge proceed hand in hand. If a sense of social crisis presses us toward premature application of knowledge, some of us must hold this sense of emergency at bay to explore alternative ways of looking at the problem of man and nature. Empirical research, engendered and interpreted by theoretical formulations, can produce new sociological knowledge and guide planners in improving the habitability of the earth.

I was encouraged to think sociologically about the natural environment during four enjoyable spring and summer months as a sociological-psychological consultant to Resources for the Future, Inc. (RFF). Initially, I examined some social and psychological dimensions of the demand for outdoor recreation. A more general consideration of the natural environment developed when my economist colleagues began asking for a sociologist's thoughts on

Preface

urban and marine environments and on the quality of our air and water.

The men who are RFF personally and professionally absorbed me as if I were a regular member of the staff. Blair Bower, Michael Brewer, Robert Davis, Charles Howe, and Allen Kneese will recognize the influence of their comments in the following pages. Continuous help with economic problems by my monitor, John Krutilla, kept the discussion on the intersect of economics and sociology from being more crude than it is. Neither he nor RFF should be called to account for what I have elected to say here. My good assistants, Sandra Bouxsein and Christine Rupard, helped me review work of earlier scholars in the field. My amanuenses, Vera Ullrich at RFF and Candace P. Cole, Gail W. Donner, and Judith Thomas at the Center for Research on the Acts of Man at the University of Pennsylvania labored over the manuscript.

Several of my colleagues have taken time from busy schedules to comment on an earlier draft of this report. Charles Y. Glock of the University of California, Berkeley, and William Burch of Yale University pointed to some weaknesses in my discussion of recreation. Lincoln Day of Yale noted some of the more serious defects in the chapter on demography and ecology. William E. Henry of the University of Chicago and Renée C. Fox and William L. Kissick of the University of Pennsylvania were perceptive critics of my policy statement. My deepest gratitude is due Albert Gollin of the Bureau of Social Science Research who reviewed the entire manuscript as a conscientious professor would that of a fumbling graduate student.

The editing by Carol Talpers of Jossey-Bass Publishers made many of my awkward sentences articulate. My wife, Madeleine, brought that measure of order into my life and work without which no manuscript could have emerged.

I dedicate the book to Madeleine Zipporah, a fortress for the earth transcended in the sky.

Philadelphia
November 1970

Samuel Z. Klausner

Contents

Contents

✿✿✿✿✿✿✿✿✿✿✿✿✿✿✿✿✿✿✿✿✿✿✿✿✿

On Man in His Environment

Social Scientific
Foundations for
Research and Policy

How desolate is the populous city!
Lamentations 1:1

The abundance of the sea shall
be turned to you,
The wealth of the nations shall
come to you.
Isaiah 60:5

✢✢✢✢✢✢✢✢✢✢✢✢✢✢✢✢✢✢✢✢✢

Chapter I

Retreat from Man-
Environment Studies

The sociological field of man-environment relations, cultivated with some élan for nearly a century, today lies fallow. Now and then an anthropologist or a human ecologist who is committed to holism surveys the territory. An earlier environmentalism encourages some psychologists to experiment with the stimulus value and symbolic meaning of light, sound, space, or temperature. For the decade or so after Hiroshima, a small eddy of disaster research projects took the truculence of nature as a proxy for the ferocity of man. Encouraged by the Committee on Disaster Studies of the National Academy of Sciences–National

Research Council and the Federal Civil Defense Administration, sociologists studied individual and communal responses to tornadoes, floods, and earthquakes (Klausner and Kincaid, 1956; Baker and Chapman, 1962).

Two wide-angle surveys of sociology attest to the limited interest in the relations of man and nature. One of these is a collection of thematic papers from the 1957 meeting of the American Sociological Association (Merton, Broom, and Cottrell, 1959) and the other a similar collection from the 1962 meeting of that association (Larzarsfeld, Sewell, and Wilensky, 1967). Neither collection demonstrates any significant interest in transposing physical environmental variables onto sociological coordinates. No references are found under such traditional index classifications as natural environment or natural resources. A single paragraph on man-land relations appears in the latter volume in the chapter on rural sociology, a branch of the field with older roots than most.

Lack of academic interest does not mean a lack of concern with palpable ties between human society and its nonhuman environment. No sociologist questions the fact that societies, as concrete organizations, shape and are shaped by their natural environment. All agree that technology transforms the environment and induces changes in social organization. All agree that each form of social organization imposes its own demands upon the environment. Most sociologists—especially since the Great Depression—have ignored the physical environment, not as unimportant in human action but as irrelevant to a sociological analysis of action. These sociologists have chosen to ignore physical objects because they feel they are not relevant to the abstractions needed to understand society. Our best contemporary student of sociological theorizing (Parsons, 1949, p. 47) states this case:

> Certainly the situation of action includes parts of what is called in common-sense terms the physical environment and the biological organism—to mention only two points. With equal certainty these elements of the situation of action are capable of analysis in terms of the physical and biological sciences. . . . But for purposes of the theory of action it is not necessary or

2

desirable to carry such analyses as far as science in general is capable of doing. A limit is set by the frame of reference with which the student of action is working. That is, he is interested in phenomena with an aspect not reducible to action terms only insofar as they impinge on the schema of action in a relevant way—in the role of conditions or means. So long as their properties, which are important in this context, can be accurately determined, these may be taken as data without further analysis.

Contemporary sociological analysis gives little attention to the physical world either as "conditions or means" or "as data without further analysis." Often physical conditions have been dissolved in a residual category under the pseudonyms of *ceteris paribus* and community.

Paradoxically, academic sociological interest in the environment has declined at a time of growing popular interest. Environmental management programs are instituted without the benefit of sociological counsel; and despite the failure of some programs to articulate with the needs of the communities they are designed to serve, they continue without sociological counsel. A disparity between sociological and popular social interest is not inconsistent with a philosophy of scientific purism. Nevertheless, this disparity is unusual in the history of sociology. Theoretical developments in sociology have tended to follow public definitions of social problems. For example, the theory of social stratification developed when an economic depression strained relations among the classes and at a time when sociological practitioners were socially mobile. Concern with the sociology of deviance and theories of social control has accompanied public concern about crime and revolutionary change.

Why, in this case, has interest waned while the problem waxed? The seeming exception of the man-environment field may be traced, in part, to nineteenth-century disciplinary fallacies and, in part, to changing social characteristics of sociologists. To explain what has diverted sociologists from an interest in the environment and to explore ways of renewing that interest, some past thinking—both sociological and presociological—on man-environment relations is reviewed.

The history of theories of the relation of man and nature

3

may be traced from index entries under *environment* in the *Encyclopedia of the Social Sciences* (Seligman and Johnson, 1934). The new *International Encyclopedia of the Social Sciences* (Sills, 1968) with its column and a half of index entries under *environment* and *environmentalism* and additional entries under *natural resources* points to more recent developments. Pursuit of the references cited in both of those encyclopedias leads more often to economics and anthropology than to sociology—but field boundaries have not been that clear.

Two perspectives on man and nature have persisted in social thought. From one perspective the relation appears deterministic. Natural events determine or cause human behavioral events. Individual and social behavior are traced directly to physical characteristics of the environment—to its chemical composition, temperature, or the spatial relation between people. From a second perspective human behavior is traced to a negotiation between man and environment. The physical environment constrains behavior but is not its cause. The human actor defines and shapes the environment and is defined and shaped in the encounter. The former perspective dominated social thought in this field until fairly recently. Its history, largely a record of theories that failed, is documented here. Theories of man as a negotiator with nature are precursive to a new environmental sociology. This second line of development is traced in Chapter Three.

The deterministic image of the relation of man and nature has been bound to physicalist conceptions of the wellsprings of human behavior. The ancient Greeks set the paradigm. Four primordial elements—earth, air, fire, and water—constitute the physical world. Man's health depends on the ratios in which these elements combine in his body. Blood, phlegm, black bile, and yellow bile—the humors of temperament—are produced by particular proportions of fire and water, of moistness and dryness, or of heat and cold. The joint action of these elements supports life. Their separation means death. From this physically based psychology, it was only a small step to the belief that man could control his personality. Greek theoreticians argued that man could control the

4

balance among his humors by inserting himself into an environment containing the appropriate proportions of heat and moisture or other primordial elements. Man's ability to control his behavior is circumscribed only by his freedom to choose his environment.

St. Thomas Aquinas (1938, Book II, Ch. 1, pp. 110f) elaborated this thinking into a theory of social character. His advice to a ruler on selecting a site for a city tells how climate shapes character:

> A temperate climate is most conducive to fitness for war by which human society is kept in security. For as Begetius tells us, all people that live near the sun and are dried up by the excessive heat have keener intellects, it is true, but they have less blood, and consequently have no constancy of self-reliance in hand-to-hand fighting, for knowing that they have but little blood, they have a great fear of wounds. On the other hand, northern tribes, far removed from the burning rays of the sun, are more dull-witted, indeed, but, because they have an ample flow of blood, they are ever ready for war. Those who dwell in temperate climes have, on the one hand, an abundance of blood and thus make light of wounds or death and, on the other hand, do not lack prudence, which puts the proper restraint on them in camp and helps them in using strategy in the field.

The empirical invalidity to which this reasoning leads may titillate the contemporary reader. In a more subtle form, however, such hypothetical linkages from climate to physiology to personality and finally to war and politics have been widely accepted over the centuries by our literati. Ibn Khaldûn (1958), writing in fourteenth-century North Africa, appealed to geographic (oceans, rivers) and climatic (air, temperature, and humidity) factors to account for differences in the characters of peoples and in their sentiments of social commitment. Jean Bodin (1945), in sixteenth-century France, examined the psychological impacts of climate. Hot climates produce inner passion and cold climates outer ferocity. Charles Louis Montesquieu (1964), interpolating the more advanced physiology of his age, believed inhabitants of cold climates to be brave and vigorous because cold air "constringes the external fibers of the body," increasing their elasticity and favoring the return of the blood from the extreme parts to the heart. This tradition reached into the French school of human geography developed by Frederick LePlay during the middle of the nineteenth century (Zimmerman and Frampton, 1935).

Anthropogeographers in Germany, including Karl Ritter (1861) and Friedrich Ratzel (1921–1922), sustained this physicalist tradition into the early twentieth century. Armed with the experimental method and nascent statistical theory, they proposed to document and confirm the traditional expectation that physical and geographic features could determine conduct.

In England, Albert Leffingwell (1892) correlated the seasonal variation of solar light and heat with the incidence of passionate behavior. Suicides, murders, crimes against chastity, and other acts of passion increased between March and August, the period of high solar heat. A numerical correlation between the incidence of these behaviors and the two seasons was interpreted as evidence of cause. The rudimentary and inaccurate physiological notion that solar heat and light, as they vary from winter to summer, increase the blood flow was chosen as an explanatory variable. Increased blood flow excites the nervous system, which, in turn, generates passionate behavior. These correlations, and, even more, Leffingwell's interpretation of them, remain unreplicated. Yet his reasoning is instructive. Leffingwell passed directly from a physically conceptualized climatic fact, hypothetically translated into a biological fact, to a socially conceptualized behavioral fact. He failed to show how the physical fact of climate is interpreted by individuals engaging in a range of social activity. Emile Durkheim (1951) also found more suicides in July than in January. But, unlike Leffingwell, he interpreted this finding in the light of a social contextual fact. "If voluntary deaths increase from January to July, it is not because heat disturbs the organism but because social life is more intense" (p. 121f). Suicides, being social acts, increase when social life in general increases. Had Leffingwell considered such social and psychological mediators, his would-be replicators—instead of reexamining the relation of temperature to suicide—would have tested hypotheses about general social activity and suicide.

6

On Man in His Environment

Charles Woodruff (1905), an American physician, combined Leffingwell's physico-bio-behavioral reasoning with a teleological interpretation of evolutionary theory that was popular at the turn of the century. White men cannot survive in the tropics, he maintained, because they lack the skin pigmentation which had evolved among Negroes to exclude the actinic, or short, rays of the sun. Systematic data collection is all that is needed to undo this hypothesis. Caucasians in Iran, for instance, under some of the strongest sunlight on earth have impressive ability to survive.

Edwin Dexter (1904) is responsible for the most thorough attempt in the serious literature of this century to correlate weather and behavior. Influenced by the environmentalist school in criminology, he correlated—among other things—deportment in New York public schools, number of murders in Denver, and number of males arrested for drunkenness in New York City with meteorological conditions during the 1890s. Physiology provided the explanation. Low temperatures, low winds, and dryness produce anabolic, or rapid, metabolism. The assumption was that an individual with high metabolism is more likely, other things being equal, to be active than is an individual with low metabolism and thus to become delinquent. High temperatures, high barometric pressure, and high humidity produce katabolic, or low, metabolism, which lessens the quantity of energy and thus the propensity for crime. The hypothesized intervening physiological condition—the influence of climate upon metabolic rates—was, as in the case of Leffingwell, never tested. Had he tested it, Dexter would have discovered that the homeostatic mechanisms of the body are adequate to maintain a relatively steady physiological state across the range of climatic change in either Denver of New York. The distribution of metabolic rates of murderers, drunks, and classroom delinquents does not differ significantly from that of pacifists, teetotalers, and teacher's pets.

Henry L. Moore (1923), an American founder of statistical economics, correlated economic cycles with an eight-year cycle of rainfall. The reasoning was traditional. The amount of rainfall influenced the yield per acre of crops. This yearly yield was correlated

with prices of food, organic raw materials, and manufactured commodities—his indicators of economic cycles. Moore, however, did
not stop at relating rainfall to food prices. He explored the rainfall
cycle in terms of an eight-year cycle of interpositions of Venus between the sun and the earth. His study provided a shot in the arm
to astrology. An astronomical occurrence had been related scientifically to human weal and woe.

Empirical correlations between substantively unconnected
events were offered in the name of science. The lack of internal
logic in this research tradition could not but have a negative impact
on the social scientific community, particularly upon young sociologists inured against statistical abracadabra. Poor conceptualization
and a too mechanical application of statistical technique, both
found here in surfeit, can drive out good theory. The sterility of
some of these propositions was nearly enough to discourage further
inquiry into the relation of man to his environment. In reviewing
man-environment theories, Pitirim Sorokin (1928) wrote:

> At the beginning of a study of these theories one is impressed by
> their brilliancy and originality; continuing the study one is per-
> plexed and bewildered by their contradiction and vagueness; and
> finally he is lost in the sea of these theories, not knowing what
> in them is valid and what is wrong or doubtful. This explains
> why the primary need in this field at the present moment con-
> sists not so much in a formulation of a new geographical theory
> or a new "correlation" between geographical factors and social
> phenomena as in a most rigorous analysis and sifting of what is
> valid and what is childish in these numerous hypotheses.

These scholars assumed that the analytic schema for studying the behavior of men were continuous with those for studying
physical nature. They presumed that one could correlate a natural
physical fact with a social or psychological one just as one might
correlate two physical facts, and their theories failed. If man were
exceptional, if his mind and his social behavior were *not* merely
extensions of the physical, if the same laws could not be established
in the physical-biological realm as in the social-psychological realm,
then the expectation of direct correlation between facts in the two

realms was naive. Evolutionary theory seemed to cast doubt on a doctrine of the *exceptionalism* of man. This doubt stirred a malaise among some nineteenth-century Christian theologians. St. Thomas Aquinas was not discomfited by holding to propositions which spanned the mundane primordial elements and the human personality. He, however, did not try empirically to establish linking propositions. Scientists have not been of one mind on this issue.

If one key attitude again and again distinguishes scientific styles, it is what William James called "tough mindedness" and "tender mindedness." The tough and the tender minded do not differ so much in the rigor of their arguments as in their choices of scientific frames of reference. Many late nineteenth-century authors of the theories that failed were tough minded scientists attending to the physical continuities between man and animal. Social scientific interpretation borrowed the imagery Darwinism had introduced in the biological sciences. The growing prestige of medicine as a scientifically rooted, independent profession also helped thrust biological models—especially evolutionary models—to the fore. Many nineteenth-century psychologists, consistent with this outlook, drew philosophical breath from David Hume and proposed taking the measure of man almost exclusively through his sensory responses and physical mobility. Some environmentalist social theories, rejecting any natural exceptionalism, maintained that man could be thought of simply as a complex animal. A father of contemporary human geography, Ellsworth Huntington (1926, p. 2), wrote, "Although man has powers far beyond those of the animals, he is not essentially different from his fellow creatures in his primal relationships to heat, cold, and moisture; to food, drink, and shelter; to mountains, rivers, plains, and seas; and to vegetation, animals, insects, and bacterial parasites." Such tough minded scientists relegated the idea of evolutionary discontinuity between man and other organisms to the realm of theological argument.

Both the assertion and the denial that the psychological and social characteristics of man are continuous with those of the simpler biota function as profound working assumptions. The assumption of continuity permits the extension, with slight modifications, of the concepts and methods of natural science to the social sciences. The assumption of discontinuity calls for the development of methods for the study of man. As in so many of these controversies, the resolution is that some aspects of man are better understood if man is considered a member of the animal kingdom and some aspects are better clarified by considering man exceptional.

Among psychologists, the notion of human exceptionalism appears in the realization that the relation between an environmental stimulus and a behavioral response depends on the subject's interpretation of both the stimulus and the impending response (Hilgard, 1956). This type of observation has diverted tender minded psychologists from the study of environmental stimuli to the systems of meaning—of interpretations—which organize behavior with respect to stimuli.

Tough minded psychologists have continued to explore the impact of environmental segments—schedules of reinforcement threshold phenomena or tachistoscopically controlled flickers—segments now abstracted from the natural environment and brought under laboratory control. They promise a new man-nature field in the tough minded image. This work attends especially to those changes which act directly, without symbolic intervention, upon limited physical responses. As Bernice Kaplan (1954) shows, diet and altitude influence growth patterns. Physical inputs induce identifiable microphysiological responses. Changes in noise levels, temperature, or atmospheric pressure affect cardiovascular performance, for instance. Simple psychological responses, such as reaction time, muscular coordination, and perceptual speed, respond to variations in laboratory environmental conditions. However, in all these cases the magnitudes of the environmental changes needed to produce noticeable direct responses exceed those encountered in the normal physical environment (Burns, Chambers, and Hendler, 1963). Thus, these environmental-physical response factors would not often concern the sociologist.

It is not the interiority of the responses which excludes them from sociological purview. The internal environment of bodily sensations is also subject to symbolic interpretation and thus takes on a specifically human and even social character. Stanley Schachter (1964), in a brilliant series of studies, shows that the physiologically aroused individual interprets his sensations as either anger or joy depending on his perception of the social context in which they occur.

Exceptionalists have been in the majority among sociologists. George H. Mead (1934), the philosopher of symbolic interactionism, justified this approach theoretically. There may be "great cataclysms like earthquakes, events which lift the organism into different environments," but under more usual circumstances the animal constitutes its environment "by its sensitivity, by its movement toward the objects, by its reactions. We can see that the human form constitutes its environment in terms of those physical things, which are in a real sense the products of our own hands. . . . We then break up our world, not physical objects, into an environment of things that we can manipulate and utilize for our final ends and purposes" (pp. 245ff). Later followers focused on the "ends and purposes" and ignored the manipulating "hand" which was so important in Mead's thinking. The notion that the ability to symbolize sets man apart from the rest of nature had already been formalized for philosophy by Immanuel Kant and his precursors. Belief in an evolutionary discontinuity between man the symbolizer and other biological creatures came to be the preponderant, though not the unanimous, opinion of contemporary sociologists.

These last paragraphs hint at the sociology of man and nature to be discussed in Chapter Three. However to argue that scientists have shifted their attention to the problem of meaning, of interpretation, and have neglected the environmental stimuli that were being interpreted, the vehicle which carries the symbol, does not explain why this has happened. To seek some reasons we leave intellectual history for an excursion through the history of some intellectuals into the sociology of knowledge.

The academic lameness of the theories that failed is but a partial explanation for the waning of sociological interest in the physical environment. Few scientists adopt a theory on the weight of evidence or abandon it under the press of negative cases. The

11

scientific enterprise is fostered and husbanded by men seeking support for hypotheses already espoused (Kuhn, 1962). Scientific positions are responsive to the social philosophies of their proponents. The disappearance of a scientific concern, in this as in any other academic area, is likely to be related to the abandonment of the social philosophies in which that concern was formulated.

The concern of the French geographer Jean Reclus (see Thomas, 1925) with physical environmental influences on behavior was congenial to his anarchistic political position. Environmental determinism minimizes the role of the state and other artificial social institutions in human behavior. For Ellen Semple (1911), in America an environmental theory was a way of undercutting racial determinism of the type which Joseph Gobineau had advocated during the nineteenth century. If different races living under similar geographic conditions develop similarly, then, Semple could conclude, social development is not due to race but to geographic conditions.

The position of a scientist, as of a layman, in the social structure influences the perspective from which he views the world about him. The ideology of his social stratum influences his social philosophy and his social theory. If the social source of professional recruitment to a field changes from one to another stratum, the social philosophy current among scholars in that field changes. Scientific concerns in that field may also change. The changing backgrounds of sociologists have probably been a significant influence on the waning of interest in man-environment relations. Reference to the disciplinary problems, the absurd contentions of some anthropogeographers, for instance, may rationalize the changing interest.

During the first decades of this century, the backbone of American sociology was rural. Today a growing proportion of sociologists are recruited from cities. The natural environment escapes the attention of urban men unless they become specialists in the environment. The social problems which grip their attention seem less directly dependent on a bounteous or miserly nature than on the ebbing and surging in relations among groups. Even the cultivated milieus and technological systems of urban society receive only scant sociological notice. These become the specialized concerns of engineers and social planners.

Scientists, like their fellow beings, locate problems by their relevance to their own interests. Social scientists seem to have a penchant for locating problems relevant to their own suffering. The suffering to which urban man is peculiarly subject—the sense of loneliness among the multitude—draws attention to the problem of man's relations to man rather than to the problem of man and nature. This feeling may have been sharpened in these post-Depression years by the realization that distorted human relationships are the ultimate ground of woe—that the evils both of depression and of war are manufactured within the social organization of men. If men starve and slaughter one another against the serene backdrop of nature—"where poppies grow"—it is men who need to be studied, not nature.

There has been another change in the recruitment of sociologists. Like most academicians a half century ago, sociologists belonged to a small elite of the university who were educated and tended to identify with an established class. Today sociologists are more likely to be children or grandchildren of immigrants. They are socially mobile, struggling against established class barriers. This struggle entices analysis of the human matrix which forms those barriers to mobility. They pay less attention to the natural matrix of human society and tend to assume the principle of exceptionalism, the discontinuity between men and physical nature. Meanings and symbols become important. In the extreme, disembodied meanings and symbols become the subjects for analysis.

Two social developments may be assisting the process. The first, modern technology, increases man's ability to manipulate his environment through operations performed at a great distance from that environment. No longer do his muscles feel the resistance of the earth to his shovel or plow. Power exerted at an Olympian distance is a good basis for the idea of exceptionalism.

The second social development assisting the process is the mixing of the ideas of diverse peoples through migration and improved communication. Each people carries its own definition of the environment, rooted in its own history. Karl Mannheim (1936) has pointed out how exposure to these contending definitions of the social environment—and, by extension, of the physical environment —creates doubts as to the real nature of that environment. The existence of alternative definitions draws attention to the definitions per se, to the symbolic screens men interpose between themselves and the environment.

Social theoretical attention to the human-symbolic or to the natural environment is also associated with the relationship which the theorist as researcher establishes between himself and his subjects. This social relationship affects the scholar's perspective on his data (Klausner, 1966a). When communication between subjects and researcher is minimal, the researcher is likely to attend to physical environmental conditions. Significantly, it is often the anthropologists dealing with nonliterate societies, or with people whose language they understand poorly, who maintain interest in the natural environment. It is now a fashion among anthropologists to report social and cultural diversity among people living under ostensibly similar physical circumstances and, consequently, to derogate the influence of nature. Diversity is located in culture, in the variety of adaptations people make to these similar circumstances. The cultural or interpretive element intervening between man and nature asserts its centrality in anthropological theory, but no anthropological field report would be considered complete without a description of the natural setting.

An increasing tendency among sociologists to regard man as a symbolizing creature is also traceable in part to the research relationship maintained. Earlier environmental theorists did not talk with their subjects. They recorded global attributes of groups. When they measured individual members of groups, they tended to amass classificatory data from records such as school reports of delinquencies and birth records. With the rise of the social survey and the aggregation of the responses of individual interviewees, the tendency to interpret behavior in symbolic interactionist terms has become overwhelming. One cannot say, however, whether the interview situation and interview data predispose to symbolic interactionism or whether symbolic interactionists are more likely to find the interview the method of choice.

Broad social factors, and the research structure itself, interact with the influence of current academic structure. The way physical environmental considerations enter the analysis defines disciplines. The physical environment becomes a special province of physicists and engineers in science faculties. Sociology has been academically interwoven with social thought, social philosophy, and history. This specialization reflects broader divisions of societal concern and is not restricted to the secular academy. The divines who explore cosmological questions in theology differ from those who develop the social gospel.

The social distance between members of these disciplines can be quite great. A contemporary interdisciplinary meeting is more likely to bring a social psychologist together with an organizational sociologist than to bring a sociologist together with a linguist. Of greater pertinence, the contemporary sociologist is unlikely to rub academic shoulders with engineers and physicists, the environmental scientists. Thus, location of sociologists within the university removes them further from environmental questions.

While most sociologists are ignoring physical environmental factors in the structuring of societies and cultures, physical scientists and engineers have not been too troubled by the sociocultural and psychological implications of environmental change. Some physical scientists, with atomic scientists in the lead, have been horrified by the hiatus between the maturity of our control over the physical environment and our stunted social-moral growth. Managers of natural resources, deploring the inefficient use and misuse of resources, are concerning themselves with the character of the society responsible for resource decisions. Agricultural specialists in international aid programs, frustrated by the reluctance of the potential beneficiaries to adopt their advice on rational techniques of planting and harvesting, look to cultural scientists for insight into this self-defeating obtuseness.

The reconciliation of physical scientists with social reality is not the focus of this book. Its aim is to stimulate sociological interest in the exploration of man-nature relations. Among sociologists, interest in the physical environment has remained alive mainly in the work of human ecologists and demographers. Location theorists, primarily economists, have also offered sociologically relevant observations in this area. All three of these groups have, to a greater or lesser degree, set values or symbols outside their analytic concern. Chapter Two explores, in the work of demographers, ecologists, and location theorists, some intellectual directions that sociologists might follow. Chapter Three introduces a *voluntaristic* model which explicitly considers values and symbols mediating the man-nature relation.

CHAPTER II

Populations and Their Resources

Students of the relation between man and nature have tended to think in terms of human survival. Most sociological issues are couched in less extreme terms. The problem of survival is translated in sociological analysis into the problem of social order. Few sociologists have concerned themselves with the very existence of a social order. The debate is more often about the type of social order which may obtain. For instance, is political authority legitimated by rational or traditional norms? What implication has this for the integration of ethnic groups or the stability of the family?

Samuel Z. Klausner

The man-nature question was raised in an ultimate form by Thomas Malthus in his *Essay on Population*. The principle of population is a principle of survival resting on the relation of numbers of people to food. Population, unless checked, increases in a geometrical ratio while the food supply increases in an arithmetical ratio. Malthus said that the ultimate check to population is never the immediate check. Population does not increase to its limit, to the point at which the means of subsistence are exhausted. "Vice, misery and moral restraint" check its growth. Vice is a Malthusian reference to practices such as birth control; misery refers to diseases, war, and famine; and moral restraint refers to delay in marriage from prudential motives, with conduct strictly moral during this period of restraint.

Three elements in the Malthusian argument serve as guides for the sociological study of man-nature relationships. First, by extending his argument from food supplies to any natural resource on which society depends, we have a general model of the relation of population and a resource base. Some modification in the theory would be required. Few resources are tied as directly to survival as is food, and the ratio of labor to the production of other resources is not the same as it is in the case of food. The arithmetic increase law would not necessarily hold for other resources, especially with improvement in technology. Malthus' focus on the problem of resource scarcity and his neglect of the problem of resource allocation under conditions of abundance limit the theory.

Second, the emergence of the checks of vice and moral restraint, and to some extent misery too, is a cultural adaptation of a population to a resource problem. This adaptation opens the way to a theory of culture as an emergent in problem solving. His use of the term *vice* reflects his personal evaluation of contraception and abortion, but it too is nonetheless a cultural emergent. Third, Malthus set a pattern for analyzing man-nature relations quantitatively—in terms of numbers of people and quantities of consumables. In this model, people are treated as equivalent and interchangeable units. The problem is to count these population units and trace their distribution in space against the distribution of a

18

second set of objects, food. This model of objects distributed in space mapped on a second distribution of objects has worked well in the physical sciences. For this reason, we will call it a physicalist model.

Contemporary demographers have maintained Malthus' physicalist model. More specialized today than Malthus was, they have concentrated on the third problem mentioned above, the enumeration of people—no simple problem—to a greater extent than they have on the first two, the study of resources and culture. Demographers employ two kinds of data to study the distribution and the composition of populations. One type of data refers to persons as units as, for example, in censuses. The other refers to events in the lives of persons such as births, deaths, and migrations—attributes ordinarily found in community registers. Three measures— migration, fertility, and mortality—are sufficient, along with information on age and sex composition, for describing changes in the size of a population. These three parameters exhaust the ways the number of objects in a set can change. Inferences from underlying nondemographic variables have not, until recently, been extensively relied upon. Predictions of future population trends can be extrapolated from current and past data. By making certain assumptions about future trends in mortality, it is possible to construct a *life table* showing the expected size of an initial population cohort in succeeding years.

Demographers devote considerable effort to the accurate measurement of migration, fertility, and mortality and to precision in extrapolating from these measures. The many ways of constructing these measures introduce a problem of validity, of knowing what the measure does indeed measure. For example, in assessing fertility for various purposes it may be legitimate to use the crude birth rate (the number of births registered in a given calendar year per one thousand population at the midpoint of that year); the age-specific birth rates (the ratio of births to women in some particular age interval); the cohort fertility (the sum of age-specific birth rates over time of women in the same age or duration of marriage grouping); or the child-woman ratio (the ratio of the number of children under five years to the number of women between fifteen and forty-four). This last ratio reflects survivors rather than simply births.

Reasonable inferences depend also on the reliability of the data sources. The registered cause of death may not be the actual cause, especially when suicide is the correct category. The comparability of data from several sources may also be troublesome. Definitions of categories change over time and differ from one country to another.

The care exerted by demographers here is not due to the fact that they have more severe problems of reliability and validity than other behavioral scientists endure. A census report is, if anything, more reliable than the responses to a public opinion poll and a more ready source of valid inferences than an anthropologist's field notes. As Wilbert Moore (1959) has said, because demography emphasizes quantitative variables and measurement, it is recognized by sociologists as one of the advanced specialties in the field. Such care and accuracy are common accompaniments of a physicalist model.

The method itself, for all its superiority in reliability and validity, has certain substantive limitations. Users of the physicalist model tend to deal with each unit or individual in a population as if it stood alone. The classificatory attributes are considered to be attached to the individual rather than being a function of that individual relative to other individuals. Age tends to be used as a calendaric category to indicate the point of entry into a population cohort and, when aggregated, the proportion in a population that may be expected to die at a given time. Rarely is age treated in terms of its social or psychological meanings. Malthus, as mentioned above, did not exclude extrademographic factors. Social checks on population, especially moral restraint, assumed the relevance of such factors. He shunted extrademographic factors aside, in part, by not developing quantitatively rigorous ways of dealing with them. Technology, a cultural element, he considered relatively static. The arithmetical increase in agricultural production related principally to the refusal of nature to respond proportionately to the increase in tillers of the soil. Perhaps, had Malthus seen the manner in which technology could act as capital input by increasing the productivity of both land and labor, he might have been led to a more thorough investigation of habitat—as were later human ecologists.

Some later imitative followers, however, have been more purist than Malthus in their use of the physicalist model. Oddly, in a sociologically oriented work on demography, William Petersen (1961) argues that it is not necessary to take explicit account of psychological variables because they are implicitly assumed in a standard differential analysis. It is not necessary to go into the life conditions, aspirations, and possibilities of city dwellers to explain why urban families are smaller than rural ones. It is better to study what people do than what they think. Population forecasters may, according to Petersen, legitimately hold socioeconomic factors constant. Population analysts should not be expected to consider an economic depression, a war, a cure for cancer, or any of the other hundred significant changes in the economy, technology, society, and cultural patterns that are relevant to population growth.

Other demographers, truer sons of Malthus, temper their physicalist purism. Wilbert Moore (1959) stated the population problem of Malthus in more general terms as involving the interrelation between demographic phenomena and their social settings. From this point of view, demographers could explore the relation between migrations and wars and the relation between fertility and economics. The organization of a population—its structure of roles and its manner of establishing authority—influences the likelihood of war and the chances of turning an environment into a source of economic affluence.

More and more sociological demography has been appearing in recent years. This literature has addressed itself to the question of population policy. Kingsley Davis and Judith Blake (1956) have analyzed the relation between social organization and fertility in terms of cultural factors which affect the likelihood and the outcomes of intercourse, conception, and gestation. For instance, the exposure to the possibility of conception is governed by the formation and dissolution of unions in the reproductive period, which in turn depend on social norms governing age of entry into sexual unions, permanent celibacy, proportion of women never entering sexual unions, and so forth. This reasoning is the obverse of that of Leon Festinger, Stanley Schachter, and Kurt Back (1950) regarding the relation between physical and social factors. In that study spatial arrangement—the physical factor—was a prior condition or occasion permitting certain social arrangements. The Davis and Blake argument reasons from the sociocultural factors which control the occasions for physical union. Each examines a different phase of a continuing series. One can imagine social factors leading to residential propinquity, which, in turn, increases the likelihood of friendships, and so on. Ray Abrams (1943) began with residential propinquity as a factor in marriage selection, thus entering the action series leading to fertility with consideration of a physical-spatial feature.

Lincoln Day and Alice Day (1964) are engaged in sociological demography as they sketch public attitudes toward population growth. Such attitudes reflect broad cultural positions—ideas on life and death, belief that man is an agent of social change, or attitudes about individual rights. The notion of an optimum population for a country is an amalgam of these attitudes with economic criteria. The Days suggest that extension of a current social attitude —the ideal of the small family—would effectively slow population growth.

Demographers concerned with population control have been modifying the physicalist model by introducing social-psychological and cultural factors. Those demographers who have given attention to the relation of population to natural resources have preferred economic measures. Sometimes the language of economic research in resources is such that the physical element itself seems to be the variable considered. Actually the variable is the value or utility of a good as assessed in some real or simulated market. In primitive societies, says Edward Ackerman (1959, pp. 621–648), men are found in numbers only where there is a supply of fresh water. In mature agrarian civilizations, numbers are a function of the amount of level land in combination with the amount of water available.

22

In industrial cultures, the important factors are the amount and quality of industrially usable minerals available to the area, particularly iron and coal, and the technical attributes of the prevailing cultural setting (to use Ackerman's phrase). Number of people is a direct function of resource conditions only when the group is isolated from trade, has a standard of living near the subsistence level, and has little flexibility of technology. In developed societies, economic organization and cultural variables—such as the technical attributes of the prevailing cultural setting—are highly significant influences on the relations between resources and population. An economic conceptualization quickly draws attention to other sociocultural elements.

Cultural-economic factors may appear as intervening variables in equations relating population and resources. The composition of populations by age, sex, and cultural group affect consumer demand and manpower potential. Under certain assumptions about fertility, migration, and mortality, the number of women of childbearing age in a population at a point in time indicates the extent of manpower potentially available to the society some two decades hence. The availability of manpower is, in turn, a factor in the pace of industrialization.

Demography reminds the rest of sociology of an often ignored truism. Before one can say anything practical about the relations of a population to its environment, it is necessary, at the very least, to know the size and distribution of the population. Demographers have been exemplary in precise measurement. Yet, exclusive or too rigid adherence to the physicalist model introduces an assumption which, though not troublesome in the study of the physical world, circumscribes the scope of interest in the human world. The working assumptions of the physicalist model are that its objects are equivalent and interchangeable, that objects possess attributes independently of their position in relation to other objects, and that the whole is the aggregate of the constituent objects. When the units of analysis are people, they can be traced as equivalent and interchangeable objects only in a restricted sense. The cultural attributes of the individuals permit them to define and orient themselves to nature in different ways and with different impacts on the environment. People may be mapped against the cow population, but Moslems put more pressure on the population of cows than do Hindus.

The characteristics of each person are not always identifiable in isolation from the attributes of others in his environment. A man needs a partner to be a conspirator. Many human characteristics are what the philosophers of science call *disposition properties*. They become manifest only in certain situations. The quality of brittleness in physics is of this nature. It has no meaning unless the material is subject to stress. In social science an attitude has such a character. Further, in moving from a consideration of the parts to the whole, the pattern of relationships among the parts can be important. The modes of organization among people affect their impacts on nature. A number of people managing individual farms may consume more water than they would if organized in agricultural communes irrigating a smaller number of larger plots. Organization changes the meaning of a population for its environment. Human ecologists, using more of a biologistic than a physicalistic framework, make the concept of organization central.

The field of human ecology is by definition concerned with man and his environment, including his natural environment. Terms like *whole* and *total* appear frequently in the writings of ecologists. One cannot, they argue, appreciate an element in nature without considering its surroundings. Like all scientific perspectival totalities, ecology conceptualizes from a concrete totality. Although not limiting the scope of its view, ecology limits the aspects from which the world is viewed. The limitation is expressed in what may be called its *biologistic* framework. Substantively, ecologists draw upon biological analogies to understand social processes. Methodologically, ecologists, like biologists prior to the flowering of biochemistry and molecular biology, focus on patterns of organization among elements constituting an identifiable living organism. For human ecology, society or the community is the organism, and the person is the element.

24

On Man in His Environment

Charles Darwin and Alfred Wallace, fathers of evolutionary biology, were patriarchs of human ecologists as Malthus was a patriarch of demographers. Communities are not simply aggregates of their individual elements, as the physicalist model tends to have it. The elements, individually, are organized in what Darwin described as the "web of life." The struggle for existence is one of the processes organizing this web. Environmental conditions govern the struggle. Communities, too, struggle with one another. Organisms and, in turn, their constituent elements must adapt to environmental conditions to survive in the struggle with other organisms. The overarching process is adaptation, a kind of referee to the struggle. Ecologists attend to the totality through their two concepts: adaptation—a concept of process—and organization—a concept of structure. Biological categories used to explain adaptation of organisms to the physical environment are transferred to analyze the adaptation of society to its environment. Generally, the elements of the environment are categorized in common-sense physical terms.

Most human ecologists assume a parallelism of the life patterns of all organic forms, including that of the human community. Human social patterns are thus more complex versions of social patterns observed among animals. The doctrine of human exceptionalism is denied. Philosophically, ecologists fit comfortably in this respect with psychologists such as B. F. Skinner (1938). His theory of learning through operant conditioning, although developed in experiments with rats, is generalized to human learning.

Most contemporary sociologists, consistent with the social theories of Max Weber (1947), are concerned with the meaning of an environmental element to an actor. The ecologist skirts this problem as the demographer does. Processes, such as individual interpretations or meanings occurring within the personality, are irrelevant at the chosen level of analysis. The ecologist studies the organized structure of activity—the morphology of a community, the spatial patterns of urban settlement—without reference to the motivations or attitudes of the acting agents. Meaning is to be found in the patterns of organization on the principle that an organized community has properties, meanings, not found in its component elements separately (Duncan, 1959). The ecologist excludes only subjective meanings.

Early human ecological studies correlated regularities in shapes of settlement with physical features of the terrain and possibilities of communication, particularly transportation, between the sectors. The horizontal organization of a community, in this frame of reference, may be described in terms of distances between individuals and their spatial clustering. Bioecologists are famous for their analyses of vertical organization, the organization among various biological levels. Building on the notion of the parallelism of organic forms, the human ecologist describes human ties to other biological communities through food chains. This food chain is analogous to that by which insects contribute to the support of the raccoon by way of the garter snake and the toad. Following the model of evolutionary biology, the size of man's communities—at least in his primitive state—is set by analogy to the size of animal communities in balanced predator-prey relationships. The eater and the eaten, in vital cooperation, achieve an optimum numerical relation to one another. So human communities may be thought of as approaching some optimum size in balance with the rest of the natural world.

The balance of relationships, forms of organization, or patterns of settlement are adaptations of systems—including social systems—to their environments. Animals adapt to the conditions imposed by the physical environment and by other living creatures. On the biological level, survival depends on some prior forms of organization, the tendency of wolves to join packs and of ants to divide their labor. Survival is also dependent on characteristics of individuals in the population, the night vision of the bat or the swiftness of the hare. The equivalents of these adaptations on the human level are the patterns of community organization and the demographic characteristics of individuals. Organization and adaptation, the two central concepts, are linked together. Along with population size and amount of subsistence material or resources available, the way the population is organized influences the level of living attained by it and, in the extreme, its very survival—that is, its adaptation.

Amos Hawley (1950) treats resources and forms of social organization as independent factors. The amount of resources may vary with no change in social organization. This might be the case if it were possible to identify resources independently of the perception of the user population, that is, if one did not have to consider subjective meanings. The mere presence of resources, their availability, does not determine the way they influence human action or whether they do so at all. The perception of the same physical objects may vary with the culture of the group and the type of social organization. Consequently they exist in different amounts under these various conditions. Almost the only way contemporary ecologists allow for culturally influenced definitions of resources is by including technology along with organization as a factor influencing the adaptation of a population to its environment.

Adaptation is the most important dynamic concept in human ecology. According to Hawley, by adapting an organism gains control over its environment and may change its own character in the process. Adaptations may be classified according to the ways the character of the organism changes. Genetic adaptations are changes in the morphology of the species. Man's erect bipedal position is an adaptation which, Hawley notes, leaves the arms free for manipulatory activities. Somatic adaptations—such as immunity to disease—develop in the life of an individual. From an ecological point of view the important adaptations are the communal or genetic ones. Culture is one of these communal adaptations. But culture does not mean the same thing to ecologists as it does to anthropologists.

Hawley defines culture as the prevailing techniques of adjustment by which a population maintains itself in its habitat. The elements of culture become identical in principle with the intense desire of the bee for honey, the nest-building activities of birds, and the hunting habits of carnivora. This view is consistent with that of ethologists such as Konrad Lorenz (1966), who infer the roots of human social attributes from zoological data. Inferences about the behavior of human populations under conditions of spatial crowding have been derived from studies such as those of John Calhoun (1962) on Norway rats. The population growth of the rats stabilized because of increasing infant mortality, failure to carry pregnancies to term, sexual deviation, and cannibalism. While some of these processes follow crowding in human populations, the incidence and mechanisms are quite different.

By ignoring the symbolic, interpretive, or subjective aspects of meaning, both ecologists and ethologists reduce culture to patterns of instinctual or conditioned responses to environmental conditions. If this were true, cultural variability could be predicted from physical environmental variability. That the environment alone is not determinative of the cultural solution to the problem it sets is apparent from the variety of cultural responses to the same environment. Ruth Benedict (1934), for instance, showed how one group could develop a Dionysian culture and another group under similar geographic conditions could develop an Apollonian culture. Some littoral peoples develop fishing industries, but others treat the sea as a wall.

As the illustration from Benedict suggests, human ecology in its anthropological incarnation is more concerned with symbolic culture than is human ecology in its sociological incarnation. Culture as a product of adaptation comprises some behavioral relationship, or norms governing such a relationship, between man and an environmental feature. The older evolutionary framework is thus modified. Environmental conditions cannot directly account for the emergent adaptation. The anthropological ecologist introduces a symbolic or interpretive process by which the individual or community first defines its environmental condition and then proceeds to adapt to the condition as defined.

Laura Thompson (1949) illustrates how culture, in the anthropologist's sense, emerges as a community adapts to a natural condition. She describes a community in Fiji living on several islands. Some are limestone islands covered with forests, while others are volcanic islands having good garden land. The forest and garden resources are conplementary. Ceremonial exchange systems evolved in which food from the volcanic islands was exchanged

28

for forest craft goods from the limestone islands. Food-related roles, such as that of crop custodian and of master fisherman, emerged in this society. These roles were a cultural solution to the problem set by the two natural environments. The solutions did not come simply from the environments but from a meshing of the environmental givens with the social relations manifest in the exchange system.

Problems of food have been salient for ecological theorists. They describe social organizations in relation to sustenance-producing activities. The problem of self-preservation is solved by adapting and exploiting an environment (Sayce, 1938). As among some Malthusians, this orientation leads to concern with ultimate rather than proximate adaptations. Typical is Waldo Wedel's (1953) study of prehistoric life in the Central Plains. He looks at the basic subsistence techniques enabling man to survive and function: the use of water holes, hunting, and food collection. Although survival of the species is an ultimate function of such social processes as economic exchange, education, and socialization, the variety of ways man can exchange, educate, and socialize are sociologically important. Attention to adaptation over extended time spans, as in the Fiji study of Thompson, should not exclude short term human action, which may itself be crucial both for social policy and for testing sociological theory.

The concept of adaptation sometimes tempts its users from a factual into an evaluative stance—the successful adaptations may be classed as the good, or desirable. This adaptation is illustrated by the caricature of evolutionary theory which Richard Hofstadter (1955) called Social Darwinism. Here scientific theory together with social philosophy affirmed that the social and economic success of capitalist tycoons and the dominance of the imperialist-militarist phalanxes proved the moral superiority of these classes. Writers of the opposite political strain, for whom cultural imperialism is anathema, sometimes accept the same premise about the goodness of the outcome of a natural process. Thompson (1949)— in her study of relations of men, animals, and plants in Fiji referred to above—describes a "balanced, functional ecocultural structure" which from time to time resists the intrusion of foreign or extraneous patterns of belief, thought, and behavior. Natural ecocultural processes, if undisturbed by foreign cultural interests, foster the development and maintenance of a "balanced, healthy, total community" of plants and animals as well as of human groups. She thus restates in secular terms an earlier theological opposition to disturbing God's plans. The notion of the moral value of the successful adaptation, or of the natural balance, echoes Adam Smith's "invisible hand."

The problem is strikingly driven home by René Dubos (1965), who points out that so-called successful adaptations might well be harmful in the long run. Since environments may change and man is very adaptable, he may adapt to situations that destroy his values. Insofar as human adaptation to the environment implies change in the individual or in group life, man may judge whether he would choose such changes to attain the adaptation. One can, for instance, ignore a high concentration of sulphur dioxide in the air. After several generations, a new population balance will have been achieved. Those with weaker lungs will have succumbed to respiratory diseases, while a new tougher-lunged population will have survived. Were adaptational theorists to apply their moral instincts automatically to this type of natural balance, the ethically positive magic of that phrase might evanesce. Technically, the concept of adaptation is ethically neutral; especially in the biological realm its processes are morally silent.

Part of the problem may be methodological. We do not have available for examination a range of different adaptations and their consequences. The evidence available is generally that of successful adaptations. Unsuccessfully adapted types may have disappeared. What criteria can be used to assess their value? To discover the unsuccessful adaptations takes archaeological digging. Physical evidence of bones or potsherds tells something of the adaptations of earlier societies even if these adaptations did not guarantee the survival of the society. The problem of inferring a human relationship or a social organization from such remains should not be underestimated. One cannot assume that a prehistoric tool played the same role in a previous society that its descendant plays today (Anderson, 1969).

Sociologists, sensitive to this methodological problem and the limits it imposes on data for the sociologist of organizations, have been studying social organizations which have failed. Typically, these are organizations that adapted, as the evolutionary theorists would say, to a narrow niche. The conditions of the niche changed, compelling the organizations to change or disappear. David Sills (1957) showed how the March of Dimes organization sought a new function when polio vaccine appeared, rather than accept its demise as an organization. In another context, Festinger, Riecken, and Schachter (1956) traced the adaptations of a religious sectarian movement after its predicted apocalypse failed to occur.

All the adaptations discussed reflect the evolutionary concept of the struggle for existence. Cooperative aspects of both animal and human relations, those involving what the Russian social thinker Peter Kropotkin (1955) called "mutual aid," tend to be left out of the equation. Hawley introduces a concept of social integration on the basis of likenesses. In the Darwinist tradition, mutual dependence is epitomized by a prey-predator relationship. Consequently, the model is better suited to the analysis of interindividual or intersocietal relations, where conflict is salient, than to intrasocietal relations, where institutionalized or shared norms coordinate behavior.

The concept of adaptation is not inherently bound to long-range changes, to ethical judgments, or to the conflictual aspects of life. The adaptation need not be an automatic response to environmental conditions. Neither is the central ecological concept—organization—restricted to physical spatial patternings. Individuals and societies can decide upon the organization with which they face the natural world. They can even regulate the demographic characteristics of a population encountering a selected environmental feature. Students of human ecology can study these designed adaptations. Much more could be done in bringing symbolic processes into the picture as they define the environment to be adapted to.

Samuel Z. Klausner

The ecologist has developed a methodology for focusing on the organization of societal units in their encounter with the environment. The next step here is to look at some theories which take symbolic behavior into account. Location theory, constructed on a rationalistic model, is one example.

Location theorists—like ecologists and demographers—map the distribution of social units in physical space. They have concerned themselves primarily with economic influences on location. The social units traditionally examined have been industrial firms, retail stores, or family residences. For all of these, economic considerations are manifest in the locational decision.

Location theory differs from ecology and demography in several respects. First, though concerned with the location of an array of units—such as a set of factories and stores or residences and markets—its logic has been to focus on factors influencing the location of a single unit at a time. Second, location theory—in establishing the linkages (usually expressed as algebraic equations) between the unit in question and other relevant units—is dealing with an array of two-part or possibly three-part relationships. These location theorists stand on a middle ground between demographers who aggregate single population units and ecologists who look for an overall organizing principle. Third, location theory interposes a rational decision between the objective forces impinging on the unit and its resulting location. An entrepreneur assumedly examines the equations and selects an optimum location in terms of rational decision rules. The principal rule is to maximize the profit of the enterprise. Because of this characteristic, I call the model guiding location theory a *rationalistic* model.

We have discussed the role of interpretation of the environment in the ecological adaptation of a community. This interpretation rests on social values. These values are also decision rules, but they are not all rational. A rational principle is one which leads to the selection of a means perceived as instrumentally related to its intended goal. Location theory permits the application of this single social value, the value of cognitive rationality. This step, however, marks a sharp break with those adaptive theories in which no place

32

was left for the intervention of symbolic processes of any kind and in which, as mentioned above, the adaptations were functions solely of the environmental conditions.

A theory of location of industries was pioneered by Alfred Weber (Friedrich, 1929). He conceived of an imaginary industrialist arriving at a rational decision on the basis of three variables: transportation costs, labor costs, and what he called "material index." The material index he defined as the weight of local materials relative to the weight of the product. When labor costs cannot be considered constant, a labor coefficient enters the calculations. A labor coefficient is the ratio of the cost of labor per ton based on the weight of goods transported. A social actor makes decisions around economic givens. He has a scale of economic utility values. Material resources or other physical environmental objects are evaluated against a scale of economic utility. The meaning of these objects can then be expressed in a cost calculus. Thus, location theory, as a theory in economics, breaks with the sheer common-sense physical meanings of nature in defining the environment in terms of its economic significance.

Weber intentionally excluded other noneconomic social and cultural meanings from a pure theory of location. Later location theorists, such as Walter Isard (1956), recommend considering certain sociopsychological and biological forces. In view of the abstract nature of the theory, Isard considers it of little direct utility for handling real problems. Rather, it is designed to express an ideal economic decision. Nevertheless, a normative implication that the rational plant owner should employ these decision rules is conveyed.

Weber wrote primarily of the location of industries and consequently, within the whole realm of nature, he was concerned with material resources and land features which might affect transportation rates and land usage. Isard has extended the theory to residential location as an aspect of the development of an urban metropolitan region. This region is a multinuclear body involving a network of transport interconnections and hence of interstitial areas, each subject to hierarchical order. Factors entering Isard's equations include the cost relations of economic activities, the spatial and product preferences of consumers of familial and of various associational units, and the "friction of distance" expressed in economic terms.

Isard has indicated the need for an extension of the rationalistic model of location theory to a broad range of values. He has not shown how these values could be incorporated. Working in sociology rather than economics, Walter Firey (1947) analyzed the economic values of residential and commercial properties in Boston. Firey was a student of Talcott Parsons. Parsons was originally trained as an economist and had studied with Weber. Firey criticized ecological theories, such as Ernest Burgess' theory of concentric zones, because of the failure to consider social and cultural values, and he also criticized the rationalistic character of Weber's location theory. He argued that social groups locate in particular residential areas because those areas are symbols for their cultural values. Thus Firey attempted the next step, introducing other values beyond the rational cognitive one into the decision.

Leon Moses (1958), a student of Isard's, proposed modifying the traditional economic framework by taking alternative sources for the inputs into consideration in the decision to locate an individual firm. Since the optimum location varies with the level of output, which is related to demand, there is no single optimum location along the arc of equal distances from the market. The demand function is computed in economic terms but could be extended to consider the social-psychological aspects of demand. Location theory shows how rational man would develop resources on the assumption that the meaning of those resources was given and fixed—specifically, given in terms of their costs at some time and place. Different social groups may perceive different resources, not simply different values of the same resource.

The element of rational decision making is a stepping stone from the physicalist and biologistic to a voluntaristic theory of man-environment relations. The previous chapter reviews some of the theories in which men entered these relations as objects of environmental action. A voluntaristic theory conceives of a negotiation between man and environment. A voluntaristic model draws on the models just discussed: of aggregating units in space with the precision and objectivity of measurement developed by demographers; of the holistic perspective on community organization and adaptation of the ecologists; of the rational decisions of people and the cognitive interpretations of the environment—perhaps mathematically summarized—of the location theorists.

The possibilities of and the reasons for breaking with the notion that an environmental event may be conceptualized only in a common-sense physical frame of reference have been suggested. The economists have pointed the way by translating physical factors into economic factors and by introducing the image of an actor considering these factors in a frame of rational values. Just as the physical fact may be evaluated in terms of its relevance for economic action, it may also be evaluated in its relevance for political, religious, recreational, or esthetic action, among others.

How Physical Facts Become Social Facts

M*an* and *environment* are terms freighted with enough colloquial meaning to reduce their usefulness as scientific concepts. Both terms need conceptual respecification before they can be admitted as elements in a theoretical net. To resolve the ambiguity about the term *man* would require a dissertation in philosophical anthropology, a task beyond this book. For sociological purposes, *man* refers to a participant in society, an occupant of a socially defined position, or an enactor of a socially defined role. Our analysis here does not turn on man but rather on the social norms which define a status, or position, in society as well as the behavior expected of an occupant of such a position. The analysis also examines institutions comprising a network of such statuses. The term *organization* refers to a group of social actors bound together in pursuit of a goal. The economy and the polity are social institutions. Business firms and the governments are social organizations. The term *social organization* is borrowed from the British anthropologists as a generic term referring to the whole complex of relations which connect members of a society. A sociological theory of man-environment relations, in the tradition which informs this book, is limited to the interaction of a *social actor* and his physical *environment*.

The term *environment* is not easily submitted to classical definitional procedure, which requires that environment be defined separately from the social actor who participates in that environment. Independent measures taken on each may then be correlated to attest to their association. This procedure would be feasible were man and environment related as parts of a mechanical system. In a mechanical system, as in a machine, each part can be defined independently. A steam generator has the same internal characteristics whether or not it is mounted on the engine. Pitirim Sorokin (1928) defines the geographic environment as the cosmic conditions and phenomena which exist independent of man's activity and which change and vary through their own spontaneity. Sorokin achieves this independence of definition by examining the relation from the physical environmental perspective. His definition does not exclude change in geographic conditions through human intervention as, for instance, when human activities affect the balance of atmospheric gases or the chemistry of water. Sorokin is here counterposing physical and social concepts rather than defining the environment by its sociological significance.

If man and nature are considered to be related as parts of an organic system, independent definitions are not feasible. For example, in a biological system each part has meaning only in its relation to its functioning context. A synapse has meaning in relation to a dendrite but not in abstraction from it.

Sociologists are accustomed to organic systems. Economic

exchange does not take place independently of a body of implicitly understood noneconomic norms. In a social system analysis, the environment is defined by or with reference to a social actor, not independently of him. The social actor interprets an aspect of environment relevant for his action. He defines the significance of the environment for his action. The current tradition in sociology is to treat the environment—part of the situation of action—in terms of the meaning it has to the participants in the action rather than to some objective observer.

Each entity in the world could be conceived as an aspect of the environment of every other entity. Such literalism would be misleading. The environment has both proximal and distal aspects. Only aspects of an environment which noticeably influence the state of an environed entity are scientifically relevant. "Noticeably influence" implies "functional distance." Physical measures of distance are appropriate in physics because relations between bodies, such as the mutual attraction of masses, are a direct function of the spatial separation between the bodies. There, physical distance is functional distance. This coincidence of measures rarely occurs in sociology.

Which of the two related entities is the environment and which the environed? A man watering a flower is part of the environment of the flower. And the flower is part of the man's environment. The observer's interest, focus, or point of view determines which is called environment. Colloquial speech designates the larger of two related entities—in a sense, that which envelops—as the environmental entity. This bias of spatial magnitude is irrelevant, or merely a parameter, in a scientific proposition stating the interdependence of the entities. However, the relative degrees of impact of each entity on the other are important for engineering or other practical purposes. A change in the state of a man in a gas filled room has little impact on the gas, but a change in the density of the gas may be crucial for the man. The gas, then, is clearly the environmental factor for practical purposes.

Scientifically, it is helpful to think of the environed and its environment as constituting separate clusterings of events, each cluster with its own focus of organization. If the degree of organization drops very low, the *cluster* becomes a *congeries*. If the degree of organization is high, the term *system* becomes appropriate. The existence of several foci for specifying separate clusters of events of a multinuclear cell may be thought of as a single system with several foci of organization.

Environed and environing systems may differ in the principle according to which their constituent events are organized. In a microcosm-macrocosm relationship, the two clusters of events differ in scope and in their foci, but each is organized according to the same principle. City in an environment of cities illustrates this.

The constituent elements of the environmental and the environed systems not only may have separate foci of organization but may be organized according to distinctly different principles. A personality viewed in the light of its social environment is a case in point. The personality is organized around an individual body according to biopsychological principles. The society is organized around a set of interaction norms according to sociological principles. When systems are organized according to different principles, their treatment as a single system of environed and environing events becomes problematic.

To speak, for example, of a man-machine system is to be imprecise. The elements constituting man are organized according to biological or psychosocial principles. The elements constituting machine are organized according to mechanical and physical principles. If one system is an environment for another, they must "naturally influence" each other—there must be an interchange across a common boundary: A climate of opinion is an environment for the behavior of individuals, not an environment for a geographic feature. Boundary interchange mechanisms must be specified (Klausner, 1967). Man and machine may be related through boundary interchanges. Their common boundary is the site of an input-output relation. An example is the interpretation the individual makes of the constraints he must impose on himself to operate the machine. Then, loosely speaking, the man and the machine may be conceived as a single system containing two subsystems.

Similarly, carbon monoxide fumes are part of an individual's environment because this gaseous chemical may enter the bloodstream, affecting the ability of blood cells to take up oxygen and thus denying oxygen support of the physiological system. The boundary interchange is a chemical one, a relation between the chemical processes of the fumes and the chemical processes of the body. When translated in this way, and only by means of such translation, man-environment may be treated as a single system. The same fumes are not a relevant environment for the individual's clothing. Most fabrics and gas, though spatially interpenetrating, are inert with respect to one another.

The absorption of gas in the bloodstream is but one boundary interchange between man and certain monoxide fumes. Posit a chemical change at the olfactory nerve receptors. Then, shifting to a psychosocial boundary, the individual may interpret the stimulus and don a gas mask. In this latter case, the meaning of the gas —its relevance for action—makes it a part of the environment for action. Because of man's ability to symbolize, he may don a gas mask in expectation of gas, without olfactory stimulation. Thus, in the case of man, a physical environment may be relevant even if not present at the moment.

Most of the studies cited earlier conceptualize the physical and social worlds in separate frames of reference without specifying the nature of the boundary processes. The meaning of an association between the physical and the human is thereby hidden from the analyst. A physical fact has a physical environment; a chemical fact a chemical environment; a social fact a social environment; and a psychological fact a psychological environment. Physical and chemical facts may, through interpretation by people, come to share a boundary with social and psychological facts. Neither the common-sense notion of water nor the chemical notion of H_2O is relevant for a sociocultural analysis. Socially, water provides a medium for swimming, fishing, or baptizing; as a physical object it is a social symbol. The physical environmental fact enters social analysis through its transformation into a social fact. The relationship analyzed is that between the socially interpreted physical environment and social action. These two systems are related organically, not mechanically. While water can exist without society, the swimming pool, fishing rod, and baptismal font cannot be conceived independently of social action. From these general definitional considerations we turn to some substantive theories.

The history of theories treating man as an initiator of action in the environment is a record of precursors of an environmental sociology conceived in a voluntaristic framework. This history is shorter than that of the deterministic theories reviewed in the first chapter. While the earlier tradition began with the question of the power of the environment to shape man, this tradition seeks to judge the goodness or evil of man's impact on the environment. Environment, called upon to serve, sometimes responds with expected and at other times with surprising answers.

Geography was the key to understanding universal history according to George Louis Leclere de Buffon's massive *Histoire Naturelle,* published in the late eighteenth century. De Buffon documented the fact that the shaping of the environment did not lead inevitably to social progress. Environmental control can have ambiguous consequences. A paper by Hugh Williamson, a physician, published in 1789 in the *Transactions of the American Philosophical Society,* reported a warming climate in the northern colonies as a result of man-produced deforestation (Glacken, 1960).

George P. Marsh's (1864, p. 43) compendium on the relations of man and nature is subtitled "Physical Geography as Modified by Human Action." His warning against the dangers of imprudent interference with spontaneous arrangements of the organic and inorganic worlds heralds a theme of later human ecologists.

> The ravages committed by man subvert the relations and destroy the balance which nature has established between her organized and inorganic creations; and she avenges herself upon the intruder, by letting loose upon her defaced provinces destructive energies hitherto kept in check by organic forces destined to be

41

his best auxiliaries, but which he has unwisely dispersed and driven from the field of action. When the forest is gone, the great reservoir of moisture stored up in its vegetable mold is evaporated and returns only in deluges of rain to wash away the parched dust into which that mold has been converted.

Marsh had experienced some of man's ravages. He knew of the aridity of the once-forested eastern Mediterranean and was familiar with the smoky pall deposited over London by inefficient coal burners. However, he only guessed at the fury of nature's vengeance for environmental disturbance. Disturbance of that magnitude occurred in the following century. Therefore, it may be inferred that his prophetic admonitions derived less from his observations of environmental pollution and deforestation than from the spirit of cultural ambivalence surrounding man's attempts to control nature. A civilization which was drawing its strength from the taming of nature still carried the ethic of an earlier age and, in the residual light of that earlier ethic, judged its own acts as heresy—an attempt to control God by controling His works. Lynn White (1967) cites a religious root of this "attack on nature." Pagan animism had restrained man. Before one cut a tree it was important to placate the spirit in charge. By destroying pagan animism and rejecting pantheism for a transcendent God, Christianity made it possible to exploit nature. Nature has no reason for existence save to serve man. St. Francis of Assisi sounded a minor theme of protest in preaching to the birds and talking to the wolf, proclaiming the spiritual autonomy of all parts of nature.

The theological objection is based on a failure to assume a spatially and temporally holistic view of the nature upon which man exerts his strength. Short range benefits of segmental environmental control are sometimes "washed away," to borrow Marsh's image, by longer range "unintended consequences."

Such cultural ambivalence and mystery could not but prompt scholarly interest. The theories that failed sought the direct cultural and psychological impacts of a physically conceived environment. Sometimes the line is thin between the theories that fail and those that might not. The difference may be a slight turn of perspective, a small change in the reasoning. The geographer R. H. Whitbeck (1918) observed that religious creeds of forest dwellers are not the same as those of plains people. He concluded that geography predisposes to certain religious forms. Whitbeck reasoned that geographic conditions affect the manner of cultural adaptation, in general, and thus predispose, in particular, to peculiar religious formulations. The slight turn of perspective from that of some other adaptation theories is revealed in Whitbeck's term *predispose*. Adaptation is not a direct function of the physical environmental conditions and of the struggle among species, as the classical model of evolutionary biology suggested. These conditions merely predispose to one or another adaptation. Whitbeck did not carry his insight to its conclusion, to the role of the symbolism of social relations in the selection among possible adaptations.

The resultant shortcomings of Whitbeck's analysis are apparent. The same geographic conditions may support or even stimulate different religions. The Phoenicians, who went to sea, incorporated a fish among their deities. The Sumerians, living not far away on another body of water, infused their worship with concern about the fertility of the land. Societies choose from a repertoire of possible adaptations to any particular environment. The physical character of the environment suggests religious metaphors. Gods would not be placed in the sky by a people confined to subterranean caves. Ancient Israelite and Greek gods resided in mountains. Arabian gods preferred green watering places, and some Assyrian gods thirsted for treed oases.

Geographers Ellsworth Huntington and Sumner Cushing (1921) took the next step in describing social institutions as social adaptations to geography. The physical conditions of location, land forms, bodies of water, soil, and minerals constrain the ways people meet their needs. People meet physical needs—develop occupations —in ways having the greatest promise of success. By interpolating the term *promise of success,* Huntington and Cushing verged on recognition of the decisional act in the adaptational process. By interpolating emergent *occupations,* they prepared the way for the study of the intervention of social roles and the structure of those roles between man and environment.

As has often happened in the history of science, this vista opened by the geographers in the first quarter of the twentieth century had already been explored in the last quarter of the nineteenth century. Frederick LePlay linked geographic conditions to social institutions. He reasoned that the physical environment dictates the economic life that develops, and then economic institutions influence other social institutions (Zimmerman and Frampton, 1935). A theory of this genre accounts for the emergence of a political structure as an adaptation to geography. Publicized by Max Weber nearly half a century ago and more recently developed by Karl Wittfogel (1957), this theory—taking Weber's example— claims that the centralized political system of ancient Egypt grew out of the socioeconomic problems of maintaining the Nile canal system. The interdependence of the canals, and thus of the farmers on their banks, generated a tolerance for central supervision to maintain them and to protect the water rights of communities along the canal.

No doubt the canal, or resource system, and the political system were interdependent. However, the Egyptian decision to develop a canal system presupposed the conception and even the existence of unified political control. The process of developing the canals, involving recruitment and organization of labor as well as conflict among the now riparian settlements, may have induced the government to centralize further. The possibilities of new routes of commerce created by the canal system and the resulting interaction among people from various parts of the littoral region would also help unite them under a central regime. The religious institutions were also affected. Weber argues that a centralized political arrangement provided the basis for the Egyptian notion of a supreme deity (Weber, 1951, p. 20ff).

Sorokin (1928), noting that centralized regimes have arisen under quite varied conditions, treats the theory lightly. Centralization emerged in China with a different form of irrigation system.

Contrariwise, given the conditions of Egypt, other systems of political control could have emerged. The Tigris-Euphrates valley, also dependent on a river system and a net of irrigation canals, was dominated by city states.

Weber's reasoning, from geographic to social conditions, was more sophisticated than that of Whitbeck, LePlay, or Huntington and Cushing. He described social mechanisms intervening between the physical character of the canals and the consequent social organization. Weber's analysis is limited by its commitment to a single line of development. Egyptian political form was one of many possible under the given conditions. Such chain linking of variables through intervening mechanisms was not uncommon during the early twentieth century. A linear theory of evolution was also in vogue then. The possibility of moving in several directions from each point of linkage, the stochastic character of the boundary transition points, was insufficiently appreciated.

Franklin Thomas' (1925) review of an argument relating natural bounty to social stratification illustrates the issue. The argument is that cheap food leads to a population increase, which decreases wages. This drop in wages means decline in the average wealth of laborers, impoverishment of the masses. Impoverishment creates a division of society into rich and poor. Social division opens the way to the subjection of the lower classes. Thomas describes how the potato in Ireland, rice in India, and the date in Egypt— all cheap foods—generated such dismal results.

Herbert Spencer, reasoning from the same initial point, reached the opposite conclusion. Abundance and variety of flora lead to an increase in population. The argument reviewed by Thomas also anticipates this consequence, but there the similarity stops. Thomas continues to reason from a population increase to a drop in wages. Spencer argues that a larger population permits the development of the arts of civilization. This development raises the standard of living. The end is affluence rather than impoverishment.

The two arguments are not totally incompatible because the division of labor—the basis for the development of the arts of civilization—may be organized into a castelike stratification system, as in ancient Greece. The essential point is that a range of social possibilities follows from a population increase. The development of civilization and the lowering of wages are but two sequels. A comparison of the economies and cultures of densely populated Belgium and India illustrates this range. The direction a country takes depends upon other cultural and social factors, including the norms of social organization, the intensity of concern with a productive goal, and the rate of technological innovation.

These theoretical precursors to a new environmental sociology explored the subjective meanings that physical environmental elements might have for social action. The classification of current environmental problem areas has followed some common-sense meanings of physical environmental features—space, air pollution, aridity, wild lands, and altitude. The preface to this book promised a reversal of the perspective—toward a classification of environmentally implicated social action rather than a classification of physical environmental features. However, the tendency to look at the social from the perspective of a physical environmental classification has remained predominant. We would be remiss not to give it more attention here. While a hindrance to the sociological reconceptualization of this field, the physical perspective by no means dampens the effort. The treatment of man-nature relationships as conditioned by the distribution of men in space illustrates this tendency, its possibilities, and its limitations.

Not surprisingly, studies on the relation of man to physical space have appeared in all the social science fields. The philosophical conceptions of Immanuel Kant and David Hume regarding objects in space were the intellectual inheritance of the infant sciences of man. The psychology of space perception has developed its own tradition. Anomalies in the perception of space in psychopathological states or under the influence of drugs are studied for their contribution to the understanding of normal spatial orientation. Jean Piaget (1956) studied the development of space perception in the child. Social psychologists have dealt with space as a perceived field of action. Physical space is converted into social psychological space in the studies of Emory Bogardus (1959). In his work, the physical proximity to which individuals are prepared to admit members of another group becomes an indicator of feelings of identification or sympathy with them. In Kurt Lewin's (1959) graphic presentation of his conception of *life space,* distance in physical space represents the perception of the difficulties to be encountered in the attainment of a personal goal. Social psychologists, influenced partly by territorialist concepts of ethologists and partly by the demands of technology and public policy, have been concerned with the distribution of social activities in a confined space such as a submarine or a space capsule (Altman, 1968).

Sparked by the interest of civil defense authorities in air-raid shelter behavior, by problems of crowding such as occur in concentration camps or ships of the slave trade, investigators have explored the relations among people packed together. The same space may feel more or less crowded depending on how its occupants organize themselves. The concept of *crowded* may be attitudinal rather than simply physical. Families sharing a kitchen may fall over one another. If they set up schedules or organize themselves for mass eating with consolidated cooking, they are less crowded. Crowding is also a function of the number and type of activities, not only the number of people, in a particular area (Klausner and Kincaid, 1956).

The density of social activities within physical space may influence the structuring of those activities. Emile Durkheim, in his *Division of Labor* (1933), recognized physical density as one aspect of moral density or social density. Social density refers to the number of interrelationships within a population, the interaction among partners. The number of relationships, of course, may vary without the physical boundaries of that population varying. However, when the population is more crowded together physically, more opportunities arise for interaction, and thus social density may increase. An increase in social density induces, according to Durkheim, social or structural differentiation, the splitting of tasks into new specialties or occupations.

Current empirical work on the structuring of relations within a spatial area suggests that people seem to arrange themselves at rather regular distances from one another, the distance depending on the social action taking place. Michael Argyle and Janet Dean (1965) found that an individual will stand closer to a person whose eyes are shut than to a person whose eyes are open. Erving Goffman (1963) describes spatial clustering as a *situation*. He defines a *situation* as the "full spatial environment anywhere within which a person becomes a member of a gathering." Rules emerge controlling access to such bounded regions. Within the region, participants tend to distribute themselves cooperatively in the available space. In both the Argyle and Dean and the Goffman illustrations, physical distance is given specific social interactional meaning.

Spatial distance not only is a basis for meaning per se but also controls the occasion for social events. This, too, is implicit in Durkheim's analysis. Placement in space affects the probabilities of encounters which, in turn, affect the likelihood of establishing social relations. Leon Festinger, Stanley Schachter, and Kurt Back (1950) studied two student housing projects. The relative positions of entrances to various houses affected the chances that the occupants would encounter one another and develop passive contacts, nodding acquaintanceships. Friendships tended to grow out of those passive contacts, so that the people living in the same building or court were more likely to work and play together than were people in different buildings or courts. This generalization is most meaningful for predicting face to face relationships where groups have already been established on the basis of some common interest. In the Goffman example, space is a facility possessing meanings of social acceptance. In the Festinger et al. (1950) example, space is a condition providing opportunities for establishing social relations. In both cases space enters as a physical parameter, and its effects vary with a physical measure of distance. In neither case is the relation of space to action deterministic. An element of decision enters.

Ecologists, graphing the development of cities, describe the spatial distribution of a population around a central place. For the ecologist, *friction of space* is something to be overcome through transportation and communication. Here physical space changes its functional characteristics under the impact of a cultural condition.

On Man in His Environment

As transportation technology improves, the same physical distance offers less friction. Attitudinal interpretations of friction, such as the differential willingness of people in Tucson and in Boston to drive distances or their attitudes toward different modes of transportation, receive scant notice in the ecological literature. But, if space were interpreted in the light of such attitudinal factors, the variation in densities of population around central places would be better explained. Culture and attitudes influence the distribution of people in space.

Ecologists and anthropologists have examined this last proposition in reverse. The way population is distributed in space affects the speed of cultural diffusion. Ecological studies have placed the physical term between two cultural ones. Transportation and communication—cultural developments—allow man to participate in a progressively wider habitat. As a result, populations occupying radically different natural areas may come to have similar consuming and occupational habits (Hawley, 1950).

The way a people relates itself to space influences other aspects of its culture. The sparse population of a forest may engage in hunting but is not likely to build Aztec-like pyramids, unless that population collects itself in urban centers. Lawrence Krader (1955), an anthropologist, studied the relation of Central Asian nomadic pastoralism to the natural environment. The sparsely settled steppe of Central Asia is "filled" by its nomadic occupants, who recognize rights to pasturages and fix seasonal movements. Turkic and Mongol nomads keep different proportions of cattle, goats, and sheep. Among Turkic nomads, sheep are relatively more frequent than goats. Among the Mongols, the reverse is the case. This difference is explained in terms of differences in pasturages. The pig does not appear in either group because it is incompatible with nomadic pastoralism. Secondarily, among the Mongols, Islam discourages pig raising.

Krader does not arrive at firmly supported generalizations because too few classes of environment are included. Would the negative correlation between nomadism and pig raising hold for a number of nomadic peoples under various spatial environmental conditions? Krader's work, while not leading to easy generalizations, exemplifies an important type of case study on the relation between economy and habitat. Clifford Geertz (1963), also an anthropologist, provides another illustration of the cultural mediation of the man-space relationship. Geertz defined space in terms of the activities which fill it. Despite a burgeoning population, the Javanese still maintain the overall outlines of traditional agriculture. In adapting to population pressure, they drive the elements of traditional agriculture to even higher degrees of ornate elaboration. He terms the resulting intensive labor method *agricultural involution.*

Walter Firey's (1960) theory of man-environment relations tempers an ecological with a sociocultural perspective. He uses the concept of a *resource process* to refer to recurrent events involving the same combination of human and biophysical factors. The habit of plowing with oxen exemplifies a resource process. A resource process may be analyzed into its ecological, ethnological, and economic aspects. Ecologically, a resource process tends toward equilibrium with the physical constraints of a habitat. Some processes— fishing, for example—are not possible in some habitats, such as deserts. Ethnologically, the beliefs and techniques—including technology—which define the meaning of a resource must be consistent with the values of the people engaged in that process. Economically, the resource process must be gainful. The successful resource process would be the optimum one on all these levels at once. A set of resource processes constitutes a *resource system.* A resource system is, to follow the title of Firey's book, a man-mind-land system. Man's adaptation to the characteristics of a resource system follows a principle of willing conformity, a voluntarism under certain physical and social constraints.

Reference to a resource system is loose use of language in the terms of our earlier discussion of the concept of environment. Each of the three interrelated aspects is itself a system integrated in its own way. The resource system is a product of boundary interchanges between the other three systems. The ecological system is integrated around exchanges among its members. Man cannot withdraw produce from the field faster than processes of organic decay restore the chemical composition of the land unless man adds organic or other fertilizers. Firey's focus is on bioecology rather than human ecology. An ethnological system emerges from a tendency toward consistency among the norms or standards which govern various activities. A form of animal husbandry in a society tends to be consistent with religious rules. The economic system focuses around the allocation of goods and facilities. The results of the allocation process register as gains and losses to various participants in the system.

Firey presents the case of the Tiv in Nigeria to illustrate the interaction of ecological, ethnological, and economic demands. Ecologically, the land of the Tiv should remain fallow for certain periods and be planted with regenerative bush. The economic requirement of the Tiv society is for maximum cash crops at any given time. Ethnologically, Tiv values direct that land is to be exchanged outside the line of immediate kinship. The result of the combination of the economic and ethnological requirements is that each family group tries to get as much as possible out of the land during its tenure. Since it will pass to another family group, there is less incentive to allow it to lie fallow; thus, the ecological need is not met. The land is eventually exhausted and the whole resource system breaks down, leaving the Tiv impoverished.

Firey's broad designations—ecological, ethnological, and economic—signify three conceptualized elements in a resource system. Research requires further specification and operationalization of these concepts. Firey includes meanings derived from values but gives less attention to those resting on social organization and social institutions. His analysis considers economic aspects of social interaction. The analysis could be extended to other forms of social organization. The political system—the structure of power—influences environmental definitions. Acts contributing to the solidarity and differentiation of the social system, the bases of system integration, also affect resource systems. Mechanisms within the social system which regulate tensions and assure the continuity of its fundamental values also define the meaning of its physical environment. Finally, although he uses the term *mind* in his title, Firey does not develop a very probing psychological analysis. Personality factors enter into the perception of the environment and so select the resource processes that may emerge over the actors' personal horizons.

The work of Piaget, Bogardus, Lewin, and others in psychology, of Durkheim, Festinger et al., Firey, and Goffman among others in social psychology and sociology, and of Krader and Geertz among others in anthropology brings us to the heart of a voluntaristic conception of the relation of man and nature. Durkheim's conception of moral density, Krader's conception of the exigencies of a nomadic existence, and Geertz's treatment of agricultural technology under increasing population pressure all have a common theme. Human action develops, fundamentally, in terms of its own exigencies—out of the problems of human beings attempting to live in conflict or concert. The problems presented by the natural world emerge in human action. They appear on this level as sociocultural or psychological problems, not as physical problems per se. Man interprets the physical datum by applying values and motives which have been generated in human interaction. Physical facts are, by means of these interpretations, transformed into social facts. The model may be called voluntaristic because elements of choice and judgment are crucial to understanding the many ways man orients and organizes himself vis à vis the world of nature.

CHAPTER IV

☆☆☆☆☆☆☆☆☆☆☆☆☆☆☆☆☆☆☆☆☆☆

Elements for an Environmental Theory

🌳🌳🌳🌳🌳🌳🌳🌳🌳🌳🌳🌳🌳🌳🌳

S ociologists, when thinking substantively, tend to distinguish physical from social environmental objects on the grounds that the former do not literally interact or assume independent attitudes in the action sequence. This distinction cannot be maintained sharply. First, the actor—in planning his action—adapts attitudinally to constraints imposed by physical objects. The constraints themselves, however, are a function of the perception of the actor as well as of the physically defined characteristics of the object. A hero may jump a hurdle which a coward of equal physical competence finds insuperable. Second, characteristics of the

53

actor's personality or of his group may be attached to physical objects. In totemic systems, animals, plants, and geological features represent aspects of group life. The ways human beings define and act with reference to physical facts transform them into social facts. The meaning of the physical world is, of course, not exhausted in its symbolization in human action.

Sociologists, when thinking methodologically, tend to distinguish between physical and social action on the basis of the frames of reference used in physical and sociological analyses. A physical analysis locates its objects on space-time coordinates and classifies them in terms of quantified units of mass, length, and time. A sociological analysis locates its phenomena on coordinates of symbolic meaning, as acts and actors and structures of acts and actors, and classifies them in terms of quantified attributes such as choice, relative power, approach-avoidance, and motivational interest. The term *role* as defined by the sociologist does not exist in the repertoire of biological or physical concepts, just as the term *atomic weight* does not fit as an element in the theoretical net drawn by sociologists. Talcott Parsons (1949, p. 47) considered the relevance of the physical to the social schemata in the continuation of the quotation cited at the beginning of Chapter One.

> The student of action . . . is interested in phenomena with an aspect not reducible to action terms only in so far as they impinge on the schema of action in a relevant way—in the role or conditions or means. . . . Above all, atoms, electrons or cells are not to be regarded as units for the purpose of the theory of action. Unit analysis of any phenomenon beyond the point where it constitutes an integral means or condition of action leads over into terms of another theoretical scheme.

Parsons' model includes among its terms an *actor* (individual or collective) who evaluates, on the basis of social norms, the subjective *end*—or future state toward which action is oriented—as well as the choice among ends, and among *means* for attaining these ends. The choice is made in the context of a *situation* of action which includes other actors and their actions as well as physical objects. These physical objects enter the analysis, however, only insofar as they are "reducible to action terms."

Like the substantive distinction, the methodological one can be strictly held only as a heuristic device. A condition is an element which remains constant throughout the process. Remaining constant in the methodological sense means being considered outside the system of interest. The physical condition does not remain constant with reference to action in several senses. First, if action continues over time, the physical objects may change—perhaps as a result of the action itself. Second, to the extent that there are changes in the *actor, end,* or *norm,* the meaning of the physical object for action changes. Manhattan Island has played a different role for its current inhabitants than for their Indian predecessors. Third, several participant actors may differ in their interpretations of the physical object and may teach these variant meanings to one another, each discovering new aspects of the object. Fourth, where a concrete sequence of acts is being analyzed, the actor may be dealing with the physical object from several perspectives. For example, a terrain imposes certain conditions which affect the tactics of a military commander who thereby discovers a new aspect of the object. Land contours influence communications between his men, the form and intensity of contact with the enemy, and the casualty rate. These factors influence his deployment decisions and the structure of command. In trying to incorporate the factor of terrain, the tactician must allow for the changing definitions of terrain and the changing of the terrain itself. As the troops move across terrain, it sets new problems for the commander and his men. As he takes casualties, the use of terrain must be reassessed. Deployment, command structure, and casualty rates are not a direct function of the physical character of terrain but depend on the way the military action is organized with respect to the terrain. The way the action is organized depends—among other things—on military doctrine, a sociocultural factor.

All of these elements affect the meaning of action. To discover the meaning, the analyst asks several questions: What does the actor think he is accomplishing? What does he think are the roles of others and of physical objects in his plan to accomplish that end? Why does he choose to strive to accomplish one rather than another end? How does this particular selected goal fit into other goals he or other actors may have?

Answers to these questions are sought on three levels of abstraction beyond that of the manifest replies. One level of meaning derives from the organization of acts around given individuals. This is a personality analysis. The second derives from the ordering of interaction among numbers of individuals. This is a societal analysis. A third focus is on the world of meanings in themselves— the way in which they are ordered as they are internalized in the personality and institutionalized in the social system. This is a cultural analysis. On each of these levels, three modes of meaning may be discerned—cognitive, affective, and evaluative.

The following pages illustrate these modes of meaning in social action oriented toward the natural environment. Then analysis on the three levels of meaning—personality, society, and culture—will be illustrated. The discussions of the modes of meaning and of meaning on the societal level will be phrased in the language of Parsons' general theory of action. The relevance of natural environmental events for the study of human action will be specified in more detail than in Parsons' basic schema (Parsons and Shils, 1951). Although the Parsons framework is applicable for cultural and personality analysis, it is rarely employed by the anthropologist and psychologist. Consequently, those presentations will follow the more customary language of workers in those fields.

A social meaning is composed of three types of judgments. In one respect, the meaning consists of factual, objective, or cognitive information about the environment. Cognition of environmental potentialities are preconditions for action with respect to the environment. The body of knowledge called natural science and the knowledge of technology are the repositories of formal and publicly shared cognitions of the physical environment. A cognition defines the instrumental role of an environmental feature in the cultural system. Inca culture used gold ornamentally. Pizarro saw it as a

56

source of power. Oil can be thought of as a source of annoying sludge puddles or as fuel for lamps. These various cognitions relate some abstracted attribute of the physical fact of social actions. The meanings are primarily rooted in and controlled by the exigencies of the social action. The different interpretations reflect everyday cultural interests of various societies.

Academic disciplines are more consciously and formally constructed knowledge. The theoretical framework of a discipline is its formal culture. Disciplinary interpretations of the environment are also rooted in the social backgrounds of the disciplinarian and, at the same time, reflect the interests of the special academic community. A sociologist or psychologist may ask whether the oil appears as sludge to be cleared from property, as fuel for the lamps of scholars, or as a lubricant for factory machinery. An economist may begin his analysis after the attribute has been defined. If the event is called sludge, how much expense will people incur to remove it? If it is a fuel for lamps or a lubricant, what is the level of demand for these attributes? While the sociologist seeks to account for the type of meaning, the economist's measure of demand —or the derivative measure of elasticity of demand—reflects the importance and intensity of a particular meaning (utility) at a time and place. The economist, like the sociologist, does not deal directly with oil as a physical fact but with the demand for sludge removal, fuel, or lubricant. As a practical ellipsis, he reads the aggregate results of the demand for these economically relevant attributes as a demand for oil.

Environmental meaning also involves emotions about the environment. Is the environment emotionally intimate or distant? Is it friendly or hostile? If the environment is considered hostile— either because it is damaging or because the individual projects his own hostility toward it—he may be inclined to conquer, tame, or develop it. The reverse is not necessarily true. An individual may seek to develop the environment without feeling hostility towards it.

Cognitive and emotional components are intertwined in the question of environmental control. Robert Kates (1962) found that people in a flood plain differed in their expectation of future flooding. This judgment depended more on their past direct experience than on indirect experience through information provided by others. An individual's own experience involves a self-relating emotional as well as a cognitive component. Information communicated by others is primarily cognitive and less likely to crystallize into a judgment to act. Kates (1962, p. 140) says "a major limitation to human ability to use improved flood hazard information is the basic reliance on experience."

In a similar study by Thomas Saarinen (1966) on the perception of drought hazard, TAT-type picture stories were used to elicit attitudes toward the environmental threat. This method of data gathering is especially suited to reveal emotional as well as cognitive meanings. Saarinen found that personal past experience significantly influenced farmers' estimation of the frequency of past drought. But he added another personality dimension. Farmers were generally overly optimistic and underestimated the frequency with which droughts had occurred (compared with a physical measure of aridity). This optimism was consistent with their self-images as resolute, determined individuals standing up to environmental buffeting, fighting back, and refusing to give in.

In addition to the cognitive and emotional components, there is a third component of an environmental meaning, an appreciative or evaluative one. Is the environment beautiful or ugly, crowded or spacious? The same physical feature may esthetically irritate one and please another. Gilbert White (1966), a geographer sensitive to perceptual factors in environmental interpretation, illustrated this with respect to decisions to act on an air or water pollution problem. People disagree as to whether a given body of water is dirty, whether a body of air is hazy or murky. Individuals apply different standards in assessing the satisfactory or unsatisfactory quality of environments.

An appreciative judgment does not directly dictate the character of action. Some judge their environment dirty and love it, even obstruct efforts to change its soiled condition. Some social groups perceive themselves as waste producers, and others take the role of waste receivers. The latter feel culturally bound to have waste cast upon them. Indian untouchables assume this role. If people dirty their environment and remain part of it, the dirt may have a meaning for them dfferent from what it has for proponents of a clean-up campaign. Clean-up programs would not evoke enthusiasm in a group that feels a place is sterile and cold if it is too spick and span. The terms *dirt* and *filth* may not always be appropriate for disorder as perceived by outsiders.

The meanings of environment for the individual and for society—as well as the cultural symbols themselves—may be analyzed into their cognitive, affective, and evaluative modes. The organization of meaning with reference to personality, culture, and society will now be illustrated. This will be followed by some notes on analysis of its cultural and societal organization.

Individuals interpret the meaning of a resource process in its relevance to the self. Some of these interpretations are given by the culture and internalized by the individual. Primitive notions of history evolve around an identification between the self and a physical feature, a place or sign of a place where something of significance to the self has occurred. Thus a holy mountain, site of a theophany, perhaps associated with a myth of origin, takes on a special significance for a whole group.

Such identifications involve a self and an object separate but related. When boundaries between self and the outer world become blurred, identification gives way to an identity of the two. At the beginning of life, this is the natural state. The neonate does not seem to recognize boundaries between self and world. Gradually, with experiences, the infant learns to distinguish itself from other human beings and from its nonhuman environment. Certain psychopathological conditions institute a regressive process in which the sense of this distinction is lost. In this magic view, events happening to outside objects are experienced as happening to the self.

Harold Searles (1960), a psychiatrist, discovered through his clinical practice that even normal individuals may suffer anxiety about losing the ability to distinguish between themselves and their environment. For this reason some people fear encounters with the natural environment. A regressive process which blurs the boundary between the self and the natural environment touches even deeper layers of the personality than one which confuses boundaries between the self and other people. For this reason, becoming one with nature, according to Searles, is a more sublime or oceanic feeling than being one with another person.

Michael Balint (1959) found that personalities could be classified in terms of whether they wanted to grasp onto objects or to escape from them. This personality classification helped explain thrill seeking through flying, parachuting, or at fun fairs. Herbert Wright and Roger Barker's (1950) study of psychological ecology is one of the most systematic enterprises to gather data on environmental interpretations by the individual. They recorded the daily activities of the total child population in a small midwestern town to "measure the parameters" of psychological laws for different "cultures and conditions of life." Behavior is embedded in a "psychological habitat" which includes all the things and events in a child's environment that have meaning for him. Through psychological interpretations the material-cultural world becomes part of this habitat. At the center of this environment is the child himself, a unique organization of abilities and needs. Particular "behavior settings" such as the drug store or the 4-H Club come to be perceived by the people of the community as appropriate for particular kinds of behavior. With this observation the Wright-Barker analysis passes from the personality to the social or cultural levels.

Neither the outside world of objects nor the self is of one piece. Individuals relate different aspects of their personalities to selected external objects. The self image is, in general, composed of several identifications, some corresponding to the liked "good me" and others to the disliked "bad me" (Sullivan, 1953, p. 61ff). The characters in a dream, for instance, may stand for several formulations of the self, some characters representing the liked and others the disliked self. Socially, one may be attracted to persons who stimulate the liked and repelled by those who stimulate the disliked parts of the self.

Identification with the natural may complement identification with the human environment. Some individuals identify the natural environment with the good and approved part of the self while identifying the social environment with the rejected images of the self. The myth of withdrawal and return is often played out as withdrawal from a difficult social environment to a resuscitating natural environment to obtain strength for the renewed social engagement. J. K. Galbraith reports this dichotomous attitude among some conservationists. He says, "The conservationist is a man who concerns himself with the beauties of nature in roughly inverse proportion to the number of people who can enjoy them" (Jarrett, 1958). Contrariwise, some individuals show marked social consciousness while rejecting the world of nature. Which aspect of an individual's self is identified with or stimulated by the natural environment is an empirical question.

Aside from good and bad selves, all individuals harbor—in varying ratios—both a feminine and a masculine principle (Freud, 1927; Fromm, 1943). The feminine principle interprets the self as a passive recipient in need of defense. The masculine principle interprets the self as the locus of struggle and active design. The natural environment is sometimes identified with the feminine and the social environment with the masculine principles.

The imagery is ancient. In the metaphor *motherland,* the earth is mother; in the metaphor *fatherland,* reference is to the fathers who possessed the land. David Lowenthal and Hugh Prince (1964) capture this image along with a strong evaluative component in reporting attitudes of the partisans of the English countryside. They have personified Britain as Beauty, a goddess in the clutches of the Beast, the British people. "The Beast is a litter lout, foul industrialist, landed oligarch or pretentious suburbanite, townsman, intellectual, sportsman, raucous hiker, bluebell picker, sunbather, and—most hated of all—a motorist" (p. 327).

The imagery is also reflected in the term virginal as applied to untouched land. Calvin Stillman's (1966) plea that natural beauty requires leaving a place alone carries this image. The protected wife image of nature may supplant that of the virgin when a user seeks exclusive rights. The individual who seeks to enjoy nature while hindering others from sharing that enjoyment may be expressing an almost sexual jealousy. The created and protected artificial beauty of a Japanese garden may be an appropriate cultural variant of the wifely imagery. The rugged, possessive individualism of the frontier, as depicted by Evon Vogt (1955), suggests the image of subduing or taming a woman. The fear of exhausting nature by use, the elitist (keeping out the masses) attitude, and the desire for isolation (from the masses who pollute) may also have some roots in this feminine conception of nature. These images of nature are developed more sensitively by some novelists and poets than by scientific writers.

An association of feminine imagery with nature is significant for the present study insofar as it is reified and influences human action toward nature. Theodore Roosevelt archetypically related to nature as if it were a woman to be subdued and protected. He was a man who despised other men, stoutly defended womanhood, conquered the wildlands, and gave a strong impetus to the conservation movement. These personal images are drawn from the culture's repertoire.

Anthropologists have studied religious and magical symbols based on nature. As noted in the earlier chapters, they have also documented survival-linked cultural adaptations to natural conditions. Anthropological research also produced its share of theories that failed to establish an association between environmental features and culture. Betty Meggars (1954) recalls how Clark Wissler had proposed that the cultures of tribal groups living on the same continent will differ according to the climate, the flora, and the fauna of their habitats. Subsequent researchers failed to verify this hypothesis. Meggars attributed the failure to their use of the geographer's landscape classifications. Climate, flora, and fauna must be reclassified socially in order to assess their impact on the cultural norms and values governing social life.

Climate, flora, and fauna on the one hand, and the state of technology on the other jointly determine agricultural productivity. Increased agricultural productivity in a nonindustrial setting allows a greater density of population. The denser a population, the greater the tendency to more specialized division of labor. New occupational roles emerge with their concomitant cultural patterns. Thus, the significant correlation is between culture and the socio-culturally relevant concept of agricultural productivity rather than between culture and the environment as classified by geographers and naturalists. Meggars reports that when the land occupied by the tribal groups studied by Wissler was classified in terms of pro-ductive agricultural potential, including the cultural factor of tech-nology, and the division of labor was treated as an intervening vari-able, the Wissler hypothesis was sustained. The transforming bound-ary mechanism is the cultural interpretation of the environment based on a mix of technology and land, the aggregating of people, the resultant change in social organization, and the new cultural norms accompanying the new social structure. Here, at least three boundary concepts intervene between a physical and a cultural fact.

There is a long history, some of which is cited above, of at-tempts to relate major geographic features and culture. A geo-graphic feature, under given conditions of technology, affects the movement and settlement of members of a society. This influence has a number of cultural implications. A physical barrier to com-merce retards cultural diffusion. A small body of water is less a barrier to cultural diffusion than a large one, other factors held constant. Even modern transportation and communication do not entirely negate this influence. It is important to remember that the facts that enter the cultural equation are rate of social interaction, technological advance, or change in attitude toward crossing the water. These facts change the sociocultural meaning of the body of water without changing its physical meaning.

However, the less extreme the feature, the more leeway there is for social variability. Some miniature geographic situations illustrate this well. As noted earlier, the arrangement of residential buildings influences the pattern of neighborhood interaction (Fes-tinger, et al., 1950). Architectural arrangement of offices influences communication patterns between the members of a firm simply by weighting the probabilities of face to face encounters. The rate of communication flow, in turn, influences the nature and degree of the firm's productive activities.

63

In both of these miniature cases, interests or statuses of individuals may override the influence of spatial layout on interaction and communication patterns. A vice-president of a corporation will wend his way to the president's office more often than would the branch manager even if the first route is more roundabout. New residents meet neighbors with similar political sympathies (perhaps because a friend and veteran resident introduces them to others in his circle).

The human ecological pattern is more affected by a physical feature when the culture is less developed. The correlation that Wissler anticipated between culture and habitat is more marked at a low level of cultural development. A study by Joseph Birdsell (Bressler, 1966) demonstrated an inverse relation between the size of an Australian aborigine tribal area and the amount of rainfall. A. I. Hallowell (1949) found that the size of Algonkian hunting grounds varied with the abundance of game, a physical characteristic of the habitat. However in Algonkian society—more culturally developed than that of Australian aborigines—the size of hunting grounds also depended on the degree of competition for fur-bearing animals between the Indians and the white trappers, a factor meshing physical characteristics and social relations. Frank Speck (1915) found that—among the Algonkian—property claims reflected the relation of the claimant to the consanguinous family through which the land was inherited. The concept *property* is an extension of the rules of ownership and thus of social organization. The meaning of land is its interpretation by such cultural rules.

In modern society cultural factors reach their greatest importance, relative to physical conditions, in explaining action. Walter Firey (1947) showed that the value of land in Boston was not simply a function of location with respect to natural features or to the remainder of the city. Land value was also a function of symbolic meanings with which properties had become invested through the social character of the population residing in the area. The Beacon Hill area, the locus of a social elite, consistently drew high rent although the shape of the city about it changed. In Firey's words, "the characteristics of space are not those belonging to it as a natural object of the physical world but are those which result from its being a symbol for a cultural system" (p. 33). Thus, the importance of the cultural relative to the physical element varies positively with the sophistication of the technical culture and negatively with the extremity of the environmental feature.

In the above illustration it is not easy to grasp what is meant by *extremity* of a physical feature. An additional illustration from acoustics may help, because the physical intensity of sound is given to precise measurement. The *annoyingness* of a low intensity sound is due primarily to the meanings the sound carries. A dripping faucet or a neighbor's radio may induce a sharp reaction. In the first case an acoustic rhythm imprisons attention, and in the second there is a violation of notions of acoustical privacy. A high intensity sound, however, may have physiological effects largely independent of the symbolic meaning of the sound. For example, nerve endings can be deadened, or—if a person is enveloped in sound—ego barriers may be broken down and the person can become stupefied.

In all of the above examples, the physical was treated as prior in time to the symbolic element. The physical feature was presented and responded to interpretively. The reasoning may be reversed. The environment may be fashioned so as to serve as a symbol expressing what man conceives of himself to be. Here psychological and cultural analyses converge. David Lowenthal and Hugh Prince (1964, 1965) sensitively illustrate the symbolic idolization of self in the environmental medium. The English, Lowenthal and Prince remark, think of themselves as admirers of a bucolic past. They recreate their self-image by creating a landscape tamed, trimmed, and humanized on the one hand, and on the other hand irregular and picturesque—an "elegant pastoral" framed in deciduous trees. Litter is removed. The unsightly is concealed behind facades.

Nations probably differ in the extent to which they shape a cultural self image out of environmental clay. The English illustration is repeated in the clean geometric landscapes of mechanically-minded Americans and in the elaborate landscapes of the convoluted

French and Spanish selves. René Dubos' (1965, p. xviii) phrase "use of the environment for self actualization" expresses this effort.

Environmental sculpting is not unrequited. The environment resists being shaped. The sculptor compromises and changes himself in the process. To express his self through a garden, man becomes a gardener, organizing his activity around fertile times and places. Man offers the self-change as a contribution in his negotiation with nature. This is part of what may be meant by the term *adaptation* if it is withdrawn from the deterministic context in which it was discussed in Chapter Two. Franklin Thomas (1925) argues that the environment's principal social role is to create cultural conditions to which man adapts. One might say that man adapts by evolving cultural forms which prescribe interpretations of the environment, including the formal development of interpretations through science and technology; by evolving forms of social organization which—considering environmental constraints—employ environment as a means to the attainment of social goals; and by evolving psychological attitudes toward the environment congruent with these social and cultural forms, especially as they are reflected in his personality.

The way some physical *fact* of the environment is enveloped by cultural meanings is documented by cultural anthropologists. Psychologists describe the processes by which these meanings are internalized by individuals. It is necessary to refer to lingusitic philosophers—including semanticists—who provide a technical analysis of the process on the cultural level by which *word* and *object* are related. Charles Morris (1946) calls attention to the requirement that "signs" be borne by "sign vehicles" or material objects. Willard Quine (1960) argues that our understanding of physical things is only initially referable to the sensory stimuli they produce in our receptors. The meaning of what we perceive is conditioned by the confirmation of those perceptions which we enjoy from others. Thus, the meanings are not literally objective but are intersubjective. They depend on the prior linguistic or cultural matrix into which they are introduced—on what Quine calls the "interanimation of sentences." These are philosophical leads for the empirical analysis of man's cultural relation to nature.

The meaning of environmental objects may be considered in the light of the function they subserve for the system in which they participate. Generally, this is a physical, scientific, or engineering system or the practical, mechanical system of everyday life. Physical objects were considered above in terms of their function for the self in a personality system and for the social relational rules in a cultural system. We turn now to the function or meaning of physical facts for the social system.

Subserving a function implies an impact on the working of its system. It may involve the contribution of some action, say a resource process, to the solution of system problems. A resource process is tied to a particular form of social organization. The election of one or another process depends upon whether the society is organized to exploit the resource or is capable of reconstructing itself to do so. James Downs (1960) provides an example of social organizational change imposed by the domestication of animals. A hunting society that would domesticate animals must become sufficiently sedentary to tend the animals in one place or—as a pastoral people—in an organized sequence of places. The society must also be affluent enough to divert energy from food production to the domestic experiment. In the process of domestication, members of the society develop new skills and living patterns. These may include changes in concepts of property and wealth. Domestication has a number of social functions—some economic, some political, and some religious. Each social institution interprets physical facts in terms of its own exigencies.

Talcott Parsons, Robert Bales and Edward Shils (1953) distinguish four problems in the maintenance of any social system. Two of these concern the relation between the system in question and external systems, that is, input-output relations. The first of these two involves input of environmental information to the system to enable it to adapt to its environment. This is the *adaptive* problem. The second problem is to engage the environment in such a way as to enable the system to attain its goals, to interact with other social systems. This is the *goal attainment* problem. The other two problems are internal to the social system in question. Thus, the third problem is to regulate relationships among the elements which constitute the system. This is the system *integrative* problem. The fourth problem concerns the need of an ongoing system for background support. On the one hand the background consists of a fund of basic knowledge, values, and norms to direct the system. These factors provide a latent resource of symbolic objects for solution of the previous three types of system problems. On the other hand, the system requires energy regulation, mechanisms to provide momentum in the chosen direction. Parsons refers to this fourth problem, in terms of its value, orientational, and motivational aspects, as a *pattern maintenance–tension management* problem.

If an act, or set of acts, contributes to the solution of any of these problems, Parsons speaks of the act as subserving an adaptive, goal attaining, integrative or pattern maintaining–tension management function for the social system. Social institutions are large patterns of such acts which—as a pattern—can subserve any of these functions. Institutions may be classified by the functions they subserve for the larger society. Economic institutions, concerned with the organization of environmental inputs to society, contribute particularly to the adaptive functions. Physical objects are relevant in terms of their significance as goods or services. (*Significance* is a key word in the previous sentence. The significance of goods is their meaning in an economic frame of reference—primarily, their price, supply, etc.) Economic institutions, acting politically as well as economically, regulate the allocation of goods and services between a society and other societies and among the various sectors within a society. Sociological research in this area is illustrated by Neil Smelser's (1959) study of the British cotton industry. He analyzed such social phenomena as the developing division of factory labor, changes in the structure of the family, and the growth of trade unions in the light of the industrial conversion and marketing of a physical object, cotton.

Political institutions, or the polity, subserve the goal attainment function of the broader society. Here physical objects are relevant in terms of their significances as sources of power. Political institutions use territory as an arena of power and employ physical force to gain compliance. Halford Mackinder's (1942) geopolitical theory that to rule East Europe is to command the heartland, a center from which dominance may be further extended, exemplifies a relation between the use of space and power. Ralf Dahrendorf (1959) treats the structuring of society in terms of conflict theory and of power based in part on the control of resources. Recent work in military sociology such as that of Stanislaw Andrzejewski (1954) relates the internal power structure of a society to the way it uses violence for internal control and to impose its will on other societies.

Social integration is a matter of ordering elements within the system. Mechanisms of social control contribute to social integration. Systems of social stratification, in that they regulate positions and the occupants of positions relative to one another, are also integrative in function. Physical objects in their significance as weapons are part of social control. Bounded territories defining areas of group habitation function integratively. Forms of social organization necessary for coping with disruptive environmental events maintain social integration in the face of special stress. The field of disaster research, as summarized by George Baker and Dwight Chapman (1962), deals with the appearance of an emergency social system, a mechanism for maintaining social order in response to sudden natural environmental change.

Juridical, educational, and, in some respects, religious institutions contribute to the solution of pattern maintenance and tension management problems. Here the physical object enters in its significance as a reducer of social tensions or an object of knowledge. Studies in the relation of drugs and society—such as Howard Becker's study (1963) of the social control of marijuana use—as well as recreation research relate to the maintenance of motivation to fill social roles. Lee Benson's work (1960) on the role of land as a resource treats it in terms of its pattern maintenance function. The existence of *free land,* a frontier, has implications for the viability of a capitalistic property system. Benson shows how, at the close of the last century, an ideology emerged around the notion that public land would be exhausted. Populations which were difficult to assimilate would pile up in urban areas and present a threat to our institutions. This led to a demand for immigration restriction, a basic reordering of national values.

These four functional-institutional categories force the analyst to think of the relation of an act, a role, or an institution to the broad social system. Physical facts are then interpreted with reference to their significance for the function of the institution in which they participate. A similar analysis could be pursued on a more microscopic level, showing the significance of physical facts for the roles and statuses which constitute the institutions or even for the norms which define the behavior constituting the roles.

A fictitious example of a resource-related decision in terms of its social and personal meanings may help to clarify some of the abstract definitions above as well as to illustrate ways of systematizing thought about the relation of man and nature. This is but one of a large variety of scenarios which might be developed from the same initial point, because the consequence of each step is stochastic.

Let us suppose that a mineral resource is discovered in a remote African kingdom. A foreign investor finds it economically more profitable to extract and reduce the ore on the spot than to incur the larger transportation costs for the raw material. The indigenous population, traditionally engaged in homecrafts, is judged to have good potential for mastering extractive and reductive tasks. The investor builds his plant and establishes training centers for personnel.

Some impacts on the society are felt almost immediately. Young men are drawn from villages into a growing urban center near the plant (a change in the allocation or distribution of personnel in the kingdom is a societal pattern maintenance problem). With new technical knowledge and the wealth and expanded social horizons which follow from it, the young men assert independence of patriarchal familial control. They establish nuclear families, setting up independent households with their wives and a smaller than usual number of children. (The change in family structure has implications for the stratification system, specifically the bases of legitimating prestige and social authority, and so affects the form of integration of the society.) The years pass. The legitimacy of patriarchal authority becomes questionable. Struggles between sons and fathers ensue, creating a family condition which David McClelland (1961) argues produces achievement-oriented personalities (an impact on the personality level which will have further societal implications). Achievement-oriented young men, products of these families, congregate in the new cities.

New forms of organization and authority have not yet crystallized to replace the traditional social ties and communal norms rapidly being abandoned. A rising rate of delinquency reflects this transition in the social structure. (Lack of legitimate norms and ineffective mechanisms of social control are dysfunctional for system integration.) The technologically trained men constitute a new elite who, finding the road to monarchical government positions blocked by members of the traditional elite, press for a greater share of political power. They succeed in overthrowing the king and installing a military junta. (Change in source of recruitment of ruling class and installation of a new government is a change in the polity or goal attainment system of the society.) The junta promulgates a law nationalizing the industry and expelling the foreign investors. (A change in economic rules affects the pattern maintenance system of the society.) The government of the foreign investor sends warships to prevent export of the metal to other countries. (From the point of view of the investors' country, social control is being extended with a colonially integrative aim. The economic blockade, from the internal point of view of the African state, affects its adaptation to its external environment.)

With the exception of the reference to socialization of achievement-oriented children, this scenario has been restricted to societal meanings of the resource process. Development of the resources meant a change in the population ecology, the power structure of the kingdom, and the rules under which it lived. The physical objects—the ore in this case—derive their meanings from the way they are embedded in these social action systems. The physical properties of the ore, its location, or the ratio of metal to waste are constraints upon the social meanings it may acquire. With respect to the original economic decision, the ore is relevant in terms of the demand for it in particular markets. As labor is organized around it, it comes to be significant as part of the pattern maintenance system, in this case an occasion for urbanization. The various significances which the ore might have for these action systems are not all direct. In the last case, the implication of the ore for the redistribution of manpower has to do with its location. However, even more fundamentally, this pattern maintenance significance is derivative from the significance of the ore in an economic frame of reference as a marketable commodity. This is what is meant by the interdependence of conceptual terms in a theoretical net or—to borrow Quine's felicitous phrase cited above—the interanimation of sentences.

The scenario could have dealt with other levels of meaning. For instance, on the psychological level, the initial redistribution of the society's personnel involves individual migration decisions. These decisional meanings may be analyzed with reference to individual personality systems. The same four types of system problems arise. A village youth may hear of the opportunities offered by the new plant and gather information (information gathering is relevant to the adaptation of the personality to its social environment). He may then apply to the recruiting agent and decide to migrate (goal attainment). Later, he may face the break with the family by rationalizing about the money he will be sending home (a mechanism of defense as a tension management device). Finally, upon arriving at the factory, he may find that he must relinquish satisfaction of needs for affection while he earns esteem in the new relationship and develops a new self-image around his occupational role (a way of dealing with personality integration).

Each element in the scenario could be conceptually specified and indicators for it devised for research purposes. Societal data could be gathered regarding the changing distribution of population in specified age groups, the proportion of grown sons residing in their father's homes, and the number of government positions held by individuals from various occupational groups. Psychological tests, appropriately validated for the culture in question, could reveal the changing personalities of industrial workers. Crime statistics might reflect the degree of integration in the new urban center.

It is difficult to develop measures of cohesiveness precise enough to signal the degree of change in social cohesion which might spark political change. With the help of a computer, the complex relations among these variables could be assessed simultaneously in a total systems analysis. The Yale Political Data Program is an attempt to develop methods and collect indicators for such a systems analysis. Research focused on restricted aspects of the problem is more feasible for most scholars. The impact of the introduction of the factory on the residential distribution of manpower might circumscribe one research project. The physical fact of ore enters primarily as an economic factor and derivatively as an aspect of occupational roles.

A planner must be sensitive to the implications of an introduced change for different parts of the society, for its culture, and for the personalities of its members. This analysis suggests what might happen under given conditions. No criteria for deciding whether the changes are desirable or undesirable—whether the military junta is better or worse than the monarchy—are inherent in the sociological research framework, at least not properly so. Such evaluation properly requires the application of social philosophical criteria to the facts. This does not mean that the analysis itself is in a practical sense free from the influence of social values (Klausner, 1966 and 1968). Social interests guide the very formulation of the problem, even influencing the meaning of the concepts. The point is, as Max Weber (1949) stated some decades ago, such value biases are not legitimate and should be consciously recognized to reduce the probability of their insidious intrusion into the planning process.

The discussion to this point has revolved about ways of studying everyday meanings of man-environment relations. The illustrations have involved the social action consequences of environmental knowledge and techniques for controlling the environment available to *everyman*. Certain subgroups in society, particularly engineers and scientists, devote themselves to formalized procedures for gaining an understanding of the environment and for developing control techniques. Science and technology are bodies of systematic knowledge, all in the cognitive mode, which define significances of the environment for man. This knowledge mediates between man and the natural environment. Science and technology are themselves subjects of sociological interest.

The institutional structures created to apply this knowledge to environmental management also influence the kinds of knowledge selected and the kinds of applications preferred. The next section deals with the conditions for discovering scientific and technological knowledge and with the conscious construction of institutions to apply knowledge to the environment.

CHAPTER V

✦✦✦✦✦✦✦✦✦✦✦✦✦✦✦✦✦✦✦✦✦✦✦✦

Rediscovery of
the Environment

Personal, societal and cultural analyses have helped us understand the way everyman discovers his environment. Everyman learns to interpret nature as he encounters it and has social experiences with reference to it. Western civilization is almost epitomized by its formal procedures for generating new conceptions of the environment. Beyond the common sense of everyman and beyond the naturally occurring learning experiences, we seek to deepen our understanding and control of the environment. Formal procedures for going beyond the obvious and the circumstantial are implemented through the social organization of science, technology, and resource management. These institutions plan the rediscovery of everyman's environment. Science rediscovers the environment by means of a rational plan to control encounters of man and his environment and for organizing thought about these encounters. Technology rediscovers the environment by working upon it in a planful way—especially by means of tools—and, in the process, by collecting information useful for technical manipulation of the environment. Resource management organizations rediscover the environment through rational bureaucratic procedures for making environmental policy and implementing it through rational management techniques. Because science, technology, and resource management are also human endeavors, the thought and behaviors of their participants—like those of everyman—may also be analyzed psychologically, sociologically, and culturally. This chapter will review some recent sociological studies of technology, science, and resource management.

In the public mind and sometimes among professionals too, technological knowledge has been confused with scientific knowledge. Both are bodies of ideas which mediate the relationship of men to the natural environment and both discover those ideas through planned, rational procedures. Both are rooted in the human tendency, which Hans Reichenbach (1961) has called the "search for generality." Technological ideas are intended to be embodied in devices and in operational procedures for applying those devices either to change or to measure environment. Science consists of an abstract body of cognitive conceptions which contribute an understanding of the environment. The referents of technological ideas are processes of material and energy transformation which may be subjected to human control. The referents of scientific conceptions need not even be observable and certainly need not be subject to control. An expanding edge of the universe is unobservable for technical reasons. Libido processes in the personality are unobservable in principle.

Though technology and science are related, that relationship is by no means obvious. As Robert Merrill (1968) says, there is a widespread notion in the social sciences that the cognitive structure of technology is equivalent to that of the empirical sciences, that one need only convert the if-then statements of science into practical operations. This is nearly possible for scientific statements which are empirical generalizations, such as Boyle's law. Abstract analytical propositions, such as a psychological statement about the mechanisms of defense in relation to manifest anxiety, are not easily translatable into action directives.

Scientific and technological knowledge have, in some measure, come to us from different historical sources. Merrill points out that a significant fraction of medieval, early modern, and even some later Western technological changes grew out of diffusions from Asian societies, particularly China. They were not simply deduced from Western science. Science evolved under the influence of philosophical systems and religious notions about the cosmos. P. M. S. Blackett (1962) argues that the European scientific revolution, as well as the industrial revolution, may both rest on a high level of craft technology largely of Near and Far Eastern origin. Another source of technological knowledge is the rationalization of attempts by earlier societies to manipulate the environment magically (Malinowski, 1954). Magic, as distinguished from religion, is empirical and technical.

A history of technology, separate from that of other cultural features, is justified because technological development—besides responding to general social conditions—follows its own internal rules. John Nef (1964) has carefully and sensitively detailed stages in the history of technology. He describes how the search for an adequate means of draining coal pits led to the practical use of the force contained in jets of steam. This insight into steampower along with the need to haul the ores led to the invention of the steam engine. Were Nef to assign priority to science or to technology, he would probably place the latter first. The problems of mining and metallurgy led natural scientists into speculative thought and experiment.

Science and technology, despite some different historical roots, tend to develop in the same social settings (Merton, 1968, pp. 661–81) and thus are likely to interact at strategic points. Nef

77

explains their coincidence in the West in terms of a genius extensively awakened among the Europeans of the twelfth and thirteenth
centuries. This genius was expressed in the desire and capacity to
exploit for fresh purposes the ideas, forms, and principles—including forms of industrial organization—suggested by the experience of
earlier societies and to absorb and generalize these ideas, forms, and
principles in new ways that made them accessible to all.

Lewis Mumford (1934) locates the key development of
western technology in the application of quantitative methods of
thought to the study of nature. Religious requirements interacted
with technical insight. Clocks were developed in monasteries to syn-
chronize collective observances. The clock, not the steam engine, is
the key machine of the modern industrial age. Mumford does not
draw as sharp a line between science and technology as is being
maintained here. Unlike Nef, he believes that science rather than
technology leads the way. An initiative comes from a scientist who
establishes a general law. The invention is then a derivative product.

But cultural conditions, whether the state of scientific knowledge or the level of technological development, open only a possibility for continued technological development. This development
rests on social conditions as well. Nef points out that the growth of
the metal industry put pressure on forest timber supplies as a source
of heat for smelting. The lower efficiency of timber for this purpose
aroused fresh interest in coal seams. Timber and mining were being
developed by independent partnerships of workers. Wherever the
demand for metals grew rapidly, such independent partnerships of
working miners or smelters were placed on the defensive by larger
investors seeking to profit from this demand. With the growing need
for capital, these working people were turned into wage-earning
employees. Companies of working miners were replaced by new
companies of absentee shareholders. Regalian lords became an important competing source of capital limiting the power of private
capitalists. Eventually, the real directing unit ceased to be the individual enterprise and became the ruler's administration. In the six-
teenth century, the discovery of ores in South and Central America
struck a blow at the mining communities of Europe. In addition,

during this period warfare on the Continent became destructive and damaged heavy industry.

Nef gives less credit than did Weber to the role of the Protestant Reformation in evoking the spirit of capitalism, a cultural ground in which technology has grown. First, Weber's thesis, says Nef, is largely irrelevant to the sixteenth- and early seventeenth-century origins of capitalism. Second, Protestant culture should be credited with stimulating the notion of quantity production, large-scale private enterprises, and quantitative thinking. The Reformation limited the proprietary activities of religious orders and tended to place control of natural resources—coal, ores, and salt—in the hands of country gentlemen and merchants. When members of religious orders applied these resources to cultural and charitable pursuits, they were consumed directly. Country gentlemen and merchants were more likely to use the mineral exploitively. This exploitation was facilitated by their access to a wide range of markets. Thus, changes in the class system which place a new class with new values in a strategic position may influence the speed and direction of the development of technology.

Sociological studies of technological innovation have traced the relation between the network of social relations and the spread of technology. Many of these studies owe their inspiration to William Ogburn (1950), who analyzed the differential development of material and nonmaterial cultures. Technological innovations emerge before social institutions are prepared for them. Ogburn estimated that social institutions require some fifty years to catch up with the technology. Workmen's compensation laws, a cultural adjustment to the accident problem in modern industry, lagged legislatively behind the industrial accident rate.

Workmen's compensation laws were probably less a response to technologically generated accidents than to changing conditions of ownership. The individual craftsman who owned his tools had no thought of workmen's compensation. The idea awaited his employment with somebody else's tools and the time when the structure of social power was such as to involve the state in contracts between employers and employees. While cultural development cannot be understood simply as a laggard response to technological conditions, Ogburn's service was to direct scholarly attention to the impact of technology upon other social institutions.

Anthropologists consider technology as a cultural product emerging through interaction between man and his physical environment. The emergent technology subsequently provides a new physical environment. The encounter with this new man-created environment generates its own set of cultural problems and adaptations—in effect, adaptations to the adaptation.

Ogburn's proposition about the impact of technology on society was further specified in succeeding years. The impact of technology on the economy became a critical issue in his work. Technological innovations limit or facilitate the types and supply of and, therefore, the social acts dependent on goods and services. The technical production process also generates residuals—by-products of production such as smoke or material such as metal containers—which are not consumed along with the product. The type and amount of residuals are a function of culturally inspired demand for particular products. Factors affecting the selection or efficiency of production techniques also influence the production of residuals. The disposal of residuals calls certain institutions into play—municipal sanitation departments, air pollution controllers, and public health agencies among others.

Differences in technology from industry to industry influence the organization of work (Merrill, 1968). Particular patterns of factory size, task composition and subdivision, grouping of tasks in the job, and work arrangements are in part a consequence of the requirements of technology. The introduction of an assembly line means new social relations among workers and managers. The types of arrangements selected in response to technical requirements are influenced by implicit sociopsychological theories (March and Simon, 1958) held by workers and management. The relation between man and machine is not simply given by the imperatives of machine operation but is also a function of the mediating culture and social organization.

The influence of the relationship of the worker to the means of production upon the social relationships among workers was a central thesis of Karl Marx. Marx was concerned both with the worker's relation to machines as physical objects and with the relation of the worker to the contractual norms regulating ownership of the machines. Cultural outlooks or ideas were traced to this relation of population to technology (Marx and Engels, 1947). The occupants of the various positions within the productive process relate in ways appropriate to the accomplishment of productive goals. Their interactions form their perspectives on life.

Ogburn had been influenced by anthropological research. Yet in studying the way technology influences social change, he reversed the research focus of the anthropologists. Like the historian Nef, anthropologists have been more interested in the ways social arrangements influence technological change. The process of cultural diffusion is one way anthropologists account for technological innovation. The diffusion of cultural items—including technological items—is influenced by cultural characteristics of the receiving society, such as the consistency of the newly introduced item with the prior cultural matrix.

Influenced by the anthropological tradition, some sociologists have studied the social ecology of new inventions. The aspect in the innovative process to which sociologists attend depends on the type of innovation they are considering. In the early part of this century, rural sociologists studied how people learned about new agricultural innovations. They focused on communication processes. This direction was encouraged, in part, by the Department of Agriculture's interest in extending the application of technology. Research in educational innovation understandably turned to the question of creativity. More recently, interest in communication patterns —and particularly in the role of opinion leaders—has occupied sociologists studying the acceptance of a new drug by doctors (Menzel and Katz, 1955–56).

The adoptive or innovative process may be looked at in relation to the society as a whole, as in the anthropologists' diffusion studies. It may also be examined in relation to individual decisions, as in medical sociological studies. Everett Rogers' (1962) extensive review of studies of diffusion of innovation summarizes four aspects of the individual decision to innovate: the innovation is perceived as a new idea by the individual; there is interaction in which one person communicates new ideas to another person; the character of the social system, the norms of the social structure, and the position of the individual affect the diffusion; and an adoption occurs when there is a decision to continue full use of an innovation.

The study of resistance to innovation is the other side of the diffusion question. Innovation may be resisted on a cultural level. The new item may be inconsistent with the broader culture. This is what Walter Firey, in the above discussion, had in mind concerning the ethnological aspect of a resource process. The very attempt to innovate may generate a social movement to counter that attempt, as is illustrated by the rise of antifluoridation groups. Sociologists have interpreted resistance to innovation in terms of conflicts of social interests. Ogburn (1951) attributes cultural inertia to classes which derive differential benefits from existing conditions. They tend to resist any change which will lessen those benefits. Bernhard Stern (1959) documents cases in which industrial interests suppressed the use of inventions directly or by monopolization of patents. Bernard Barber (1961), turning the searchlight on members of the scientific community, shows how they also—guided by their perceived interests—resist scientific innovation. In essence, the sociological study of technology and its rediscovery of the environment is continuous with the sociological study of the relation of everyman to his natural environment. We turn now to science and its formal schemas of interpretation.

Societies structure their relation to their environment through culturally given paradigms, or frames of reference, which serve to interpret nature. Individual perceptions of the environment are enclosed in these cultural paradigms. Everyman's paradigms are formalized by cultural institutions. For most of human history, the significant paradigms of the environment have been formalized in religious and philosophical systems. Certain religious ideas evaluate the relation between person and environment, explain the action of the environment on man, and suggest directives for acting upon the

82

environment. Certain philosophical ideas offer cognitive maps of man and environment separately and in relationship to each other. Cosmological theories of the environment and anthropological images of man have been set against a backdrop of ontological theories of the nature of being. Ontologists have reasoned about the basic substance and/or the basic acts of which environment and man are constituted. Today in the United States, the prestigious cultural formalizations of the natural environment are those put forward by the community of scientists.

Magical and technological control of the environment are distinguished by the degree of formal rationality involved in each process. Technologists set tighter limits than do magicians on the decision rules for evaluating environmental feedback. There is a similar relation between rational and mythic ways of understanding the environment. In the mind of everyman, the environment is understood through some mixture of rational and mythic modes of thought. Religious, philosophical, and scientific knowledge are all formalizations of the rational elements in thought. Music and the graphic arts are analogous, stylized—if not formalized—expressions of mythic elements in thought. Religious thought is more intimately influenced by the mythic than by either the philosophical or the scientific. Contrasted with mythic symbols, religious, philosophical, and scientific concepts establish rather strict rules for conceptualizing the environment.

The community of scientists has provided a rather specific and strict set of rules for conceptualizing the environment. The first and perhaps the foremost rule is that of objectivity. The nature and existence of the environment are treated as independent of man's conceptualizing. Because of this, one observer may be substituted for another, and both should return with the same report. This is the attempt of science to break free of the mythic forms of everyday social action, forms in which the meanings of the environment depend upon the way it is embedded in action.

In contrast to the scientific, the mythic paradigm conceives of the environment as an extension of man. The nature of the world is peculiar for each man or each group. Information about the environment is transmitted uniquely from the creator through his oracles to an elite of prophets.

A second rule of scientific conceptualizing derives from the first. Personal value judgments belong in the personal and social realms and are irrelevant to the behavior of the environment or to theories of that behavior. The environment is value neutral. The mythic consciousness sees evil in the storms and good in the glow of the sun.

Thirdly, science defines restrictive rules for the conceptualization of space and time. Objects are located on a set of coordinates which define the space. Rotating the coordinates, and so changing locations, is not relevant to the meaning of those objects so long as their positions relative to one another do not change. In the mythic consciousness, location and direction are fraught with special meanings. There are holy places and accursed places. An object located in a high place is morally superior to one located in a low place. In the realm of social action, areas may take their names from the uses to which they are put—playgrounds, battlefields, living rooms, and dining rooms.

In the formation of scientific concepts, time is a succession of events. The lapse of time between the events defines their meaning in relation to one another. The particular position of a set of relevant events in the overall chronological flow is unimportant. A falling object behaved the same at the time of King Arthur's court as it does today. But for the mythic consciousness, the temporal location of the object between a genesis at one end and termination at the other defines its significance.

Most importantly, science abstracts. The scientist withdraws certain attributes and qualities from their concrete contexts and observes them as a series of comparable instances. The esthetic and mythic consciousnesses gather attributes into a concrete whole in which each such event has a unique significance.

Mythic ways of conceptualizing nature, while characteristic of everyday thought, are ruled out of science by fiat. The scientific formalization presents the world in what Ernst Cassirer (1957) calls a single symbolic form, a single perspective. Esthetic and mythi-

84

cal symbolism are effective rhetoric for social control but are peculiarly ineffective in explaining, predicting, and controlling events in the natural environment. In principle, a scientific paradigm stands or falls on an empirical test of its success in predicting or controlling environmental events.

There are, in fact, many scientific paradigms. The rules of objectivity, value neutrality, and abstraction have been generally accepted as goals in all of them. Various scientific paradigms may be distinguished by some peculiar ways of posing questions about the environment. The paradigms are social products. One task of the history and sociology of science is to examine the social conditions for the emergence of each scientific paradigm.

The history of western science is a record of shifting paradigms. Thomas Kuhn (1962) has called these shifts "scientific revolutions." "Normal science" takes place within a given paradigm. The scientific community knows what the world is like and has clear notions of the entities of which the universe is composed, how they interact with each other and with the senses, and what questions are legitimate. When such a view encounters anomalies— observations that cannot readily be accounted for in terms of the accepted theory—the system may be restructured. A new gestalt, a new way of looking at things, appears. The shift from Ptolemaic to Copernican astronomy was such a paradigm shift.

Within a single paradigm, science is cumulative. Scientists select problems that can be solved with conceptual and instrumental techniques close to those already in existence. However, concepts of one paradigm cannot easily be expressed in terms of another. Aristotle interpreted a pendulum as a heavy body moved by its own nature. The swinging body was simply falling with difficulty and would eventually reach the bottom of its fall. Aristotelians measured the weight of the stone and vertical height. For Galileo, the swinging body was repeating the same motion over and over again ad infinitum. He measured weight, radius, angular displacement, and time per swing. This entailed a new gestalt. The physics of Einstein is not simply broader than that of Newton but is a different way of looking at the physical world. Elements in competing paradigms are incommensurable. To make them relevant to one another, transformation concepts must be introduced. Such concepts explain the relation of the world as grasped from one perspective to the world as grasped from another.

A shift in paradigms may follow a change in the social character of the community of scientists. A paradigm shift is likely to take place when sociologists and social psychologists join the economists and engineers in environmental studies. The disciplines differ paradigmatically, in part because of their differing histories, different inherent characteristics of their objects and, in part, because of differences in the social sources of recruitment of their members. The conceptual apparatus of scientists, despite their long effort to free it of everyday mythic elements, is—like that of all men —rooted in the perspectives of their social strata.

Marx and Engels (1947) argued that all ideas, social conceptions, values, metaphysical notions, and political views are epiphenomenal to the patterns of social relations. This insight has been further developed by Karl Mannheim (1936) as a problem in the sociology of knowledge. Mannheim distinguished a *special* from a *general* conception of the sociology of knowledge. The special conception is that in which one analyzes an opponent's ideas in the light of psychological forces which distort his thinking. The general conception is that in which all thought and feeling are structured by the relations inherent in the social positions which people occupy. The view from the top is different from the view from the bottom. The sociology of science has at times been concerned with the special and at times with the general conceptions.

Psychologists of perception, such as Jerome Bruner (Bruner, Goodnow, and Austin, 1956), have studied some of the mechanisms involved in the cognitive thinking of the individual. Klausner (1966, pp. 329–41) has presented empirical evidence for the influence of the social and cultural milieus on scientific conceptualization. These milieu factors work through noncognitive elements, such as the way an individual feels about and evaluates his world. As argued in the discussions on the modes of meaning, these affective

86

and evaluative elements are intertwined with and so influence cognitions.

Individual perceptions take place within a societally given framework. Here enters the general conception of the sociology of knowledge. The development of a cultural paradigm is also a socially influenced process. Kuhn observes that when an individual or group first produces a synthesis able to attract most of the next generation's practitioners, the older schools gradually disappear. Either their members convert to the new paradigm, or—if they cling to the older views—they are simply read out of the profession which thereafter ignores their work. The transfer of allegiance from paradigm to paradigm is a conversion experience that cannot be forced. Those who resist are relying on the assurance that the older paradigm will ultimately solve the key problems. The tendency to convert, according to Kuhn, may depend on the idiosyncrasies of autobiography, nationality, or prior reputation. The man who embraces the new paradigm in its early state often does so despite the lack of evidence for it.

Scientific knowledge is affected by the internal organization among scientists. Robert Merton (1968, pp. 604–15) maintains that science develops more readily when scientists have freedom to explore. The evidence, however, is not clear that free-ranging imagination and freedom from constraints on the selection of problems produces more or better scientific findings. The opportunity to pursue a wide range of problems, though, certainly increases the probability of opening new paradigms.

The effect on science of the educational organization of the discipline is demonstrable. Joseph Ben-David (1960), measuring scientific productivity in terms of the number of scientific discoveries, found the French leading and the British following at the beginning of the nineteenth century. A preponderance of German discoveries appeared in the second half of that century. The American share rapidly increased from the eighteen-eighties onward. The superiority of Germany to France, Ben-David claims, rests upon the decentralization of academic research which gives rise to academic competition. French scientists were largely self-supporting and academic appointments were honors. Specialization was absent in France. Academic organization in the United States was similar in this respect to that in Germany. Competition developed within a decentralized system. This, in turn, encouraged the establishment of specialized research roles and facilities. These specialized roles and facilities, Ben-David suggests, account for high productivity.

The community of scientists, its perspective, and consequently the character of scientific knowledge is also influenced by the acts and expectations of the wider public. Like the scientist, attaching himself to a paradigm partly on faith, the public supports science partly on faith. Public support rests on a faith that science will have application to technology (Price, 1965) and to the solution of social problems. These expectations can, of course, be only partially met.

The public also supports science for the prestige and self-enhancement it may bring. The public support of science in the name of technology has been traced historically by Richard Shryock (1948–49). During the greater part of the nineteenth century, Americans were indifferent to basic research. Technology, inventions, and surgical practices were enthusiastically encouraged. Congress persistently refused to support a national scientific organization. Industrial leaders, anticipating a relationship between science and technology, began supporting science between 1900 and 1940. Economic organizations and business firms thus influenced the direction of science and technology.

Alvin Weinberg (1961) cites historical precedents for irrationalities in public support of science and calls attention to some consequences for science. Throughout history, societies have expressed their aspirations in large-scale monumental enterprises—such as the pyramids in Egypt—which, though not necessary for the survival of the societies, have taxed them to their physical-intellectual limits. Science may fulfill this role in the twentieth century. As a consequence of this interdependence of scientists and the public, Weinberg complains, scientific issues are too often settled in the popular press. Dealing with the public makes the professor an operator. His students and intellectual eminence suffer.

Norman Storer (1963) is even more critical. Public support, he writes, has led scientists to change their reward structure. Professional recognition becomes less important than rewards of money and prestige common in the rest of society. Public expectation increases a tendency to see basic research as a way to solve specific problems. As a result, the vital concept of the disinterested quest for knowledge is in danger of being stifled.

Generally, public impact on science depends on the social institution through which its influence is exerted. Governmental institutions have had a telling impact. An ideological position about the relation of science to other social institutions encourages certain regimes to take an interest in science and technology. Charles Gillispie (1959) draws an example from the period of the French Revolution. At the time of the Jacobin First Republic, the French scientific community was the most brilliant in the world, and the most highly institutionalized. In 1793 the Jacobin convention abolished learned academies. Jacobins supported natural history which, because of its association with biology, appeared more humane. Science stood accused as a stubborn bastion of aristocracy, a tyranny of intellectual pretension, stifling civic virtue. They erected central and normal schools—such as the Ecole Polytechnique—where science served, primarily, a pedagogical function. According to Gillispie, an emphasis on technology at the expense of science resulted.

Government science policy may also draw science onto an ideological sidetrack. David Joravsky (1961) describes how, as part of a five-year plan, Stalin pressed Soviet professors to become patriots and precipitated a struggle between scientists and ideologists. The ideologists triumphed in genetics. Scientific prestige rested on its willingness to fulfill political values.

We have been describing the relation of social structure to the development of scientific knowledge. Science, a body of knowledge and an institution that deals in that knowledge, has an impact on society. That scientific knowledge shapes man's relation to the natural environment is the rationale for this discussion of the sociology of science. The impact of science on society through scientifically inspired technological innovation is too obvious for mention and too complex for analysis here. The impact of scientific ways of thinking on many sectors of culture is almost incalculable. Scientific ways of thinking and scientific findings have become part of the ideologies of many religious institutions. The revolt of some agnostics and atheists in the eighteenth and nineteenth centuries against the established churches—as well as some fundamentalist secessions from the major denominations—have centered on the meaning of science for religion and vice versa. Scientific thought has influenced criteria of efficiency in education, as standardized testing and programmed learning bear witness. Cost/benefit analyses reflect the influence of its rational form on economic decision making. Even contemporary music and the graphic arts have not escaped its discursive rationalizations of line and tone.

Don Price (1965) has studied the impact of big science on the American polity. One of its most important effects has been to draw the public and private sectors of the society closer together. Government is entering the science business. Through large grants, institutions such as RAND have been developed to provide information important to policy. Science is changing the bases of power. Property was a prime source of power in earlier times. The technology of the industrial revolution contributed to the development of private corporations and made stocks a new kind of liquid asset. Science has made property almost ethereal. Power can rest upon what people know and the professional skills they command. All of this, Price continues, is drawing science and scientists deeper and deeper into the political arena. Scientists and professionals are being forced to make policy decisions that go beyond their competence. They are being asked to recommend purposes and values.

We have now gone full circle. Our discussion opened by distinguishing science, a mode of understanding, from the mythic and esthetic consciousness, modes of incipient social action. Science is being drawn back into the activity of the world, the arena of politics. Science becomes not only a source of paradigms for conceptualizing the natural environment but directly affects the social institutions whose members make decisions about the management and development of the natural environment.

On Man in His Environment

Resource management institutions do not simply translate everyman's environmental concepts into policy and implement his environmental decisions. Resource policies and programs are influenced by the organizational contexts in which they are forged. These organizations are rational bureaucracies; through their decisions and actions they rediscover the environment. The social organizational ties of TVA are more complex than those around an individual farmer's irrigation system. This difference implies a difference in the decisions made.

An examination of resource management organizations begins with a definition of natural resources. Earth, seas, air, flora, and fauna are usually collected under the term *natural environment*. The plowed fields, the city buildings, automobiles, coins, and the multitude of processed products and tools of contemporary living are elements in the *man-made physical environment*. Natural resources emerge between these two categories. They appear when the natural environment is perceived as malleable. An environmental element is a resource when it does, or potentially can, enter into a social action system—usually to become part of the man-made environment. A material becomes implicated in social action when people are aware of its existence, when they know how to employ it as a means or condition to facilitate the achievement of social or personal goals, and when the economic, social relational, or ethical cost of employing it is acceptable to them.

A natural resource originates independently of the agency of man. The term *natural* highlights this independence. Water—before it reaches the drinking glass, before it washes the ore and coal, before it becomes a constituent of plastic—is a natural resource. Erich Zimmerman (1963) defines natural resources as those aspects of man's environment which render possible or facilitate the satisfaction of human wants and the attainment of social objectives.

The same physical object can serve as a resource for the attainment of several social and personal goals. These usages depend on perceptions of attributes of the physical material. Gold may be a symbol of status by virtue of its rarity and slow rate of oxidation. Gold enters medical practice, for instance, in prostheses, despite its rarity but because of its other attributes. Even the notion of rarity is social since it depends on cost and amount producible under given technological conditions relative to a culturally defined requirement. Animals may be sacrificial objects in religious ceremonies or sources of food, clothing, or energy for the economy. Earth from the Holy Land is used in diaspora Jewish burial rituals and is also used to grow potatoes. Whether animals or earth are seen with reference to religious or to economic institutions has different implications for animal husbandry. The term *natural resources* is used today primarily in relation to the economic system. The role of resources in productive industries as material, as energy, and as means for transforming other products is central to most resource analyses. This institutional focus is not dictated by the requirements of a sociological theory of resources but by the characteristics of a society which places *homo economicus* ahead of *homo religiosis*.

Resources may become a problem in our particular social setting when people perceive a potential scarcity—either because of the threatened exhaustion of a natural object or because of its spoilage. A coal seam may become exhausted or its quality reduced. Quality reduction may result if materials are put in the wrong places at the wrong time. Allen Kneese and Robert Ayres (1968) discuss environmental pollution and its control as a "materials balance" problem. The residuals which remain from industrial production and create a waste disposal problem depend upon the "total materials throughput" and the efficiency with which the system (including consumption in the process of recycling) utilizes those materials. The "materials balance" problem is also a "social action balance" problem. One environmentally oriented action, such as lumber harvesting, may consume the resource needed for another, such as wildlands recreation. Resource planning emerges especially when resources become the focus of a social problem.

Typically, the planner moves either to prevent or control further deterioration, or he moves to create a situation better than that which existed before the problem was recognized. This striving for an environment superior to that of nature is characteristic of entrepreneurs in a capitalistic setting. They may "oversolve" a problem—to devise means of communication with more channels and less noise than people had ever thought they would need. Harold Gershinowitz (1969) has pressed government agencies toward positive thinking about resource problems. He proposes that government and industry together consider how the waste heat of power production might be used beneficially instead of being suppressed and how nutrients in sewage—instead of being removed—could contribute to eutrophication of lakes to stimulate growth of desired organisms. The decisions of resource management agencies often determine whether materials balance, positive thinking, or some other approach will be elected. A discussion of resource planning may be organized around the problem of resource management decisions.

Resource decisions are made by individuals and by groups in the context of organizational relationships and institutional norms. The individual farmer deciding what to plant and the forest manager deciding whether to burn off brush are constrained, by the norms and social structures of their institutions, to perceive and support certain possibilities of action rather than others. Four types of institutions—economic, political, managerial, and juridical— might hold responsibility for resource decisions as well as for the implementation of these decisions. In American society, resource decisions are most often reached in an economic and political context—by organizations in both the public and the private sectors.

A recent Congressional White Paper (Joint House-Senate Colloquium, 1968) called for creating a "carefully designed, healthful, and balanced environment" by proceeding with economic, political, and juridical planning. On the economic level, equitable ways of charging for environmental abuses could be devised; on the political level, governmental control would be extended where corporate resource development does not preserve environmental values; and on the juridical level judicial procedures would be established to assure individual rights to the environment. In practice, the relative power of the economic, political, and juridical implementing agencies would determine which of these three decision contexts would be the most salient. That managerial institutions are not mentioned is due to the fact that the group preparing the report did not perceive them as an independent type. Rather, each of the three designated institutional types would have its managerial arm. Here we hold that the exigencies of management as such provide an institutional decision context—in fact, a powerful administrator in the economic, political and juridical contexts can subvert their aims to the aims of management.

Of course, each institutional context is independent only in an analytic sense. Political institutions may rest their decisions on economic criteria as well as on criteria of the distribution of power. These institutional contexts influence conceptions by their members of the meaning of the environment both as a result of cultural orientations and as a result of the organizational forms they develop to mediate the relation of man to nature.

Economic decision criteria are central for both profit-oriented private industry and for interest-defending legislative and executive agencies. The preference for economic criteria is rooted in the fundamental status of economic motives in our culture. Within rational bureaucratic organizations, the sophistication of economic measurement techniques and the apparent close correspondence between the theoretical model and the actual situation are strong incentives to use economic criteria. While political and juridical analyses rely on rough, often nonmetricized, measures, economic analyses usually rest on quantitative measures.

The general problem for an economist is to allocate resources to different social purposes. The recent trend toward cost/benefit analysis attempts to solve the problem through an economic transform of its elements. Assessment of a project in cost/benefit terms is usually supplemented by a political decision about how the costs and benefits will be allocated among different parts of the population. Within an economic frame of reference, ideally, the idea of a resource is expressed in terms of economic factors, such as the price it brings in a market.

The economist bases a decision on the economic efficiency of an action for the broad economic system and on the utility for the individual or group, among other criteria. Economic efficiency

94

is obtained, according to John Krutilla and Otto Eckstein (1958), when productive resources are so allocated among alternative uses that any reshuffling of the pattern cannot improve an individual's position and still leave all other individuals as well off as before. When a resource allocation changes the distribution of income, the position of some individuals is improved at the expense of others.

Besides the efficiency for the aggregated economic system, the economist assesses the utilities for the actors involved. The term *utility,* following Frederick Mosteller and Philip Nogee (1951), refers to a value, usually expressible in quantitative terms, which a commodity or service has for an individual or for a group. Commodities can be compared in terms of their positions on a scale of utilities. Resource decisions can consider these relative scale positions.

In the economic theory of consumer behavior, utilities are thought of in subjective terms and assessed in terms of expressed preferences. As Kevin Lancaster (1966a) has pointed out, utilities need not be attached to a good as such but may be attached to characteristics of goods or to bundles of characteristics. Sociological analysis is relevant to economic analysis at this point. A commodity is a special case of the physical environmental element discussed above. The utility assigned any given commodity, or characteristic of a commodity, depends upon the meaning of that commodity for the person or group. Meaning, and consequently utility, depends upon the way a commodity functions in human action systems. The utility of an item is a function of the utility of the social action which it facilitates.

Members of different social categories, different classes or ethnic groups, for example, will assign the same commodities differing positions on the scale of utilities because they perceive and use them in different ways. A Cadillac has a higher utility for an American than for a Hottentot because of the additional ways it is embedded in the American's action system. That the utilities of several people or of several groups of people may not be comparable constitutes a problem for the decision maker. Not only might different people assign different positions on the scale to the same commodity but each might use a differently calibrated scale. One common assumption is that the utilities of various people are measurable in terms of the economic demand they exert. Utility is then expressed in monetary terms. Of course, money itself may vary in its utility. The utility of a monetary unit to the individual varies according to the general level of prices and the amount of income he commands or wealth he possesses.

Economists have tried to overcome the problem of the incomparability of utilities by using aggregate data. The economist is only in a limited sense concerned with the utility of a good to an individual. The object of economic analysis is the economic system —a type of social system. The market price for any good is a resultant of a large number of individual action vectors. Reasoning back from the market price to the individual acts of which it is constituted, one may say that each purchase at the price reflects the same marginal utility for the purchaser. The price then measures the marginal utility of the good for everyone who buys it. Individuals may vary in their share of the market, the amount they buy, and the demand they exert.

The economic analyst more often deals with the number of purchases than with the number of individuals making these purchases. The economic attribute *marginal utility* is not an attribute of an individual but is a membership characteristic, an attribute which this individual obtains by virtue of membership in a given market.

The economic value of a commodity is assessed through an aggregative procedure such as integrating the area under the demand curve. This shows the total of units which will be claimed at each price level and, by addition, the total value realized when all are sold. The slope or shape of the demand curve may change under various psychological and social conditions. The social and psychological variables commonly used include age, sex, ethnic group, social class, residential location, or past buying behavior (Katona, 1953, 1960, 1964). The full range of independent variables influencing utility is still open to research.

The economist's methods of dealing with extrasystemic impacts of actions are especially helpful in reaching resource decisions. The impacts are referred to as *externalities,* a concept overlapping the sociologist's concept of *unintended consequences.* Unintended consequences are impacts which have not been consciously predicted by the actors. Externalities are often predictable. Also, externalities are literally external whereas unintended consequences need not be. They may involve impacts on groups originating the action. Externalities, like unintended consequences, may refer to benefits as well as to costs. Building a storage reservoir upstream may benefit some downstream riparians who do not pay for it.

The importance of considering externalities is that benefits or costs may accrue to third parties outside of the market. They might then not enter the private calculus of the decision maker. Krutilla (January, 1966) discussed the impact of upstream water pollution on the cost of water purification in a fiscally unrelated downstream community. Orris Herfindahl and Allen Kneese (1965), in considering externalities, weigh the diseconomies imposed on potential users when a resource is destroyed.

The concepts of economic efficiency and externalities may be considered jointly. In terms of broad economic efficiency a project might be justified economically as long as the benefits, "to whomsoever they may accrue," exceed the cost, to be measured in terms of the contribution to the national product or income. Costs accruing to an actor outside the project may also be figured in the calculus by extending the boundaries of the system to redefine the economic unit so that it encompasses the affected actor.

Inclusion of externalities also contributes to understanding action within the particular unit under consideration. The relation between means and the goal of an individual, as well as the relation among the several goals of an individual, depends not only on his individual act but upon what many other individuals do—a fact recognized by economists as consumption externalities or interdependence of utility functions.

The system extension involved in bringing externalities into consideration extends consideration only to economic impacts on the wider community. In terms of the model developed earlier, economic decisions may be said to be based on certain adaptive and allocative problems of the social system. Costs and benefits associated with societal integration, goal attainment, and pattern maintenance have not generally been included in the economists' calculations. Economic analysis also tends to ignore factors related to the personalities of actors and to the culture. The precision enjoyed by the economic model is related to its readiness to treat noneconomic factors as *ceteris paribus* conditions. This limitation does not seem, in principle, to be inherent in economic analysis. The concept of externalities might be extended to noneconomic impacts if appropriate measures could be developed.

Real life resource decisions must, of course, involve these other factors. When the noneconomic aspects are considered, measures of willingness to pay or of market price may no longer represent the utilities of commodities to concrete individuals. (They will still, of course, represent the marginal utilities to economic actors.)

Confusion is likely to arise here as we cross the border from economic to sociological and psychological analysis. The prices and utilities of concern to economists are social system attributes. The shape of the demand curve—the amounts bought at particular prices—is influenced by the tastes and preferences of consumers. As mentioned above, economic analysis does not deal with tastes and preferences of individuals but with the distribution of tastes within a socioeconomic system. An economist aggregating payments or willingness to pay of many individuals obtains a measure of demand —a system attribute. A sociologist or psychologist is more likely to focus on the individual act of paying and relate it to the personality of the individual. It then becomes a proxy for a motivational state of the individual, not an attribute of a social system. When aggregated, the measure attests to the distribution of certain motives within a population. However, personal goals and preferences do not stand simply in a microcosm-macrocosm relation to social goals and preferences. Price paid is then a *preference measure* for the sociologist. A preference measure is not only a function of the characteristics of the commodity, but also a function of the personalities and social backgrounds of the individuals judging the commodity.

98

By and large, the economist measuring willingness to pay, in estimating the value of a particular commodity, service, or facility at the moment is essentially using it as a static concept which takes individual preferences—however arrived at—as given along with the goals and norms of social institutions. Resource allocation decisions in this static context may be important and numerous. They do not, however, exhaust the resource allocation decision contexts.

To consider the future, we need to understand the elements involved in preference formation and how preferences may change as a function of these elements. In clarifying the dynamics of preference formation, economic analysis may be supplemented by a sociological and psychological assessment of values, preferences, and tastes.

One way to observe how sociological and psychological factors bear on economic factors is to enter them as additional variables in a regression equation. An alternative to this multiple factor, or regression, approach to the integration of economic and other social scientific theories has been proposed by Talcott Parsons and Neil Smelser (1956). They take exception to the notion that the reason that economic theory does not adequately explain concrete facts is because it deals with only some of the variables which must be supplemented by other significant variables. They view the economy as one aspect of a social system. Its theoretical structure is a special case of the general theory of social systems. The basic variables of the economy are also variables in the more general system. The economy does not have a separate class of variables different from those of the theory of personality or of the polity. The special case is distinguished by special parameters applied to the same variables.

For example, one variable of the general theory is performance-sanction. The basic notion behind it is one of action and reaction in which the responding actor indicates to the initiating actor whether further acts of that type are desired. This variable appears in personality theory in the concept of reinforcement and in social theory as an element in social control. Parsons and Smelser maintain that within the economy, supply-demand may be seen as a special case of the performance-sanction variable in the general theory. Supply is the production of utility or economic value. The act of supplying is the performance aspect of the role relationship. Each act of the supplier is interpreted in terms of its contribution to the functioning of the economy. Demand is the disposition to pay in a process of market exchange for availability of such goods and services. Demanding is the sanction or reward aspect of the act.

The economist, say Parsons and Smelser, interprets demand in terms of its bearing on the disposition of supplying agencies to produce in the future. They treat wealth and income as disposable resources. Wealth is the aggregate economic value of goods and services of a social system. Income is the flow of command over such values per unit time in that system. Utility is the economic value of physical, social, or cultural objects in accord with their significance as facilities for solving the adaptive problems of social systems.

Again, categories of wealth, utility, and income are states or properties of social systems. The units do not apply to the personality of the individual except through the social system. Thus, Parsons and Smelser say, Adam Smith was correct to speak of the wealth of nations rather than of individual members. From this point of view, costs and benefits must be assessed with respect to a function for some social system.

The proper measures are then of collective rather than of individual properties. A collective property is an attribute of a group as such. A provisional list of group properties has been developed by Robert Merton (1968, pp. 364–79). They include such measures as shape and height of stratification and extent of social interaction in a group. Progress in the logic of measuring group properties is being made in the efforts to develop systems of social accounting (Gross, 1966; Bauer, 1966). A governmental effort to develop social measures for policy decisions has been presented in a report of the Panel on Social Indicators (1969).

The use of economic criteria for resource decisions has been discussed at some length because of the frequency with which those criteria are applied. The institution having administrative responsibility for resource management—whether that responsibility was originally delegated by political, economic or juridical institutions—may itself become the referent of decisions. Decisions may be reached in the light of organizational or administrative exigencies. Management institutions are concerned with system order or—in terms of our model—with the integrative problem. Management institutions have the most intimate acquaintance with the resource system. They are concerned with the day-to-day maintenance of physical facilities and the ordering of the activities of people with respect to resources. Their operational knowledge may not always be put into effect, because their decisions may become enmeshed in considerations of organization. The importance of undisturbed or smooth operation of the administrative machinery, the amount of paper work to be generated, the number of personnel involved, or the size of the institutional budget may loom large relative to the considerations of the role of the resource in the total society.

Herbert Kaufman's (1960) study of forest management illustrates some of these points. He was concerned with how decisions reached in Washington were implemented by 792 district rangers under a variety of local conditions. The decisions involved timber sales targets, timber cut targets, maximum acceptable burn targets for controlling fires, grazing targets, and wildlife targets among others. Kaufman found a remarkable degree of conformity, achieved through a tight set of preformed decisions and diaries, which show inspectors how each day is spent. Frequent transfer of personnel maintains organizational loyalty in the face of local ties.

The model for the contemporary sociological study of organizational bureaucracies and the way their internal exigencies influence their decisions is based on Max Weber's (1947) work on legal authority within a bureaucratic administrative staff. The ideal type of bureaucracy is characterized by a continuous organization of official functions bound by rules—specified spheres of competence for the occupants of the offices, the organization of offices following the principle of hierarchy, offices occupied by technically competent officials who are separated from ownership of the means of production, separation of official position from private life, and decisions formulated and recorded in writing.

This type of internal structure can induce the emergence of an administrative world. Michael Crozier (1964) has shown how the struggle for organizational power can lead the organization to become a cultural system in its own right. Then the decisions it generates are conditioned by the internal relations among its members. Theodore Caplow (1964) has described how the effectiveness of an organization in making and implementing its decisions depends on internal factors such as its ability to increase the status of its positions, to control the volume of interaction among occupants of its positions, and to control internal conflict.

Few sociological studies of organization have dealt specifically with resource management organizations. The production of material goods as an organizational goal has been used in sociological studies as an indicator of the social relations within the organization. The relation between the productive process and the social relations in the organization have received less attention. Sociologists have been more occupied with developing a general theory of organizational life. This would be a theory of what organizations have in common, whether they are engaged in industry or mining, in generating and communicating knowledge, or in inciting effort for political change. Amitai Etzioni's (1961) work, for example, discusses religious, political, health, and industrial organizations under the single rubric of *compliance structure*—the way low level participants are controlled. As the sociologist sees it, the resource management organization is a special case. What is special about that case still needs to be spelled out.

Resource management organizations may be classified according to whether they are part of a central planning agency or have been created to manage a specific resource. In the former case, the life of the higher level bureaucracy will have a greater impact on decisions than that of operational personnel. In the latter case, the interrelations among operational personnel will carry greater weight. The park and forest agencies tend to be single-purpose planning and programming agencies. Land and water management agencies tend to have multipurpose jurisdiction. In the latter case, they are in a better position than single purpose agencies to create economics of scale and deal with externalities (Brewer and Bordner, 1966). Planning may be geared to resource development, that is, to a change in the rate of input of a resource into some system. Resources may enter the production function itself. Their natural condition may be modified and they may be combined with other resources to yield services and benefits. Planning may also be geared to conservation. In this case, limits are set on the way the resource enters the social system. Recreational use is one of the allowable ways it may enter. Science and technology also tend to play a dominant role both in resource development and in conservation planning (Maass, 1968).

Conceivably, multipurpose jurisdiction may increase the probability of an orientation to resource development while single purpose agencies may have more of a tendency to be conservationists. This conjecture would require an empirical test.

The political is a third context in which resource decisions are reached. Political institutions, in the language developed above, contribute to the goal attainment function of the society. Political decision making may also have internal integrative functions as it weighs diverse societal interests. This is illustrated by Philip Selznick (1949) in his study of the TVA, which shows how the policy makers of a major natural resources project dealt with community power. The TVA assumed regional responsibility for electrical power and agricultural irrigation, among other things. Its official doctrine called for grass roots administration. This doctrine had emerged as an adaptation of the TVA to certain local and national interests. The commitment, however, had restrictive consequences for the policy and behavior of the Authority. The Authority met the dilemma through what Selznick describes as "coöptation"— absorbing new elements into the leadership of the organization to share the burdens of and the responsibility for power. The coöpted groups did not necessarily share power.

In a democratic social order, political decisions tend to respond primarily to current interests. In political alignments, with less than perfect diffusion of power, decisions tend to be biased in favor of individuals or groups with access to power holders. This was illustrated in Floyd Hunter's (1953) study of community power. Hunter distinguishes "men of power" from the policy makers who activate them. "Separate crowds" within the power structure control resources in which they have special interests. Whether private interests or the social will prevails in resource decisions depends on the character of the social order existing at a given time and place (Zimmerman, 1963). Considerations of group continuity exert a pressure toward a social appraisal by political decision makers.

A decision in favor of collective benefit may have paradoxical consequences. For example, Krutilla (1966a) described how flood control legislation led to an increase in the flood plain damage potential because, with flood protections, more structures were built in dangerous flood plains.

The power of decision may reside with the police operating under general directives. This is a special case of political decision making. Generally, such an arrangement is designed to meet an emergency. The police or military executor of directives has little interest beyond the control of social tensions. Decisions then are made in the light of tension-management functions as well as of goal attainment functions of the society. Barring particular political influences, police action predisposes toward conservative decisions which preserve the status quo. In special cases, of course, the police may represent a particular subcommunity and enforce decisions in the interest of that group.

Another possibility is that a society might prefer that resource decisions be juridical ones. Juridical decisions rest on the normative system and so involve the pattern maintenance function for society. The distinction between a juridical and a political decision depends somewhat on legal philosophy. If the judiciary, or judicially-acting resource commission, sees itself as an interpreter of law, then it is an arm—although a more stable arm, of the polity. If the judiciary defines its responsibility as the development of law, as a philosopher-king, the decisions would themselves create a new body of rules. Juridical decision making has the advantage of safeguarding long-term interests. A disadvantage derives from the reticence of the judiciary to bend in terms of specific cases and to consider noncodified social norms.

The distinctions between these institutional influences on decision processes are, of course, analytical. They are not identical with cognate concrete organizations. Managerial organizations, when looked at in relation to the broader society, fulfill an integrative function. However, when examined internally they have subsystems which are primarily economic (adaptive) political (goal attaining), juridical (pattern maintaining) and managerial (integrative) which contribute to the maintenance of the managerial organization itself. Thus, a decision emanating from a concrete resource management institution may be influenced by any of its subsystems. Managerial organizations consider economic and political criteria as well as the more strictly managerial decision criteria. The same may be said for the other institutional types. Only an empirical examination will show the extent to which the several criteria influence resource decisions. In common, however, all the contexts provide rational ways of planning for action on the environment. The relation of these organizations and of their members to nature may be studied with the same sociological tools as are used for the study of the relation of everyman to nature.

✿✿✿✿✿✿✿✿✿✿✿✿✿✿✿✿✿✿✿✿✿✿✿

CHAPTER VI

Social Implications
of Filth and Noise

🌳🌳🌳🌳🌳🌳🌳🌳🌳🌳🌳🌳🌳🌳🌳🌳🌳🌳🌳🌳🌳

This book has only sketched some theoretical analyses. Its armchair theorizing may still be elaborated extensively. The relation of the sociology of organizations, of law, and of religion to the study of the natural environment are obvious areas for development. Such development, however, requires a better data base. Three types of research would be worthwhile—cross-cultural and historical studies, methodological studies, and studies of specific resource systems.

Historical and cross-cultural analyses of the association between the development of resources and social organization may grow out of the sociology of technology and of science. Many significant impacts of resource systems on social organization become apparent only when viewed over relatively long periods and in different cultural settings. The ways in which particular forms of social organization (folk and urban societies, industrial and craft economies, fluid and static stratification systems) are intertwined with particular forms of resource development may be appreciated best in historical perspective.

Methodological work is needed to develop means by which the motives, sociocultural values, and forms of social organization associated with various resource systems could be scaled in relation to economic cost/benefit analyses. Economic and social-political value terms are incommensurable because each derives from a different theoretical context. They tend to be incommensurable on a practical level because social, cultural, and psychological costs and benefits involve not easily monetizable considerations—like an ethic or an affect which are not priced on any market.

A traditional solution could be achieved by developing families of demand curves with each curve expressing the demand under specific social, psychological, and cultural conditions. This is an elaboration of Robert Davis' (1967) call for an assessment of the nonmonetized utility of travel before travel can be translated into price. Another solution to this problem of metric may rest in nonmetric scaling methods. These are methods for removing nonadditivity from qualitative but ordered data (Kruskal, 1964).

Studies of specific resource systems should be pursued at the same time. Economic studies (of river systems or of water pollution) should be accompanied by social psychological studies which would look for social organization and social change implications of resource arrangements at the very time, or prior to the time, that these arrangements are being instituted. Studies of the social context in which decisions are made—of the politics of resource decisions—should be balanced against studies of changes in social organization which come about as a result of a given resource policy.

This and the following chapter illustrate sociological reconceptualizations of three environmental problems usually thought of in physical terms—air pollution, noise, and outdoor recreation. Each case is examined in more detail than the preceding one. The discussion begins with the problems as ordinarily conceptualized and then shifts from the physical phenomenon to an analysis of social action which takes place with reference to the phenomenon. The selection of these problems is not a judgment that they are the most socially or sociologically significant problems. Rather, these are the three issues through which the author has considered human action in a nonhuman environment.

The basic problem in reconceptualizing is to discover *transformation concepts* which present social, cultural, and psychological significances of physical environmental facts. The voluntaristic model described in Chapters Three and Four is recognized in these three tentative efforts.

FILTH AND SOCIAL AVOIDANCE

John Evelyn (1961) more than three hundred years ago appealed to his king to act to abate the pollution of London's air. "It is this horrid Smoake which obscures our Churches, and makes our Palaces look old, which fouls our Clothes, and corrupts the Waters, so as the very Rain, and refreshing Dews which fall in the several seasons, precipitate this impure vapour, which, with its black and tenacious quality, spots and contaminates whatever is exposed to it" (p. 18). These phrases have a contemporary ring. His abatement proposals might also be contemporary. He asked that the offending industries be removed some five miles from London. For the ensuing economic dislocation he offered a consolation. More workers would be employed bringing goods to London.

In a preindustrial age—outside of such nascent engine and hearth concentrations as were found in London—wind-borne soil, dust, or pollens were the usual air-borne particulates. The problem has become more complicated, because automobile and industrial effluents today carry particulates along with gases such as sulfur dioxide and carbon dioxide. The corrosion of materials due to sulfur dioxide increases the dirtying by particulates. There is some suspicion that the increase of carbon dioxide in the air—resulting from the burning of fossil fuels—may affect climate. Increased respiratory irritation in smog is a health hazard.

Traditionally, pollution problems have been classified in terms of the medium—either air or water—into which waste materials are discharged. Control of air pollution has largely been a matter of preventing pollutants from escaping from their source, of eliminating the sources, or of shifting location of the source or the recipient (Stern, 1968; Gilpin, 1963). This common-sense conception of the problem defines abatement in engineering terms. In fact, until recently the term used was smoke, and government interest centered in the Bureau of Mines (Davenport and Morgis, 1954).

Economists have added their analyses to those of physical scientists and engineers. They have examined the costs of reducing air pollution to specified levels and of allocating these costs among various sectors of the society. The recipients of pollutants are not necessarily related economically to the producers of pollutants (Kneese and Herfindahl, 1965; Kneese and Ayres, 1968).

Limiting attention to the question of particulates, several sociologically relevant issues are immediately apparent. The density of particulates may influence forms of social interaction. People may move gatherings—parties, picnics, or discussions—from outdoor to indoor locations. The particulates themselves are not the factors entering sociological analysis. Rather, the analysis of this problem would revolve about eating customs, esthetic values, and standards of personal comfort. (The emphases in the last sentence are on the words *customs, values,* and *standards.*) Particulate matter that has settled on a person or on household objects may also be interpreted as filth. This aspect of particulate pollution, its relevance for cleanliness, may be explored as one illustration of sociological conceptualizing in the air pollution field.

The amounts of particulate matter settling on people and in their households are, of course, functions of physical factors such as the amount of particulate matter in the air, wind velocities and directions, and characteristics of house construction. The amounts of air-borne particulates depend on the type of technology, a cultural factor. House construction also depends on technology and architecturally rendered esthetic concepts. The amounts of particulate deposited also depend on social behavioral factors such as the time people spend out of doors and their tendencies to leave windows open or closed.

Cleanliness or filth is an interpretation given to deposits of particulate matter. People and groups differ about the level of soil that they consider deserves the description *filthy*. The interpreted filthiness may depend on the type of particulate involved, which in turn depends in part on other cultural involvements of one or another particulate. Soot may be interpreted differently from organic dirt such as that deriving from garbage or bodily wastes. The levels of revulsion at any of these differ across cultural boundaries.

Several theories about the social and personal meanings of filth and cleanliness have appeared in social science literature. William James (1950, II, p. 434) debated whether the tendency to cleanliness was an inborn instinct or a learned habit. In the history of religious institutions, dirt has been associated with moral impurity. Rituals for regaining moral purity may simulate actions appropriate to the removal of physical dirt. Water and fire may be at the center of purification ceremonies. In Freudian theory, filth may be related to feelings of guilt, as in the image of Lady Macbeth at her handwashing ritual. In a medical context, dirt has been associated with disease. The responses to it have taken the form of public health measures, washing, disinfecting, and sewage disposal. This implication is carried in current air-pollution literature.

Social avoidance is a fundamental theme of all these theories. The appellation *dirty* is usually applied to another person or another group whom one rejects. The dirty object or the filthy person is to be set apart. In the case of guilt, the filthy self is to be avoided or purged.

The rejection is, fundamentally, rooted in characteristics of social relations. Dirt enters secondarily as a sign which rationalizes the rejection. The avoider expresses his reluctance to enter into a relationship by attributing a state of filth to the candidate for that relationship. The definition of filth is context-dependent. Certain body odors which are repulsive in the subway may be erogenic in bed.

The acceptance of a filthy self may mirror the avoidance response of others by asserting that the self should be rejected by others, at least by those others. In contemporary *hippie* culture, bodily filth may be a sign that the individual has separated himself from the scrubbed establishment. Filth as a signal that one wishes to be avoided may be expressed euphemistically as a wish for privacy.

Filth, personal and environmental, may also act as a social boundary-maintaining mechanism. Filth (or cleanliness) may be a symbol for structuring patterns of social avoidance. This meaning may condition individual and community response to filth deriving from particulate air pollution.

The issue of air pollution, particularly the public response to it, may be examined with reference to social cohesion. Patterns of social avoidance complement patterns of social cohesion or social integration. Social order, a fundamental sociological problem, rests upon the regulation of both avoidance and cohesion. Social avoidance is related to social integration much as, according to Georg Simmel (1955), social conflict is related to social cooperation. Conflict is one mechanism by which boundaries are maintained between social groups.

Conceivably, groups of various social ranks may be allotted residential areas with greater or lesser exposure to air pollution. If lower status groups occupy the more polluted areas, and they accept this role, it would follow that less political pressure for clean air might be expected. Particulate air pollution would more likely emerge as a social problem when upper strata are exposed to it. This is not only due to the affected population being more politically powerful, but also due to the fact that the level of particulates is culturally acceptable as a group discriminator. Certain social groups—the Shudra caste in India, for instance—assume the role of recipients of social refuse. Such groups may even resent attempts to clean them as inconsistent with their own accepted social position.

The association of cleanliness of self and of the immediate environment with social rank seems to hold cross-culturally. The higher one's rank the higher the standards of cleanliness, as defined in a particular culture. By extension, a greater effort would be expended in maintaining cleanliness by the socially mobile or by those with mobility aspirations. Contrariwise, an accumulation of dirt may be expressive of downward social mobility of individuals or communities. Other mechanisms of social avoidance such as locked doors, haughty attitudes, membership cards, socially identifiable clothing, may be used selectively. They signal avoidance to one role partner but not to another. Filth has high generality. A body odor or refuse filled room can repel all but a selected few potential role partners.

Given a culturally influenced level of cleanliness, under a given rate of particulate invasion, the effort expended in cleaning is one index of an individual's, or a family's, standard of cleanliness. The degree of achievement of cleanliness, relative to the standard, is a joint function of the available cleaning technology and the meaning of cleanliness for the person or group. A condition of dirtiness must be evaluated in terms of a discrepancy between the condition of the customary environment and the one the individual family maintains. This is a frame of reference problem.

In assessing the response to filth due to particulate matter, measures may be taken on three levels: the cleanliness of the self, the cleanliness of the interior of the house, and the cleanliness of the neighborhood. The interrelation among the standards for these three spheres provides important information. People living in squalor in an otherwise clean neighborhood differ socially, and, perhaps, psychologically, from those who live in squalor in an otherwise dirty neighborhood. In the former case, family disorganization may be a relevant variable. In the latter case, socially conforming behavior may be involved and the analysis might better proceed on the community level. People who live in clean homes in generally dirty neighborhoods may not be taking that neighborhood as their reference group (Merton, 1968, pp. 279–440). They may be a socially mobile family. A clean interior accompanied by neglect of the exterior, such as one finds in some well-to-do townhouse sections of cities, may reflect the anomic character of city living. External dirt may serve as a moat, a device by which the people in their clean houses maintain privacy by inducing communal avoidance of them. Or, contrariwise, external dirt may serve as a device by which they absolve themselves of interest in their immediate environment.

The frequency of self-ablutions and, at one remove, of the cleaning of clothing might measure the standard of personal cleanliness. Degree of effort expended in house cleaning, holding technology constant, is a useful indicator of concern with filth in that environment. Concern of people with the cleanliness of the environment is, in part, a function of the extent to which the environment is perceived as an extension of the self. A woman is more concerned with the cleanliness of her kitchen and a man with that of his automobile. Greater effort may be exerted in cleaning owned homes than in cleaning rented houses.

Neighborhoods may be classified by degree of cleanliness. This classification would refer to cleanliness of interstitial or common property, of the sidewalks, the streets, and the areas between houses. The consistency of the levels of cleanliness of these interstitial areas with that of the area within the house would depend, in part, on the sense of identification between the individual or family unit and the community as a whole.

The meaning of cleanliness of the house and community are not only functions of the extension of the self to these environmental areas. These broad areas are also the intersects of the self with other selves—the other family members who share the house or the other citizens of the neighborhood. The interest of a given individual in cleaning these areas depends on his relation to these others. Level of cleanliness of common areas is also a function of the attitude of these others to the environment. This points up the importance of keeping the unit of analysis clear—whether it be the individual, the family, or the community.

This conceptualization suggests but one type of sociological research with respect to the problem which society defines as air pollution. It is not the most important problem sociologically but is a convenient way of illustrating here how one may begin with a seemingly sociologically peripheral problem and quickly involve such a central concern as social cohesion.

NOISE OF STRANGERS

Motor noise which assures a driver that his car is working well is called the sound of an engine. A loose fitting gasket makes noise. Yet, as a warning it is a welcome, though unpleasant, sound. The term *noise,* a pejorative for *sound,* suggests a problem. Generally, any departure from some standard of system functioning is by its very nature a problem. The type of problem is given by the nature of the system being affected and the character of the standard being violated. Noise that interferes with the transmission of a message is a communications engineering problem. Vibratory noise with deleterious effect upon machinery is a physical engineering or simply physical problem. Interference with competent individual human performances may be spoken of as a psychological problem, and if noise disturbs the progress of social action toward some particular goal, it is a sociological problem.

The same noise may create all of these problems or any subset of them. Strictly speaking though, the term *noise* has a different referent in each case. In a communication system, noise refers to the overlapping of physical wave systems. Its referent is a physical event. In its effect upon machinery, the force of vibrations—a physical event—may be at issue. However, it is the meanings, the ideas, carried by the noise which constitute it as a psychological or sociological problem. The referent is symbolic. Not the physical event, but the human interpretation of it is the term which enters the analysis.

Noise as a sociological problem need not be the same as noise as a social problem. A sociological problem emerges in the course of objective dissection of social processes, in terms of some theory held by the sociological analyst. A social problem, on the other hand, is defined by an individual social actor or by a society. Corrupt political patronage may be a social problem for an enraged citizen but not a sociological problem for the analyst satisfied with

114

his understanding of the way patronage impedes, or "greases," the social machinery.

Noise, in its common-sense meaning, has become a public issue. Noise pollution lowers the quality of our environment (Bragdon, 1968; Wakstein, 1968) and noise abatement is a problem occupying the government and its science advisers (National Academy of Sciences, 1968a). Most work in this area has conceptualized noise as an acoustical problem and recommended ways of reducing its physical magnitude or of isolating it (National Academy of Sciences, 1968b). The participation of social scientists in this effort has been minimal.

Initial attempts at sociological and psychological conceptualization in this field are reminiscent of the theories that failed, described earlier. Some researchers have correlated physical noise with behavior. The results have been ambiguous. One such study reported, "Performance on vigilance, mirror tracing and anagram solving tasks was slightly poorer in intense background noise than under more quiet conditions. All such differences were statistically insignificant. . . . Repeated testing under noisy and quiet conditions on one task (anagram solving) showed insignificant differences which were reproducible from test to test" (Cohen, 1966, p. IV). H. F. Huddleston (1966) found that sound vibration impairs performance on certain types of problem solving tasks. Given our intuitive feeling that it is difficult to work in noisy surroundings along with the ambiguity in research findings, researchers are encouraged to continue this type of exploration.

Realizing that human behavior is not a simple function of noise as measured in decibels, some social scientists have interpolated the psychological concepts of *annoyance* and *perceived noise* (Kryter and Pearsons, 1963). These concepts open the possibility for investigating the complex relation between noise and annoyance. Perceived noise is not, of course, a monotonic function of the physical magnitude of noise.

A difficulty with the concept of annoyance is that it suggests evaluation of the noise phenomenon on a dimension of desirability-undesirability. This tendency dovetails with the tradition in psy-

115

chology, derived from work on our mute antecedents, to look at behavior in terms of approach and avoidance. The meanings carried by noise are, of course, more complex than this single dimension could reveal. In fact, annoyance or avoidance is conditioned by various qualitatively different meanings of noise.

Consideration of noise as an element in social action is not new to the social sciences. Although it has not received attention as a by-product of the machine age, its role as an intentional social product has been discussed. To pick up but one tradition, James Frazer's *Golden Bough*—the classic compendium of myth and folklore—is replete with examples of noise in its social context.

Frazer, through his contemporary redactor Theodore Gaster (1959), writes of a carnival in an Italian village. "The hymn of the Carnival is now thundered out, after which, amid a deafening roar, aloe leaves and cabbages are whirled aloft and descend impartially on the heads of the just and the unjust, who lend fresh zest to the proceedings by engaging in a free fight" (p. 253). The context is that of the death and resurrection of a god. The noise is publicly demanded to signify the appropriate human recognition of so cosmic an event.

Another illustration shows how noise functions in mimicking an event. The example is drawn from ancient Crete and the mimicry is that of the violent death of Dionysus at the hands of the Titans. "All that he had done or suffered in his last moments was enacted before the eyes of his worshippers, who tore a live bull to pieces with their teeth and roamed the woods with frantic shouts. In front of them was carried a casket supposed to contain the sacred heart of Dionysus and to the wild music of flutes and cymbals they mimicked the rattles by which the infant god had been lured to his doom" (p. 354).

Noise also plays a part in rituals connected with the riddance of evil. On a manifest level, its meaning rests on its supposed obnoxiousness to witches and demons. On a latent level, its production involves a joint activity through which, among other things, a community controls its collective anxiety. The following events

116

occurred on Walpurgis Night, the Eve of May Day, in Medieval Central Europe. "Always the weapons with which they fought their invisible adversaries in these grim encounters were holy water, the fumes of incense or other combustibles, and loud noises of all kinds, particularly the clashing of metal instruments, among which the ringing of church bells was perhaps the most effectual" (p. 526). Perhaps the most familiar meaning of noise in social science literature is that connected with Saturnalia or periods of license, periods in which the usual social norms are placed in abeyance—social ranks are inverted so that boys become kings and kings act as slaves, holy truths are profaned and ecclesiastical ritual is burlesqued.

These are a few meanings of noise in one social science tradition. Social science work in the noise field suggests a hypothesis about its meaning which is, in essence, an extension of the traditional hypotheses quoted from Frazer-Gaster. Whether any particular individual or group perceives sound as noise—as a social problem—depends on whether that sound interferes with the social ends the individual or group envisions. Noise, as part of a ritual for the riddance of evil, might be presumed quite as unpleasant to the witches as was the noise of Joshua for the inhabitants of Jericho. Noise associated with a period of license would be obnoxious to one not willing to accept what the licentiousness celebrates. The problem has two aspects: the sound is unpleasant when it occurs at the wrong time and wrong place—when the meaning is displaced in time and space; and the sound is unpleasant when it is generated in connection with the meanings of another group—that is, when it is the sound of strangers.

These symbolic interpretations of noise are significant for the analysis of everyday noises. As the physical noise becomes intense or acquires certain peculiar characteristics of pitch, the symbolic meaning gives way to a direct physical impact—direct in the sense that it involves not only symbolic processes but physiological processes as well. Noise which startles people—has strange frequencies, is intermittent, or is very loud—is bothersome primarily because of such direct physiological responses. This problem of high-intensity noise will be examined briefly after a discussion of some meanings of low-intensity noise.

What evidence in social research on noise suggests that one may become annoyed when noise is socially displaced or displaced in time or space in one's own group? Several kinds of evidence point up the dependence of human response to sound upon the type of meaning carried by the sound. Individual interpretations of sounds are governed by social norms. Whether the individual finds a sound or a level of sound acceptable depends in part on his expectations, in part on whether the existence of the sound is rationalized. Sound is less annoying when it is believed necessary (Cohen, 1964, p. 86).

Attitudes and feelings about noise are partly responsible for the individual differences in the effects of noise on performance (Cohen, 1968, p. 15). A study by E. V. Mech (1953) showed that performance in noise could be altered by giving the subjects different pretest briefings about the possible effects of noise on their work efficiency. "The group expecting noise to cause detriment did, in fact, show loss, whereas the group expecting noise to improve performance showed a performance gain."

Significantly, while attitudes influence the response to noise, general personality traits do not seem to do so. A trait such as passivity, which on an intuitive level might seem to make one tolerant of changing stimulus conditions, does not correlate with either verbal or physiological indices of stress response to sound deprivation (Biase and Zuckerman, 1967). Extroversion/introversion also has no relation to sound deprivation (Rossi and Solomon, 1966). Certainly the personality measures have not been exhausted. Perhaps some trait not yet measured correlates with response to noise or to sound deprivation. However, attitudes relevant to noise might be specific object-related dispositions—referring to the meaning of certain environmental objects for the person. Personality traits generally are thought to transcend specific situational contexts.

Joseph Antonitis (1965) exposed children to 1000 and 250 cycle tones as well as the sounds of breaking glass, a pencil grinder, a music box, and a voice giving a command. He found that the reinforcing (leading to learning) effect for such nonnoxious sounds was dependent on identifiability,—on whether the child knew the meaning of such sound. John Chotlos and Gerald Goldstein (1967) comparing three hospitalized patient groups on the basis of their response to sounds of weeping, tolling bells, door slamming, and tearing paper—among others—found that the association made with the sound was crucial to their response as measured by heart rate, digital temperature, and skin resistance.

The meaning of sound is to some extent culturally given. However, the physical characteristics of sound, even aside from high intensity sounds, generate their own meanings. Paul Vitz (1966) varied the amounts of information in elements making up sound sequences and found that pleasantness ratings increased up to a moderate amount of stimulus variation. This could be due in part to the contemplation by the individual of the differing characteristics of the sound and, in part, to the interpretation by the individual of physiological shifts taking place in response to shifts in the character of the auditory stimulus.

Individual attitudes about sound need not be consistent with social norms. A norm is not only a reflection of attitudes but reflects the interaction of attitude and other factors in a structure of relations. To illustrate the possible disjunction between individual attitudes and social norms, a study made by the National Academy of Sciences Committee (1968b, p. 4) supposed that a population might come to accept sonic booms of supersonic transports quite passively while suffering extensive annoyance and disturbance as individuals. Contrariwise a population might, as individuals, suffer relatively little annoyance and disturbance, yet generate such a level of complaint behavior and of community reaction as to make the situation politically difficult.

The Committee on the Problem of Noise (1963, p. 5) recommends that to mitigate the problem of noise, complaints about noise, the public should be kept informed about which noise nuisances are readily avoidable. The comparison of notes among individuals, the discovery of interindividual differences in exposure to noise, and the availability of leadership for organizing the opinions of the neighborhood can all be factors in determining a complaint rate.

Social action with regard to noise requires not only a norm for interpretation but an organization for implementation of action. Horace Parrack (1957, Ch. 36, p. 3) noted that the type and extent of group action are not related to the noise stimulus. Group action depends on the organization of a neighborhood, its leadership, and the extent of its knowledge about effective procedures. The seeming lack of concern in certain public circles about the noise problem may be understood in these terms. If noise is not defined as a social problem, and no norm exists for registering a complaint, a population is not likely to express concern.

Expressed annoyance is an indicator of the extent to which individuals and groups perceive sound as noise, as a social problem. The amount of annoyance reported by interviewees, however, is not directly proportional to the amount of physical noise to which they are exposed. The British report found that whether people live in a noisy or quiet place does not affect the proportion who say they are seriously disturbed. Distance from the airport did not appear as an important factor in the amount of annoyance attributed to airport noise. The Committee on the Problem of Noise (1963) reports 87 complaints about jet aircraft noise in 1956, 205 in 1960, and 541 in 1962, a six-fold increase. The number of jet flights rose from practically none to 52,000 per year over this period (p. 63). (A complaint may be a more conservative indicator of a social problem than annoyance expressed to an interviewer because it depends on a propensity to complain and knowledge of where to direct a complaint. On the other hand, a social climate may generate a complaining fad which escalates the number of complaints out of proportion to the bases for them.)

Individuals and groups concerned to realize different types of action in the face of noise may differ in their assessment of its annoyingness. Ervin Gross and Arnold Peterson (1963, p. 21) say, "The extent of our annoyance depends greatly on what we are trying to do at the moment. It depends on our previous conditioning, and it depends on the character of the noise." A report of the

On Man in His Environment

British Committee on the Problem of Noise (1963, p. 8) argues that the annoyance felt as a result of noise may be thought of essentially as the resentment we feel at the intrusion into our physical privacy or into our thoughts or emotions. Annoyance is a function of the emotional information which sounds carry; such information has an emotional effect far out of proportion to the physical intensity of the noise.

Noise annoyance is ordinarily not eradicable through habituation. Once noise is judged annoying, a decrease in the annoyingness of the noise requires changing its meaning for the auditor. This is accomplished not by repetition of the stimulus but by a redefinition of the situation or of the goals of the action in which it is implicated. In a literature survey (Bolt, Beranek, and Newman, 1967, p. 115), annoyance by aircraft noise was reported to be independent of the length of exposure to such noise. In fact, in the British Committee study, 34 per cent of the respondents said they had become more used to the aircraft, and 24 per cent said that they had become more bothered over the course of a year (p. 217). Rather than developing a habituation pattern, the population seems either to polarize with respect to the noise or to be randomly distributed across the three categories of response (more bothered, less bothered and no change). L. R. Lieberman and William Walters (1968) experimented with the relatively pleasant sounds of music and found that repeated listening does not always increase the enjoyment of serious music. High school and college students listened to Stravinsky each day for ten days, but their enjoyment of the music did not increase. It may be, although this is not clear, that response change does not take place even on a relatively nonsymbolic level. New born infants stimulated for five successive days by a buzzing sound showed acceleration of their heart rate. There was no change, however, in the amount of acceleration over the days except for that due to increasing maturation (Graham et al., 1968).

The National Opinion Research Center (NORC) at the University of Chicago (quoted in Clark, November 1961) found that a combination of sociopsychological factors accounted for more of the variability in annoyance than did the noise-exposure variables. A particular level of physical noise proves bothersome to certain people but not to others, in certain situations and not in others, and at certain times and not at others.

Alexander Cohen (1964, p. 86) attempted to specify the social-psychological variables at issue. He conjectured that an individual will tolerate certain sounds associated with an advantage. The comforts derived from air conditioning apparently outweigh the noise produced by the units. The economic values to the community of nearby factories or airports may partially offset the noise nuisance they produce. The British report agrees that tolerance for noise depends on its perceived usefulness. During the World War II, although the number of military aircraft increased until few parts of Great Britain were unaffected by their noise, most people welcomed the noise as a sign of allied air strength. Complaints about noise caused by aircraft began after the war.

The concept of *usefulness* in these studies assumes that individuals engage in rational accounting, developing their own cost/benefit analyses to decide whether they are annoyed and whether they choose to tolerate annoyance. The issue is more complicated. The British study compared daytime and nighttime annoyance, finding about equal numbers of complainants at both times despite the fact that there were four times as many aircraft movements by day as by night. They also found that physical locale seems to influence annoyance. Road traffic bothers 36 per cent of people who are at home, 21 per cent of those outdoors, and 7 per cent of those at work. Aircraft disturbs 9 per cent of people at home, 4 per cent of those outdoors, and one per cent of those at work (p. 63). Cohen (1964, p. 86), noting that complaints of evening noise are more numerous, hypothesized that sleep and relaxation are being interfered with. He then generalized that a sound may be judged annoying if it is inappropriate to the activity at hand.

A more general hypothesis may be suggested. The rates of social interaction follow a rhythmic pattern. At various times people enter the arena of social activity and at other times withdraw from it. There are the small day and night rhythms, the larger weekly rhythms and even larger seasonal rhythms. The pattern of bothersomeness of noise seems to constitute a counterpoint to such life rhythms. The same noise seems to be more bothersome when it occurs during a withdrawal than during an active phase. Thus, noise seems more bothersome during the evening than during the day, on weekends than on week days, and probably more so during the winter than the summer, allowing for the differential access of noise through open windows.

As a corollary, noise seems more bothersome the more the locale is withdrawn from communal social action. Thus, people are more annoyed by the same sound when they are at home than when they are outside. Pursuing this, noise might be expected to be more bothersome to people in their bedrooms than in their living rooms, irrespective of whether they are trying to sleep.

This hypothesis describes general rhythms of social engagement and withdrawal. Individuals participate or withdraw from specific social actions, and their attitudes about the sounds produced by these actions would depend on whether they are part of or approve of the actions. The nonparticipant in a noise producing activity is annoyed to the extent to which the meaning of the activity, rather than simply the volume of the noise, is bothersome. This is the problem of every staid citizen exposed to the more sonorous profligates. Noise is annoying when intruding into a social activity which is not generating it or not related to it in any functional sense. It is annoying when it communicates the presence of a disapproved activity or group. The clatter of voices belongs to the cocktail party and the rock music to the celebrants. They are not bothered by the sounds. In fact, they seek them. But noise, unlike other aspects of their activities, reaches out beyond the immediate confines of the action. The group of noise producers is, in some sense, socially distinct and may be in conflict with the group of noise receivers, who are unwilling captives of the activity. Inability to control noise may become a factor in its bothersomeness. David Glass and Jerome Singer (1968) argue that the frustration and inefficiency of people exposed to noise is related to their powerlessness to control it. The noise of aircraft is more bothersome to those at home trying to read than to those at the airport waiting for a plane. The noise of street drilling is more disturbing to the policeman on the beat, not to speak of the individual at home, than to the supervisor of the job. Noise originating in the normal activities of an individual's own group, such as his work group, is less bothersome to him than noise originating elsewhere. The study by National Academy of Sciences on the sonic boom (1968b, p. 8) found that people associated with the aircraft industry are less bothered by sonic boom.

A study by the Stanford Research Institute (1967, p. 3) also found that noise associated with one's livelihood is more tolerable. The tolerance may come from identification with the noise producers. Borsky (1961, quoted in Bolt, Beranek, and Newman, 1967, p. 65) notes that in a neighborhood where individuals are largely employed by a noise generating industry, people tend to be tolerant of that noise. The same people might not tolerate noise of an industry engaging in operations of which they did not approve or in which they were not involved. Even music from a television or a transistor radio can be bothersome to one not seeking those sounds. Annoyance is a response determined by the individual's associations with the social activity producing the sound as well as a response to the dissonant qualities of the sound. This hypothesis has been foreshadowed, though not developed, by R. D. Berendt's (1968, p. 4) concept of *acoustical privacy*. He said that a major sociological and psychological factor which often is overlooked is the need for conscious or subconscious assurance of acoustical privacy. People do not wish to hear the sounds of their neighbor's activities, nor do they want their neighbors to hear them. The ever increasing residential density in buildings makes acoustical privacy a social and personal issue for the occupants. In surveys neighbors are frequently found among the offenders. Studies in Boston, New York, and Los Angeles found that people are bothered by children and neighbors about as much as by the noise of traffic (Bolt, Beranek and Newman, 1967). D. Chapman (1948, cited in Cohen, 1964, p. 86) reports that 10 per cent of the residents of an area were troubled by the noise of delivery trucks. However, 40 per cent complained over the less intense noises produced by the neighbors' pets. Conceivably, the delivery trucks signaled a contribution to the residents. The noise of pets was considered separate and foreign, irrelevant to those without pets.

Not only social scientists have observed these facts. L. E. Farr, a physician, after reviewing five qualities that K. D. Kryter had associated with the "annoyance value of sound" (unexpectedness, interference, inappropriateness, intermittency, and reverberation) writes, ". . . one additional and very important quality should be added—the origin of sound. Self-generated sound commands a very high tolerance in the individual generating it. . . . But sound generated by another person or an impersonal sound, such as a sonic boom, has a very high annoyance value. . . ." (p. 100). Cohen (1968, p. 18), observing that some indoor noises from a neighbor's apartment are more bothersome than from one's own, introduces the picturesque image of people living in a "sound-porous fishbowl."

Following the hypothesis that it is the noise of strangers which is annoying, tolerance for an invasion of privacy might be expected to depend upon the relationship to the invader. Distress at a neighbor's noise might be a function of one's relationship to that neighbor. In studying noise as a social problem, neighborly relations rather than noise might be the first focus of study. A report of the Office of Noise Abatement (1968) states, "The problem can be classified as one of conflict between two groups—the producers of air transportation service and those people (individually and collectively) living and/or working in communities near airports" (p. 2). This report does not go on to the logical conclusion of their finding. It recommends a rational approach to resolving the conflict by reducing the adverse affect of noise to the lowest practicable level. While such a move would be salutary, it is not quite clear that it would solve the underlying problem.

People who complain about noise also complain about other things in the community. Distress at noise may be just one indicator of general alienation from the community. There may be a general relation between annoyance and nonparticipation in broad classes of social action. The above-mentioned NORC report found that complaints about noise were related to overall satisfaction with living conditions in the area. The National Academy of Sciences (1968b, p. 8) report suggested that noise complainers are those who habitually question political authority and have a history of frequent complaints. The British Committee report found that the more things informants disliked about their area, the higher their scores on the aircraft annoyance scale. Noise as a social problem is not separate from the problem of integration and alienation in the community.

These hypotheses provide a context for some other findings of noise surveys. Members of various social classes are differentially bothered by noise. This is supported by a variety of indicators of class. The British survey (referred to in Bolt, Beranek, and Newman, 1967, p. 81) found differences among social classes in susceptibility to road traffic noise. Borsky found professional, managerial and skilled nonmanual persons more susceptible to road traffic noise than manual or unskilled workers. With ascent in grade of occupation, sound seems more of a nuisance. Brain workers experience more sound nuisance than manual workers. People who owned their own homes were more likely to be complainers than people who rented their homes. Sound seems to be more a nuisance as income increases. The two most prosperous classes are more susceptible to sound than the two least prosperous classes. Higher social standing is associated with higher susceptibility to sound nuisance. People in a middle age range experience more sound nuisance. They also have higher incomes than both the preceding and the succeeding age groups. Susceptibility to sound nuisance increased among people with older children. This merely replicates the age factor. Susceptibility to sound nuisance tends to decrease with an increase in family size. Because larger families are more common in lower classes, this may replicate the class finding. Sound nuisance is experienced more by those in the highest educational groups. This too may be another social class indicator.

How are these associations between various indicators of social rank or social class and annoyance to be explained? The Stanford Research Report (1967, p. 3) points out that business leaders, engineers, architects, physicians, and attorneys have better access to the sources of political and economic power than do members of other communities. Hence, they show more rapid and massive reaction to noise. Parrack (1957, p. 36–3) argued that higher class people understand their legal rights better and possess more knowledge of ways to control the agency creating the annoyance. These explanations referring to differences in social power help explain the increased complaining more than they help explain the higher annoyance response rate of survey interviewees. A likely explanation is the idea that higher class people value their isolation more than other groups do. High incomes buy distance and isolation. Higher class people are resentful of intrusions. Basically, according to the hypothesis, a characteristic of people in regulatory or leadership positions in society is to control their social involvements. If they did not they would be inundated by information. Thus, their sharper response to noise is a reflection of the more focused environment in which they would live.

Categories which usually constitute significant independent social variables do not seem related to susceptibility to annoyance from noise. The Bolt, Beranek, and Newman, Inc., survey (1967, p. 115, quoting Robinson, Bowsher, and Copeland) found no important distinction between the judgments of men and those of women or between younger or older age groups in scores on a scale devised to rate intrusiveness or annoyance. The British survey, too, found little difference in the responses of people of various sexes and ages. Perhaps differences due to age and sex were not discovered because the noises presented, such as aircraft noise, were not differentially relevant to various age and sex groups (Clark, 1961, p. 15). Ira Berman (1961) asked men about household noises. They were most annoyed by washing machines and vacuum cleaners (p. 37). These are women's noises and so belong to another action system, another group. Would a group of women be more annoyed by the sound of a power mower, or of an all-male sporting team, than would a group of men?

A high-intensity noise crowds out much of the symbolic meaning on which the above argument depends. The psychophysio-

127

logical impact of noise overshadows its symbolic interpretation. As intensity increases, as many as 400 impulses per second may be generated in the fibers within the ear. Such a rate is maintained for only a fraction of a second after the onset of a sound. The rate then decreases to about 150-200 impulses per second. Nerve fibers differ in the specific decibel levels at which they begin to respond but most reach their peak response some 30-40 decibels beyond that initial level. The experience of intensity, or loudness, rests on two factors: The number of fibers brought into play by the stimulus and the number of impulses evoked by it (Morgan and Stellar, 1950).

There is a known relationship between the intensity of the stimulus of sound in decibels and the psychological experience of loudness. According to S. S. Stevens (1961, pp. 1–34), "sense organs serve as the transducers that convert the energies from the environment into neural form." The relationship between the psychological magnitude ψ and the physical magnitude ϕ is expressed by the equation $\psi = k\phi^n$. This exponent differs for each sensory modality. For sound, it is .6. When the decibel level is doubled, the experienced loudness is somewhat less than doubled.

Turning to more psychological terminology, it may well be that high-intensity sound produces a system overload. The system attempts to cope by shifting the sound threshold (Lebo and Oliphant, 1968). Ego boundaries may give way, releasing their surveillance of deeper emotional processes. This may be the basis of the experience reported in *Time Magazine* (August 9, 1968, p. 47) with the sounds of rock orchestras. A Florida teenager explained "the sounds embalm you. They numb you." The notion of numbing may not refer to the sedating quality but to the experience of being affectively enveloped. Battlefield roar may have a similar effect, numbing the soldier and enabling him to advance in the face of danger. Released affect might also be experienced as anxiety. Whether affect is interpreted as security or anxiety depends, in part, on the socially defined message carried by the sound—whether the siren is warning of an air raid or announcing the "all clear." It also depends, in part, on the degree of psychophysical effect and on the attitude of the individual toward this effect. This attitude is a socially influenced psychological response.

Research in the psychology of noise has just begun. The work to date in sensory psychology, in studies of the auditory sense, can be extended into personality psychology. Noise as a stress phenomenon influencing both ego and deeper level personality functioning can be explored. Studies might test the suggestions about high-intensity noise as a releaser of affect. The relation between sound and psychopathology might also merit attention. Because the structure of meanings differs among the psychopathological syndromes, one can expect differing responses to noise.

Social psychological studies can explore factors influencing public attitudes toward noise. Some studies already accomplished —which correlate social attributes of individuals with their propensity to be annoyed—should be repeated using more sophisticated measures and more delicate forms of data analysis. It is important that research move from the simple approach-avoidance dimension to a mapping of qualitative meanings.

There has been no work, known to this investigator, which would qualify as sociological. The hypotheses advanced in this paper about annoyance by low-intensity noise fall between the social psychological and the sociological. The notion that annoyance is related negatively to participation in the noise-producing social systems leads directly to explorations in community segmentation, social alienation, and social integration. Investigation might be guided by the methods of human ecology and explore the relative spatial distribution of people and of noise, the role of noise in various types of social activities, and its distribution through social strata.

The formalization of social norms into law may either follow or precede their wide social acceptance. An article in the *Columbia Journal of Law and Social Problems* (March 1968), "Urban Noise Control," reports an interview with a New York City councilman who said that the police cannot take the time to enforce the present city noise ordinance. The councilman said that the ordinance refers to unnecessary noise and that the police do not know what that means anyway. The same article also reports the comment of a noise expert: "Don't blame the policeman. He won't enforce it if there is no public support" (p. 111). Some municipalities, such as Santa Barbara, California, have reacted to mounting public pressure by passing ordinances which ban jet noise and sonic boom caused by airplanes flying over their territory (p. 117). The British report says that a noise nuisance has to be very great before most people will take it upon themselves to make a formal complaint to the authorities. One may add that a certain type of social segmentation is required. Complaints will increase when there is more community cleavage or when wider segments of the society come to accept what are today elitist norms about an appropriate environment. W. H. Ferry (1968) implicitly recognizes this sociocultural fact: "The case against noise must be based on civilized standards as much as on public health or economy. . . . We should not have to produce irrefutable evidence that our health is being impaired before action can be taken against the ever more numerous assailants of quiet. Civilized life means communities among which quiet and privacy rank high: and civilized life is one of the principal goals of all activity here below" (pp. 93–95).

Policy makers dealing with noise as a social problem should differentiate between high- and low-intensity noises. For low-intensity noise, where no physical health hazard is directly involved, the approach might be framed in terms of invasion of privacy—the freedom of the individual to decide upon the social activity in which he participates. For high-intensity noise, matters of psychophysical stress come to the fore. The issue may be approached directly in terms of mental and physical well-being. The latter problem includes the former but the former need not encompass the latter.

CHAPTER VII

�чичичичичичичичичичичичичичичичичичи

Recreation as
Social Action

🌳🌳🌳🌳🌳🌳🌳🌳🌳🌳🌳🌳🌳🌳🌳🌳

Social research in outdoor recreation has been accumulating for two decades. Rolf Meyersohn (1969) has prepared an excellent guide to the literature. Little of this research, however, rests on a sociological theory of recreational activities. As a consequence the findings have not contributed to a coherent body of knowledge. Before projecting further research, fragments of this past work will be drawn together.

For convenience, outdoor recreation research may be divided —according to its sources of data—into large-scale demographic studies and studies of specific populations. Demographic studies, in general, enumerate individuals or attributes of individuals as colloquially conceived. The underlying social and psychological meanings of their activities and the social system in which they are embedded receive less attention. Such studies sample both participants and nonparticipants in outdoor recreation. They enumerate the incidence of manifest recreational activities and classify the participants in terms of such demographic characteristics as age and sex. The second group of studies, those focusing on specific populations, although relying on small and often haphazard samples come closer to elucidating the inner character of outdoor recreational groups.

The National Recreation Survey (Ferriss et al., 1962) used the broadest sample of the population available. The data were gathered as part of a regular Current Population Survey of the Bureau of the Census, which employs a sample of one in 35,000 households in the total United States. The study directors were constrained to restrict themselves to items feasible for a door-to-door census canvass by people trained in simple enumerating rather than interviewing. Recreation activities were classified as boating, water skiing, bicycling, camping, and so on, and respondents were asked how often they took part in these activities. These popular formulations of outdoor activities are classifications of the implements used, the places where they are used, or the relation between some implement and a feature of the physical environment. Such classes might be helpful for short-range planning for manufacturers of boats and skis. They are not, however, good proxies for relevant sociological or psychological factors and give scant direction for long-range planning of recreation facilities. A given piece of equipment can be employed in a variety of social situations—the bicycle can be used for transportation to the store, in a sporting competition, as a way of expressing friendship with a group of peers or as a device for exercise. Information on the popularity of these activities—in particular social groups—along with information on the probability of bicycling combined with a prediction of future membership in those groups in stated locales would give a still firmer basis for short-term planning of bicycle manufacturing. This would, nevertheless, be insufficient information for planning recreational activities since other devices may be substituted for bicycles in the long run to serve the same social functions.

The National Recreation Survey includes a factor analysis based on frequency of participation in these popularly conceived recreational activities. By clustering recreational activities, the factor analysis allows inferences from common attributes of activities in particular clusters. Sightseeing and driving have a high loading on a factor named *passive pursuits;* water skiing and fishing have high loadings on *water-related activities;* sports and bicycling have a high factor-loading on *physically demanding activities.* This factor analysis shows the likelihood that individuals who engage in one also engage in another activity—that is, people who drive for pleasure are more likely to sightsee than they are to go water skiing, and people who fish are more likely to go boating than they are to go hiking. This information leads to social and psychological analysis if we assume that the vacationer chooses among such activities in a cluster in terms of some underlying predisposition. Then the researcher, scanning the items in one cluster of activities and contrasting them with the items in another, can define the relevant dimension or predisposition responsible for the particular clustering. Some options, of course, mechanically imply others—having arrived at the water for boating, one is more likely to swim than if he had gone backpacking.

Sociologists have found certain population measures to be generally useful and rather easy to obtain. These include measures of level of income, education, age, and sex, among others. In the National Recreation Survey, and in many like it, the researchers have opted to follow this traditional list of demographic variables. These measures of members of a population are correlated with the activities of those individuals. If the correlation is statistically significant, these traditional measures are accepted as successfully dividing the population in ways relevant to the activities under consideration. Income, for example, has been found in other studies to be correlated with level of education, political attitudes and the choice

133

of a church. In this case, it is correlated with the propensity to hike. The reason for such associations with income may be different in each case.

The correlation coefficient alone reveals too little. A finding that participation in active sports depends more on age than any other measured factor provides little insight. Time and budget pressures prevented analysts of the National Recreation Study from pursuing most of the data beyond zero order correlations. The intervening mechanisms which can explain the associations between activities and demographic classes are hidden. Without knowing the underlying meanings of recreational activities, it is not possible to extrapolate reliably to future demand for outdoor recreation.

The National Recreation Survey was selected for purposes of illustration because of its breadth and the quality of its sample. The comments above are relevant to most social research in outdoor recreation. Gerald Gurin and Eva Mueller (1962), also employing a national sample, attempted to assess the demand for outdoor recreation. Their principal dependent variable is a constructed *activities scale*. Eleven activities including swimming, boating, hunting, driving for relaxation, and nature walking enter the scale. Each respondent received a score of "1" for each activity in which he participated four or less times and a score of "2" for participating over four times during the preceding year. Some extra points were granted for spontaneous mention of participation. The sum of these credits constituted the activities score.

Combining the activities arithmetically assumes them to be mutually substitutable—a one-time participation in skiing has the same effect on the score as a one-time participation in sightseeing. Picnicking is equated with hunting in its activity value. There is little hint as to what these activities might mean to the participants. A multivariate analysis using nine variables such as income, education, and length of paid vacation explained 30 per cent of the variance in the activity score. The composition of the activities score makes it difficult to know what this could mean. Gurin and Mueller also correlate some demographic variables with the individual activities. Here their findings essentially support those of the National Recreation Survey.

In both of the above studies, it would have been helpful if demographic variables had been selected that were specifically relevant to the meanings of the various activities. Income is a predictor of political preference because it indicates membership in certain interest groups. A negative correlation between income and hiking might mean only that hiking is inexpensive and so more likely to occur in lower income groups. The income variable would be more significant if it were shown that hiking expresses an element in a particular culture or set of social relations and that people with lower incomes are more likely to possess that kind of culture or to have those types of social relations.

Philip Hauser (1962) has criticized the mechanical use of demographic variables, suggesting that the usual rural-urban classification, based on the size of the respondent's city of residence, is insufficient for recreation studies. Urban residents might better be classified by the degree to which they assimilate the urban way of life. Hauser's proposal is that urbanism, as an ethos, is the relevant variable. He hypothesizes that the degree of acculturation to urban life affects the way outdoors is experienced. Specifically, greater acculturation to urbanism is associated with less interest in outdoor activities.

William Burch, Jr. (1966) says that instead of the usual classification by age, and perhaps by number of children in the family, families might be classified by their position in the family life cycle, a combined measure of the age of parents and of children. He found in his own research that the age of a family's children influenced the type of camping the parents elected to pursue. At various stages in the family life cycle, camping activity assumed different meanings for the family.

A second group of outdoor recreation studies has drawn data from specific recreational populations. Typically a researcher interviews, either in person or by mail questionnaire, persons or families using a particular facility at some given time and place.

Data are assembled on both the preferences and the social characteristics of the respondents. These populations tend to be small, although at times the size of the sample analyzed is not appreciably below that of some of the large scale studies. However, sample selection is not subject to the same statistical control. Leslie Reid (1963) distributed over 49,000 questionnaires to people entering twenty-two summer and two winter recreation areas in various parts of the country. The low response rate makes it difficult to generalize even to the population found entering the areas. Those who return mail questionnaires tend to differ from those who receive and fail to return them. Reid's method, by relying on the population of users, precludes the comparison of background characteristics and preferences of recreationists with those of non-recreationists. Recreationists with various preferences and characteristics are compared with one another. This may be said about nearly all of the published studies of specific recreational populations. This approach is efficient for studies designed to probe the bases of preferences.

In 1960 Charles Glock and Gertrude Selznick (1962) interviewed 491 respondents in seven wilderness areas. They found that by classifying respondents according to their social backgrounds—including whether they were church members—it was possible to explain the types of meanings the wilderness experience held for respondents. The meanings were classified as exit-civilization (to get away from people or the work-a-day world), aesthetic-religious (to observe the beauty of nature), health (to restore health), sociability (to enjoy companionship) and pioneer spirit (to experience the feeling of being able to survive alone). Nonchurch members, for example, were more likely to find an exit-civilization appeal in the wilderness than were church members. This study—a rather sophisticated application of survey research methods—combines numerous items into useful indices of the strength of each appeal of the wilderness and the degree of commitment to the wilderness and relates these indices, for instance, to early camping experience. This work, too, cannot be generalized to a larger population and certainly not to the population of nonusers of the areas. However, Glock and

Selznick go far in applying a cross-tabular method to explain the preferences in the study of population.

Robert Davis (1967) intensively interviewed a small sample of hunters and campers to gather information to construct a measure of the demand for outdoor recreation in the Maine woods. L. C. Merriman, Jr. and R. B. Ammons (1965) studied recreationists in the Bob Marshall Mission Mountain Primitive Area and Glacier National Park. Both studies located slightly over one hundred respondents. While the unrepresentative character of their samples precludes generalization of the results to a broader population—including the population of users of these areas—these investigators could probe attitudes toward terrain, conditions of crowding, and the availability of facilities. Davis recorded information on the nature of the groups in which these recreationists traveled. He examined and then monetized the time and driving effort expended.

The cost of face-to-face interviewing makes the mail questionnaire attractive. However, nonresponse rate then becomes a problem—in Reid's study only 22 per cent of the original population responded. Wiley Wenger and H. M. Gregersen (1964) have shown that the rate of nonresponse differs quite drastically among participants in various recreational activities. The traditional way to handle this problem is to interview a subsample of the nonrespondents, compare their characteristics with those of the respondents, and then apply appropriate correction factors to the population of respondents.

Introducing Reid's study, Marion Clawson writes that interviews of individuals regarding recreational experiences they have not yet had are limited for estimating demand because the users can evaluate only what they have known. The interviewee expresses choices without appreciating the costs of the choice. This criticism does not apply intrinsically to the interview as a method of data gathering but may apply to inferences carelessly drawn from interview data. If the respondent is asked about his own experiences and these experiences are aggregated uncritically, then Clawson's critique is valid. If, however, the reported experiences are interpreted in terms of underlying attitudes regarding recreation, treated as indicators of underlying meanings, then the data can be extrapolated to predict behavior in situations which the interviewee has neither experienced nor known. This is sometimes done intuitively. A psychoanalyst, for instance, may infer an underlying motive from a series of expressions. In quantitative survey research, the underlying meanings are more often discovered through scaling techniques. Guttman scales, the Lazarsfeld latent structure models, and paired comparison techniques, among others, use a mathematical model to identify an underlying theme of a series of items (Stouffer et al., 1950).

Nothing prevents an interviewer from instructing his respondent in the costs of alternative actions. However, the discrepancy between an interviewee's assertion that he will incur a cost of a given magnitude and his actually doing so plagues interpretation of all verbal data. Market researchers have developed some techniques for coping with this problem. These include the development of methods of reason analysis or accounting schemes which direct the interviewer to inquire about each of the steps in a decision, for instance, to buy or to take a vacation (Lazarsfeld, 1954).

Most social scientific studies of outdoor recreation are executed in an economic frame of reference. Their concern is with estimating the demands for outdoor recreation. The demand for an environmental resource will vary depending on the way the resource enters systems of action and on the size and character of the social systems with which it is involved. Sociological and psychological factors may affect the shape, slope, or the area under the economic demand curve.

Hauser (1962) argues that demand for outdoor facilities may be a function of the size, distribution, and composition of the potential user population. Demand is not a direct function of such factors but is conditioned by the way a population incorporates a resource in its action system. Arabs along the Asian and African littoral do not develop extensive sea bathing facilities, but Germans travel some distance to avail themselves of the cool waters of the North Sea. Such preference factors, rooted in cultural orientations, may be subsumed under what Hauser calls the "composition" of the population.

Demand for outdoor recreation has been estimated from participation rates. This estimate is cruder than one based on willingness to pay because it equates the payment proxy of each person. Clawson (1959), assuming that driving is a sacrifice or payment, estimates demand from the distances participants drive to a recreation area. Some recreationists drive for pleasure and some pass a recreation area near home in favor of one at a greater distance.

Demand is also related to class culture and education. Gurin and Mueller (1962) found that an increase in income is associated with an increase in picnicking and nature walking. However, an increase in income is associated with a decrease in hunting. Since hunting is the most expensive of these activities, one might have expected the demand for it to increase with income. Perhaps hunting has different meanings in the cultures characteristic of each income level. The predatory character of hunting could eliminate it as a middle class activity while it remains popular in the elite and in working classes. The number of working class individuals in the Gurin-Mueller sample is high relative to the number of elite class respondents. Thus when tabulated, the working class would express great interest, the middle class little interest, and the upper class great interest again. However, the small number at the upper end of the scale would not permit separate classification. Therefore, an inverse rather than a curvilinear correlation between hunters and income appears.

The probability of camping seems to have a curvilinear relation to income. Interest in camping increases to above the nine thousand dollar income level and then declines. Abbott Ferriss' findings (1962) differ from those of Gurin and Mueller (1962) only in detail. The income/camping curve levels off at the fifteen thousand dollar level for Ferriss' national sample. (In the South and Northeast, Ferriss also found that it leveled off in the $8,000–$9,999 income class.) Thus, the effective demand is conditioned by the high motivation among those with moderate ability to pay and lower motivation among those better able to pay. People who live in urban areas are more likely to picnic and less likely to camp. Urbanization may decrease willingness to pay for camping. People in the Northeast are more interested in swimming than are people in other parts of the country. People in the West are more interested in camping. We do not know whether this a a result of urban-rural contacts or of some regional cultural factor such as access to camping areas.

Camping is also curvilinearly related to the number of years of education. It peaks among those who completed no more than high school. Since income and education are so highly correlated, it is impossible to discern from the tables in the Ferriss report whether the contribution of education to the variance is independent of that of income. Nonwhites, compared with whites, rarely go camping. Further analysis of the data would be required to tell how much of this is due to the relative sparseness of Negroes in the West, where so much of the camping is done, and how much to their low income level. Professionals, craftsmen, foremen, and technical workers are more likely to camp than members of other occupations. A prediction of future demand would have to take into consideration the future distributions of people in these categories. Since, however, these factors do not act directly on the recreational demand but through interpreted meanings, demand could not be predicted accurately from changes in the population character alone. Perhaps in fifty years camping may be more popular among the college educated than among the high school group. Class cultures are not constant over time. The relation of camping to such underlying cultural meanings must be grasped to predict future demand.

An operational definition of outdoor recreation begins with the observation of human action set in a natural environment. Some outdoor recreation engages the natural environment. A site called a *recreational facility* is a natural environmental feature that has been socially transformed. Skis and guns are not simply physical objects but are culturally developed tools for coping with problems set by the natural environment. Implements are defined in terms of the social action in which they participate. Skis and guns may be used in a variety of social acts, only some of which are recreational. When they are part of recreational activity, they assume a special meaning. What is *recreational activity?* Does it, as Joffre Dumazedier (1967) says of leisure, have the force of an "independent fact," to be considered on its own terms, with its own dynamic?

To define recreation as leisure time activity begs the question. What is leisure or how does one "do" leisure? In everyday affairs, leisure is contrasted with work. Intuitively, this distinction is not difficult to grasp. Individuals have little difficulty in telling an interviewer whether they are working. It is more difficult to articulate the criterion by which a layman or a researcher makes this distinction. It is not possible to arrive at a viable distinction in terms of the intrinsic nature of the activities, in terms of the experience of the actor, or in terms of the productivity or rationality of the activity.

A difference in the intrinsic nature of work and of leisure activities is not a good guide. The same intrinsic activities appear under both headings. Fishing is work for one person and sport for another. Driving is work on Monday and recreation on Sunday.

The pleasure-displeasure distinction does not help. Some people find more pleasure in work than in leisure. There are certainly times when people prefer work to leisure. The contrast between effort and relaxation does not distinguish work from leisure. A girl may think of her relaxed function as a receptionist as work and of her vigorous activity in a swimming pool as recreation. A classification of acts according to their immediate productivity also will not clearly separate work from other activities. Playing golf with a client, a leisure activity, may be as income-relevant as signing a sales contract with him, a work activity. The rationality with which means are related to goals does not characterize one sphere to the exclusion of the other. Football tactics, called play, are more rationally planned than the work of a graphic artist.

Why are none of these criteria satisfactory for distinguishing between work and leisure? The reason is that the distinction between the meanings of these activities is not given on the level of individual

141

behavior. The distinction rests on social criteria. Work and leisure are distinguished by the goals of the systems, usually social, in which they are integrated. Work is an attribute of a role in a social system. The sociology of work, as understood, for instance, by Theodore Caplow (1954), is the study of the way work roles emerge and are structured relative to one another, the way role occupants are recruited, and the influence of occupying particular work roles on the individual's performance in other roles. Work is a role in a social system; one goal of that social system involves a production-consumption function. A tangible, usually marketable, product is the conscious goal of work. Leisure might produce such a product but only tangentially.

In addition, work is supported by societal sanctions. Some broader group, of which the work group is a part, rewards and punishes the worker for occupying or failing to occupy a work role and for the manner in which work is performed. These sanctions, or rewards and punishments, may take the form of money but are also at times rendered as prestige or social acceptance. The demand that one shall work is considered legitimate in most of society and is supported by moral sanctions (the virtue of work and the immorality of nonworking) and by coercion (the giving or withholding of the means of physical sustenance). Both criteria, production-consumption-relevance and social sanctions, are necessary to define the character of work. Work is the name given to all activities performed as a member of a group which is oriented to production-consumption and sanctioned by the broader society. Organized sports, for example, carry performance-contingent sanctions, but the participants are not oriented to production-consumption goals. Sports which are so oriented become professional, and participation in them defined as work.

In defining work, leisure has been defined negatively as an activity not involved in a system of production-consumption and lacking performance-dependent sanctions. Leisure then appears as part of a residual category of all activities not defined as work or not accomplished as part of one's occupation. This residual category must be further partitioned to arrive at a definition of recreation.

Nonwork activities are not all, by their very nature, recreation. The deacon of a church or the mother of a family is neither working nor playing. (In labor force statistics and economic analyses, they may be classed as working but not as gainfully employed.) Religious groups may have working leaders—who receive performance-contingent rewards—and nonworking communicants. Recreation may play a part in religious group life (the church picnic) or in family life (family camping). It may even be an adjunct to work (the company bowling team). Religious and family groups exist alongside occupational groups. They are neither work nor recreational groups.

Recreation in its pristine form may, like work, be defined in terms of a social context. This context seems to engage a group which, on the one hand, is wider than the primary group of a particular family but which, on the other hand, is narrower than the community of common economic interest, the network of occupational groups. Recreational activities take place in groups that are often culturally more homogeneous than occupational work groups and often culturally more heterogeneous than family groups. Recreational activities may follow family lines, as they do in traditional societies, or ethnic, ethnoreligious or racial lines. In a small, culturally homogeneous town, the recreation group and the community could be coterminous. In a large urban setting, recreation may be a neighborhood affair, especially where neighborhoods are also culturally homogeneous. Among those emancipated from residential constraints in establishing friendships, recreational time is shared with members of a *social circle*—a delimited community sharing some particular style of life (the country club, the Bohemians, the professional circle). The style of life may be determined by ideology or some composite of income level and ways of allocating income among consumption items.

A group assembled around a recreational activity may be called a recreational group. Recreation, however, does not generally form the sole basis of relations within such a group. Rather, recreation is one among many functional activities in such groups, just as work is one among many functional activities contributing to the goal of an occupational organization. (Some sporting or playing associations, formed specifically around the development of a particular game, exemplify a limiting case in which interest in the game provides the principal reason for the existence of the group.)

In the United States, the principal prestige ranking system, the system of authority, and the distribution of incomes are all based on work. This is a peculiar feature of certain Western societies. In Bedouin society, for example, rank, authority, and income are more closely tied to lineage than to work. The Soviet Union illustrates an extreme form of the American orientation. Recreational activities there tend to be viewed as adjuncts to occupational relations. The work group and the recreational group are often identical.

Recreational activities, like the larger class of leisure activities to which they belong, have been defined as not oriented to the goal of production-consumption and not subject to an obligation to participate. More precisely, however, recreation activities do not appear obligatory in the eyes of the broader society. No economic penalties are imposed for nonparticipation. In a society in which the occupational system is dominant, recreation may appear peripheral or even unimportant. While recreation is not geared directly to occupational goals, it does contribute to the life of certain nonoccupational social groupings. The importance of recreation rests on its contribution to such groupings and the part they play in the broader society.

Recreation meets certain of the functional requirements of these groupings and is indeed subject to obligatory norms. The affirmation of group solidarity and culture is one such functional requirement. It is a latent function rather than a manifest goal. Unlike the goals of production, solidarity is not attained by manifestly pursuing it. Group solidarity, like love, rests upon trust and commitment. Manifest pursuit vitiates it. Recreation that appears purposeless when judged in terms of the instrumental, goal-oriented action of the occupational group is far from purposeless when viewed within the context of the subgroups of which it is a part.

Further, while the broader society does not impose sanctions for recreational participation, recreational groups do require participation on the part of their members. One's office mates may not really care if one takes a vacation, but one's family may press the requirement. People in certain social positions must give dinner parties which people in related social situations must attend. In a traditional society, violation of these recreational mores could lead to economic sanctions. In our society such nonparticipation may lead to ostracism from the offended group, but would provoke economic sanctions only insofar as the recreational groups are articulated with occupational groups. (Once entering a recreational situation, one is subject to many rigid rules—the rules of play—but this is another problem.)

Our earlier definition of work may now be modified. Work is an activity within an occupational social system. Concretely, it is usually accomplished within an organization. It contributes to the attainment of a goal of that organization and to a goal of the society to which it belongs—specifically, to the goal of production. The broad society rewards this performance with goods and services. The norms of obligation are legitimated and compliance enforced by the broader society which, because of the economic interdependence of individuals and groups, has a stake in work performance.

Recreation, on the other hand, tends to take place within more culturally homogeneous subsocieties—principally, within family, ethnic, religious, and ideological groupings, including social circles composed of individuals sharing a common life style. Roger Caillois (1961), the French sociologist, defines play as an activity in which "property is exchanged but no goods are produced." It contributes, among other things, to the integration of such subsocieties. They, in turn, impose an obligation to participate in recreation. This obligation is not necessarily supported by the broader society.

145

Recreational activity is not apparent in societies at earlier stages of cultural development. While there is a prejudice in our society about the lazy and lackadaisical primitive who knows no work discipline, to term his nonworking activities recreational may be an improper borrowing of concepts from our own culture. A culture must have rationalized the concept of time to have the notion of recreation. A rational concept of time is one in which events are ordered discursively and perceived as occurring discretely in sequence. In cultures with a prerational concept of time, the continuous present is predominant. A discursive time order of activities, such as work on the one hand and recreation on the other, is difficult to imagine in these situations. Lacking the temporal distinction, work and recreation blend.

While recreation requires a temporal separation of activities, it is not necessarily spatially separated from work. Both may occur on the same precincts but not at the same time. Even outdoor recreation may not be spatially separated from work. Hunters and loggers may use the same territory. Spatial separation arises secondarily in the effort to separate recreational from production-consumption activities and from the social relationships organized around those activities.

The Dutch historian Johan Huizinga (1955) finds a play element in such serious work-like activities as law, war, and philosophy—as long as the actor is not striving for direct material profit. In effect, any absolute distinction between work and play is analytical. In actuality, work and recreation overlap to a greater or lesser degree. Perhaps the earliest distinction between work and play, more precisely between work groups and recreational groups, arose in religious contexts. In a polytheistic age, religious holy days were set aside for the worship of special deities. The sabbath was a consecrated tithe of time. It was called a time of surcease from labor but was, in effect, a shift from the usual to special labors related to worship. Religious holy days might involve communal celebrations or pilgrimages to a central shrine. Greek games formalized certain aspects of these celebrations—separating audience and participant, stressing competitiveness and excellence in performance.

146

These were no longer worshipful activities but activities under the protection of deities. Games were modeled on myths of the activities of the gods.

In early modern Europe, sports and games were disengaged from religious life and, in fact, became a competing focus of social organization. The Reformation church opposed certain sports and leisure amusement as wasteful or even sinful. James I promoted sports as part of his fight against Puritanism. The ambivalent attitude toward fun, as opposed to productive activity, reflected in the Reformation position is still with us. Today, recreational and devotional activities compete for time on the Saturday or Sunday sabbath.

Recreational activity can be thought of as a symbolic drama played by a group. In recreation, a group may be experimenting dramatically with solutions to group problems. The experiment may flow into real situations in which those solutions are applied. This is the sense in which the playing fields of Eton were related to the battle at Waterloo. Literary criticism, the sociology of literature, and the sociology and psychology of play have evolved methods for analyzing the symbolic meanings of such activities (Burke, 1941; Lowenthal, 1957). Recreation may also be a ritual drama of reaffirmation or rededication to the existence of a particular group. Models established in the sociology of religion suggest this function (Durkheim, 1954).

The dramatic meaning, the function of the drama for the group, is given by the content of recreational activity. A classification of dramatic themes could generate a typology of recreation. Such a formidable task will be deferred at this time. However, some correspondence exists between the *form* recreation takes and the *content* of the drama played through that form. A classification of forms of recreation is a fundamental requirement for research. One classification is suggested here.

Recreational form may be classified along three dimensions —one regarding the ecological relation of man to nature, a second regarding the social relation of man and man, and a third regarding the psychological relation of man to himself. All of these relations

147

rest upon a symbolic interpretation by man of his situation. In this sense, they are all mediated by culture. The following illustration is developed for the case of relatively extended vacations. With some modifications, it could be applicable to other types of recreation.

Extended vacations contain elements of a drama about residential, occupational and social mobility. They may be dry run experiments in mobility. Vacations specifically designed to keep the vacationer within a single social circle, such as the gathering at a spa of the old European elite, may be dry runs for residential mobility. Such vacations are also occasions for political sparring, matchmaking and reaffirming the integrity of one class as contrasted with other classes.

Spatial location and movement—the ecological dimension— seem to be crucial in the definition of a vacation. All vacations (with the exception of the limiting case of the homebound vacation of television watching or digging in the garden) involves some geographic and social movement. The individual or group abandons the physical and social environment of the residential community and selects a spatial and a social setting appropriate for the vacation. This appropriateness is dependent upon the dramatic content to be expressed. Spatial movement may be classified in terms of a physical characteristic of the territory toward which it is oriented. Movement may either be to *open spaces* such as the desert or the seaside, or to enclosed *inner spaces* such as forests. This defines two polar types of vacation classified in relation to topography. Dramas associated with gaiety and sexuality may tend to seek out the seaside setting, while those associated with solemnity and labor may have more affinity for the forest glen. These associations between form and content may be presumed to be culturally influenced and individually learned. The physical symbol vehicle, open or inner space, must be appropriate for the symbolic meaning which it carries. Conceivably the inner spaces offer more resistance to life and so become associated with work, while the open spaces involve the explosively creative meanings associated with water and expanse and so are associated with these activities.

On Man in His Environment

The point is that, at base, the classification is of two types of social action. The classification may be constituted in terms of the topographic features because of some widespread cultural evaluation of these features. The topographic features seem to have similar meanings, often similarly understood stage settings, for large numbers of people. The general relation between agorophobia (open space) and eroticism has been documented in psychoanalytic practice (Abraham, 1927) and that between claustrophobia (inner space) and the struggle to free oneself, archtypically, to be reborn, has been described by Bertram Lewin (1935).

Some vacation movement vacillates first to inner and then to open spaces. People travel, sometimes emerging at open land and sometimes penetrating into the woods. The process of movement itself, rather than the destination, is then the primary setting. This type may be called *nomadism*. Movement to inner and to open spaces, as opposed to nomadism, involves a sedentary relation to topography during the vacation. Movement to open space and a sedentary settling in open space is one extreme pole of the dimension and a sedentary settling in enclosed inner space is the other pole. Nomadism is an intermediate form between the two poles.

A second distinction rests upon a change in social relations —in effect, a matter of the direction of social movement. In leaving the occupationally determined community of residence, the vacationing group, or single person, may seek isolation from all other groups or persons. Such movement, from a social center outward, may, by physical analogy, be called *centrifugal*. Alternatively, the group or person may leave to join another group—go to a resort, a religious community or a summer colony of a particular political shade or to visit other members of the family. Movement that assembles vacationing persons or groups into another group may be called *centripetal*.

The South Sea island paradise, the centrifugal vacation utopia, is atypical in our culture. Literature on outdoor recreation suggests that centripetal vacations are the more popular. Margaret Mead (1962), commenting on the centrality of centripetal movement, has noted that 51 per cent of those who traveled on vacation did so to visit kin. Many outdoor activities, such as camping along the way, were secondary to this primary purpose. Gurin and Mueller also found that centripetal vacationers in America outnumber centrifugal. They say that for a minority the appeal of the outdoors is associated with getting away from people, but that for the majority it is a chance to share activity—to be gregarious.

Centripetal vacations are an occasion for reaffirming belongingness to groups not ordinarily integrated through the occupational and income stratified residential pattern of American society. These centripetally formed groups tend to be more homogeneous than the community of residence with respect to ethnic background or political ideologies, particularly minority ideologies. Most frequently, as Mead noted, they are kin groups. Perhaps for the first time in history, in America members of extended kin groups are geographically separated while still belonging to the same territorial and national society. The vacation is a way of compensating for the occupationally induced mobility and consequent separation of like-minded or otherwise related people.

Max Kaplan (1960) notes that sometimes centripetal vacationers are from different backgrounds but share leisure interests. Grouping around specialized leisure time interests, such as sports events or the intercommunity meetings of fraternal orders, may be part of the process of forming new social groups. These are affirmations of what Charles Kadushin (1968) has called "social circles, informal networks of individuals who share a common interest."

Centripetal vacations, while contributing to the integration of special groupings, have total societal functions. In strengthening the family units of which the society is composed, the centripetal vacation contributes to broad societal maintenance (a pattern maintenance-tension management function). Because families in mobile American society cut across class lines and because ideological or interest gatherings bring people together from different occupational strata, the centripetal movement may dampen a tendency for the society to polarize along social class lines (an integrative function).

On Man in His Environment

Certain broad social functions are subserved by both centripetal and centrifugal vacations. Integration of local polities is encouraged as travelers resident in one jurisdiction submit themselves to another jurisdiction. The requirement of reciprocity in the treatment of these citizens and the accompanying diffusion of ideas restrain tendencies to localism.

Vacations have been classified topographically with respect to whether open or secluded sites are sought, and then they were classified social relationally with respect to the temporary dissolution or reformation of groupings. A third general dimension for classifying outdoor vacations rests upon the allocation of individual psychological energies. A vacation may offer an opportunity to "give out" in some new setting—to expend energy, to relate actively to the environment. A vacation may, contrariwise, offer an opportunity to "take in," to relax and become reenergized, or to submit, to be soothed or passively encounter the environment. The active and the passive orientations are two forms of psychological encounter between the vacationer and his environment. The classification is based on manifest activity or passivity. In a deeper sense, of course, manifest activity toward the outer environment may cloak an attitude of "taking in," gobbling it up, while the outwardly contemplative individual may be in inner struggle.

Conceived in terms of activity/passivity, vacations may subserve a personality function. The problem of allocating energies (a tension management function with reference to the internal functioning of the personality and a goal attainment function with reference to the relation of the personality to its situation) is central to any personality. Activities induce new tensions which displace old ones. The passive vacation involves a disengagement from the sources of tension. The way tensions are related to objects has implications for a sense of ego competence. The active vacation involves a mastering orientation through which the ego develops an image of itself as more competent. It is associated with a frontier atmosphere, with ruggedly individualistic people. Ego competence is not usually at stake in the passive vacation. The passive vacationer's sense of

151

ego competence, of control, rests on submission of the self to the environment, a mystical merging with the environment to absorb its strength.

Of course, all of these meanings, whether based on a response to a physical feature or on social and psychological action, have the status of hypotheses. It remains to be determined empirically whether open space does provide a setting for more expressive behavior or whether an active camping vacation involves testing of one's sense of competence. Joseph Sonnenfeld (1969) has tested the meanings of various landscape and climatic features such as rain, fog, and sunshine for Eskimo groups by applying Osgood's semantic differential. He has begun to trace some cross-cultural differences in environmental meanings but, principally, has illustrated the need for such empirical verification of hypotheses such as those suggested here. Together, the moves to inner/outer land, centripetality/centrifugality and activity/passivity, define a three dimensional conceptual space. Values along each of the three dimensions are continuous. A recreational occasion may be located by its triplet of values, its location on these three coordinates. Thinking of the dimensions, only as a trichotomy and two dichotomies, however, twelve (2 x 2 x 3) distinct formal settings for recreation are defined. Each setting is a stage for a relatively distinct type of recreational drama.

For simplicity, here are some examples based on two of these dimensions: the psychological dimension of activity/passivity and the social dimension of centripetality/centrifugality. A cross-classification of these two dichotomies defines four *ideal typical* vacations: centripetal-passive, centrifugal-passive, centrifugal-active, and centripetal-active.

A vacation may involve centripetal social movement and place the vacationers in a passive relation to the environment. The individual or group may join another group for the purpose of relaxing together. A religious retreat exemplifies a centripetal-passive vacation. The individual may contemplate, seeking the gift of the spirit, while in a community in a quiet wooded spot. The religious centripetal-passive form is infrequent in the United States but common in Thailand where men may enter and leave a monastery by arrangement. The assembly of a regular clientele at a country hotel provides an American example.

A centrifugal-passive vacation is exemplified by a family or individual seeking to relax in isolation from others. The esthetic motif may be prominent as vacationers stroll through beautiful scenery with minimal exertion. The centrifugal-active vacation of an individual or group involves exertion in circumstances of isolation from other individuals or groups. Hunting, fishing, and hiking —involving the development and testing of skills, exemplify this type of vacation. Family members, lodging in a country cabin, may assume ordinary tasks under unusual conditions and be welded more closely together in their accomplishment. A centripetal-active vacation is exemplified by individuals gathering from all over the country for an annual sport parachuting competition. Of course, the participants rather than the observers are the active ones.

The table presents these illustrations, schematically cross-classifying the three topographic, two social and two psychological relations. Twelve basic forms of vacations are defined.

Several other attributes of vacations are subsumed by these primary dimensions. Calvin Stillman (*Black Rock Forest Papers*, No. 28, 1966) distinguishes between hunters who want a touchable environment and those who are satisfied to observe it. Touching is, manifestly, an active orientation to the environment; observing is a way of passively taking it in. Thus Stillman's distinction overlaps that between activity and passivity. Burch (1965) emphasizes the dimensions of self-sufficiency in the case of the family camping group. This is another way of stating the choice of centrifugal rather than centripetal form. The group that goes away centrifugally, to be alone, is seeking to be self-sufficient.

Elwood Shafer et al. (1969) use landscape categories in assessing preference ranks assigned by campers to scenic photographs. They classify landscapes into zones of water, sky, vegetation, and nonvegetation. Water and sky seem to be special cases of the inner-open space dimension. The matter of vegetation, degree of aridity, seems to be an additional significant dimension not con-

Samuel Z. Klausner

TYPOLOGY OF VACATION FORMS

Topographic Relation	Direction of Social Movement	Psychological Orientation		Illustration
Sedentary, Open Land	Centripetal	Active	1	Beach surfers
		Passive	2	Beach front hotel guests
	Centrifugal	Active	3	Family camping on beach
		Passive	4	Stereotyped South Sea island paradise
Nomadic	Centripetal	Active	5	Teen-age western summer tour
		Passive	6	Cruise ship
	Centrifugal	Active	7	Hiking
		Passive	8	Sightseeing
Sedentary, Inner Land	Centripetal	Active	9	Boy scout summer camp in mountains
		Passive	10	Country hotel guests
	Centrifugal	Active	11	Lone cabin in woods
		Passive	12	Private serviced lodge in mountains

sidered in our scheme. So much of human life has been organized with respect to verdant and arid conditions that these features must carry a heavy symbolic loading.

A vacation may also be described in terms of its esthetic character. Esthetic experience of nature may be associated with the psychological dimension of passivity. Franklin Thomas (1925) quotes Wilhelm von Humboldt's characterization of the appreciative vacation (from Humboldt's *Cosmos*, p. 3): "Mere communion with nature, mere contact with the free air, exercises a soothing yet strengthening influence on the wearied spirit, calms the storm of passion, and softens the heart when shaken by sorrow to its inmost depths." Stillman (*Black Rock Forest Papers,* No. 27, 1966) offers his own expression of this mood: "Any great natural phenomenon has a special meaning for persons who behold it. For many of us this meaning is positive and personal, beyond articulate expression. It is something we treasure, something dear to us; something whose preservation is important to us" (p. 4). This imagery of esthetic appreciation is inconsistent with an active manipulatory orientation. Hunting, for instance, exemplifies the active orientation. Tony Peterle (1967), studying hunters in Ohio, found that those who enjoyed the esthetics of the natural environment hunted less. This may, of course, be a special case of the inverse correlation between hunting—known to be culture-group related—and level of income. Logically, though, active exertion of effect upon environment would tend to be associated with an aggressive attitude toward that environment, a desire to change or exploit it in use rather than contemplatively enjoy it.

Three other important dimensions have not been included in our recreation typology: the length of time allocated to the recreation, its location in social time, and the size or type of the recreational group. Each of these dimensions refers to a level of analysis different from that from which our three dimensions are drawn.

Differences that follow from various lengths of time do not seem, in themselves, to involve qualitative distinctions of meaning (except, of course, insofar as they allow the selection of different options). A family picnic in the local park and an overnight family stay at a camp ground are both characterized by inner space location, centripetal social movement, and an active psychological orientation. The overnight outing would, however, provide for a more intense drama, placing both a greater strain on family relations and holding the possibility of greater integration. Length of time may affect the intensity of a particular type of vacation. It is a significant variable for economic analysis which is less concerned with the social psychological meaning of a commodity than with the demand for it. Time allocated in traveling to a site and at the site is crucial for an operations analysis of travel flow on site usage (Cesario, 1969). Abbott Ferriss (1962) also classifies activities according to the time spent in them or the money required to engage in them. He did this to measure the intensity of interest or demand for particular types of vacation. The priorities established in scarce time may be indicators of meaning. Time budgets, a well established social research tool (Sorokin and Berger, 1939), have been used to demonstrate changes in the relation of work and leisure, although they are costly to collect in a reliable way (Converse, 1968).

A classification according to the location of the vacation in social time—whether over Labor Day or in midwinter—places it in a broad cultural context, and is likely to have consequences for its meaning. Weekend recreation, summer vacations, and holiday outings are all tied to cosmic changes and to changes in the types and rates of general social interaction. The special meanings of these occasions are linked more to the content than to the form of recreation. Location in social time controls the articulation of recreation with other activities. The yearly gathering around the Christmas tree unites recreation to religious institutions; a visit to Gettysburg on Memorial Day binds it to political institutions. These cultural-content distinctions are important for analysis of the place of recreation in the broader social setting.

The cultural character of the vacationing family or club—like location in social time—defines the relation between recreation and these other social institutions. Some vacations are planned to coincide with meetings of political organizations while others are vital events in the yearly calendars of churches and families.

The size of the vacationing group is yet another important distinction. Size may simply reflect the type of group or it may be relevant in its own right. A vacation may be solitary, a small group or a mass activity. Each of the twelve settings defined above may accommodate groups of varying sizes. For the single vacationer, the proposed dimension may be used to assess the meaning of the vacation for the individual personality. For a group of vacationers, these dimensions may be used with reference to social system analysis.

Recreation may be integrative for an individual personality (helping to articulate the values or energies of a person) or for a social system (helping to articulate relations among a plurality of persons).

A typology is a first step in planning research. It defines the variables. However, a typology alone tends to have a static ring. Vacations may be conceptualized in more process-oriented terms. The moment that one's focus is shifted from the forms to the content, from topography, social movement and energy economics to the dramas being played in these settings, it is difficult to resist a sense of social process. One common vacation theme seems to be that of "rebirth." Such colloquialisms as refreshment and recharging batteries suggest this imagery. A vacationing family pulls away from its usual surroundings, isolates itself for a time in an environment with a different set of physical and social challenges and then returns to its original setting. A vacation of this type is judged successful when some relationships among family members are fortified. Max Kaplan (1960), using this rebirth imagery, writes that leisure either renews or develops personal identity.

A vacation promotes rebirth by encouraging a regressive social or personality process, a return to a simpler mode of social or personality organization. It is facilitated by withdrawal from usual role obligations, particularly the occupational, and the assumption of new, more earthy, roles. A forest is a particularly apt setting for a play around the theme of regression and rebirth. The forest has served as a secluded hideout, or a place to hide in, from time immemorial. Merriman and Ammons (1965) describe the advantage of the isolation of the forest, the charm of treading where no sign of human intrusion is found. Complex cultures have failed to develop in the depths of the forest. For Thomas (1925), it is an environment which imprisons and prevents growth of large social groups because its inhabitants must struggle for the essentials of survival. William Goode (1962) has pointed out that in such a situation individuals avoid their usual class position, with its privileges and burdens. Status in the forest depends on camping skills. There is an unmasking of the individual. This unmasking may be a prelude to social regression. The division of labor, which civilization has carried to a high degree, may be reversed with each family member taking on a wider set of tasks. The norms which, outside the forest, supported all the highly specialized statuses slip away. In a socially regressed state, with some social norms in abeyance, a reorganization of the relations of authority among members of the family is possible.

In the family camping situation, one type of reorganization is around leadership. In American society, the types of labors and skills necessary for forest survival are more likely to be possessed by males. The matriarchate, which has come to characterize the American urban family, is rejected in the wooded camp. The woman pursuing household type chores is somewhat more dependent on male assistance in the successful accomplishment of her tasks. The rebirth through camping is characterized by reassertion of patriarchal control.

Regression and rebirth under the best circumstances are not smooth processes. Families held together by routine may be strained by the travail of a vacation. With the usual authority structure disrupted, some adult campers—particularly in the absence of children—may become licentious, engaging in excessive drinking and even brawling and destroying of property. Delinquents in the camp setting, like delinquents in the city, are only a minority. Vacation delinquents are probably not the psychological and social siblings of urban delinquents. Model citizens at home may become delinquent when the authority structure and the usual role relations are placed in abeyance. Social disorganization, even in its simple, nondelinquent forms, may be needed to clear the way for a new reintegrative process. A family may emerge better integrated after working through a chaotic period to new norms. The reassertion of patriarchal authority is one resolution. If the normative disorganization is not resolved, the family may emerge weakened and the vacation considered unsuccessful—even when the weather and mosquitoes have been kind.

The paradigm presented above rests on two proposals and a suggestion about their connectedness. It is proposed that the content of recreation may be analyzed in terms of a drama in which the players symbolically deal with a life problem. This concept could be validated by establishing a classification scheme for the dramas—much as the scheme for interpreting stories in the Thematic Appreciation Test has been developed. Then, dramas of groups with different life problems might be compared in terms of some criteria of meaningful coherence between dramas and life situations. The proposal would not, however, fall on some particular classification of dramatic themes. If no themes associated with social or personal characteristics of a population could be discovered, the proposed approach would not be useful for empirical research—although it might still retain some descriptive interest.

The second proposal, for a formal typology of settings (the one elaborated in this paper), could also be tested. Coordinates might be assigned to particular vacation activities through an empirical investigation. The assumption is that the different formal settings are associated with some nearly universal symbolic significances—that entering a forest, for instance, indeed means—or is significant because it means—isolating oneself from the usual social environment or placing oneself in a situation in which one is compelled to struggle against environmental resistance. These meanings could be tested on an individual level with attitude measuring scales and on a group level by a content analysis of social communication.

These two proposals are independent. The validity of the proposal about the dramatic themes does not depend on the validity of the proposal about the formal characteristics of settings. Conceivably one proposal might prove useful and the other not. However, the third proposal that individuals seeking particular dramas are drawn to particular settings depends on the joint validity of the first two proposals. This relation could be tested by observing the statistical likelihood of certain dramatic content being played in one formal setting or another.

A few suggestions for studies in outdoor recreation that might be implemented at an early date are appropriate here. The gathering of original data is the most expensive part of social research. This fact places a premium on secondary analysis of data already available. Data gathered in the course of national sample studies, such as the National Recreation Survey (Ferriss, 1962), have not been fully exploited. Despite the misfortune that some socially relevant questions were not asked in the survey, a theoretically oriented treatment of the relation of the measured demographic factors to outdoor activity is possible. Few organizations have the resources to obtain national population samples of the quality which the Bureau of the Census provided for this survey. A secondary analysis of those data might encourage the Bureau to include more sociologically relevant indicators in future surveys. What follows are some specific leads for applied—rather than theoretical—research in outdoor recreation.

A prime research question is one of population parameters. What are the relevant recreational groups within the broad national population? As noted above, the recreational community is wider than the family and narrower than the occupational-residential community. Inner city populations consist of a multitude of recreational communities, ethnic, ethno-religious, political-ideological, and racial among others. Each community differs in the way its members distribute themselves among the types of recreation. Italo-American and Polish-American communities each congregate at different locales and engage in different activities. Both differ from the Negro community in their concepts of recreation. The Negro community itself is not homogeneous. The recent migrant from the rural South and the second or third generation city dweller are struggling with different problems which they may dramatize through the recreational medium. It would be worthwhile to explore, in depth, the meanings of outdoor recreation for each of these recreational circles.

The example of vacations away from home, one among many forms of recreation, was selected for elaboration in this paper. A conceptual scheme might begin with this broad classification of vacations and then proceed to a more specific typology of meanings of particular sites, times, and activities. What are the life problems people express in their recreational play? Through what manifest activities and in what settings do they enact these dramas? What

160

proportion of the population selects each type of vacation? What are the social, cultural, and psychological characteristics of those choosing one rather than another type?

Questions of meaning may be answered with the help of two techniques: drawing upon the tradition of clinical psychology, depth interviews could be conducted with some small samples; drawing upon the tradition of anthropology, participant-observation of people engaged in recreation could go far towards clarifying the meaning of that activity.

To extrapolate to the future, it is necessary to learn something of the laws of development of recreational patterns of individuals. This might be done in two ways. A less exacting but also less expensive way would be to collect recreational life histories and subject these to sociological and psychological analysis. A preferable approach, and a more time-consuming one, would be to repeatedly interview the same panels (a selected group or sample) of vacationers over several years. Both these approaches could produce developmental data on the recreation life of a population.

The life dramas of low-income Negroes are different from those of the white middle class. Their recreational preferences may also differ. The association between recreation and sexuality differs across class lines. Sex-homogeneous recreational activities, such as hunting by males and card playing by females, are common in the white middle class. Among low-income Negroes, sex-heterogeneous recreation is relatively more frequent. Family picnicking may also be assuming greater importance in the urban Negro than in the urban white populations. Some recreational activities even take their name from the type of food consumed—beer parties, weiner roasts.

Among youth using recreational facilities one observes a good deal of aggressive (not necessarily hostile) behavior. This drama may have to do, in part, with the establishment of dominance-submission relations—at least micro-orders of dominance or submission. (The macro-order is set in the larger social system.) Youths also seem to enjoy testing themselves against some natural barrier—the seeking of stress (Klausner, 1968). Stress seeking is not

161

classbound but is probably differentially distributed among classes. Facilities might make provision for such activities. The functional equivalent of the mountain for the mountain climber may be needed—at a lower cost than access to the mountain entails—in the more congested city environment.

A conceptual distinction has been drawn between work and recreation. What, however, is the relationship between these two worlds, the world of work and the world of recreation. One might think that the unemployed, having more leisure time, would participate more in available free recreation in the park or playground than would their employed brethren. This would lead one to expect a positive correlation between use of local facilities and unemployment. More likely, unemployment and recreational participation are negatively correlated. In the American situation, where status and rank—even in primary groups such as the family—are contingent upon position in the occupational structure, it is likely that alienation from one's occupation would imply alienation from the social relations of the recreational community. Such a study could elucidate some links between recreational and vocational rehabilitation. It might throw light, not only on the case of the unemployed but also on the problem of the role of recreation in the rehabilitation of socially, culturally, or physically handicapped persons in general.

The typology of vacations presented above deals with meanings sought by vacationers. Vacationing could be examined as a system in its own right. The community of vacationers and the community of suppliers of vacation facilities are bound together in a broader system of vacationing. A study of this sort, in tandem with studies of vacationers, would be necessary background for rational planning of the social-organizational and physical facilities of vacationing.

Each type of vacation makes its own demands on facilities. Behavior of the suppliers is not independent of the behavior of the vacationers. Facilities are required for the meeting and mingling of groups of people and for opportunities for isolated living. Suppliers provide the raw material for people to act upon, such as wilderness or lakes, and equipment for engaging in the activities, such as skis and canoes. They also provide amenities which minimize the vacationer's need to look after his own comforts. Knowledge of the interaction of suppliers and consumers of recreational services and goods is an initial requirement for predicting future recreational demand.

The classification of vacation spots into inner and open space was based on some general meanings which such places might assume. A playground or a park becomes endowed with certain more specific social meanings by virtue of the social activity that takes place on it. Various locales become associated with specific groups. Davis (1967) hypothesizes "that one chooses the campground where he will take up more than transient residence with the same social considerations (and possibly with a higher degree of realization) that guide his choice of neighborhood, club, and other associations." In some cases the social criteria applied might, of course, differ for home and for camp.

The relations among the groups associated with various locales may not be peaceable. Locations, say within a park, become territories for which social groups may compete. When the group controlling the facility commands overwhelming social power and uses this power to exclude another group, the question becomes one of discrimination in the use of public and quasi-public facilities. The less powerful—excluded—group may appeal for admission to outside forces such as the constitution or the judiciary.

When the groups are more nearly matched in power, an outright conflict over the facility may erupt. Such conflicts are extensions of broader social conflict. The facility is merely one battleground. The current struggle over public accommodations is a case in point. Gang fights in public parks are another. Under what conditions does violence erupt in a recreational facility and how can it be managed? An answer may be approached by collecting and analyzing a series of case studies of violent incidents in such facilities.

Sometimes facilities shift "ownership." A kind of Gresham's law, not necessarily related to the relative power of the groups involved, seems to operate. The arrival of one social group may lead to peaceable evacuation of the territory by another social group. The shifting of the population of users of a recreational facility may be a miniature example of the invasion and succession rule of urban residential shifts.

The type of activity in an area may change. At one time a forest may be a locale for isolated backwoods camping and at another time for social campgrounds. The direction of change is probably from isolated to social use. At one time, a site may serve people interested in active vacations; and at another time, it may serve people interested in passive relaxation. Commercial development would induce or reflect a change in that direction.

The same physical facility may serve more than one type of vacationer without conflict when their needs are complementary. Davis (1967) found that the Maine woods serve hunters at one season and family campers at another. All of this suggests the importance of studies of the natural history of recreational facilities.

The inner city has a special problem with facilities, resulting from the mobility of its population. The demand for given facilities in given locales may change over time. One population may want rocks to romp over. City parks across the country attest to this demand. City Negroes are less likely than their white fellow citizens to attend the carefully developed zoos and art museums of the cities. Facilities must be constantly reassessed with respect to current client populations.

In sum, outdoor recreation invites historical, methodological, and substantive studies. Vacation, as a meaningful man-environment relation, may be studied in terms of the types of meaning the vacation has for individuals and groups, the structure of the relations between vacationers and suppliers of vacation facilities, and the natural history of the vacation sites. These studies can draw on the theoretical insights of the sociological fields sketched in the earlier chapters. We have not discussed all of the relevant sociological fields that seem pertinent to such an enterprise. Considering the history of neglect, however, this attempt to plot a set of directions will, it is hoped, serve as a new beginning in the study of human action in the nonhuman environment.

Let us assume that a variety of recreational possibilities for a population is visible above its cultural horizon. Then if, as has been argued, recreation expresses a life drama, and if various subgroups—differently situated in society—have their own interest-detetrmined dramatic problems, then each subgroup might seek different types of recreation. Each group might even seek different formal settings for their recreation.

This seems to be the case. Urban Negroes (even with income held constant) are rarely found among backwoods campers. Bowling attracts more of the working class than of the social elite. Sports participation is related to class and ethnic position. Games, for cultural-historical reasons, are associated with certain social groups—tennis with the English and baseball with the Americans. Some games are associated with regional cultures—sport flying with the western United States and scuba diving with the Florida Coast.

This fact of class and regional recreational bias has a consequence for governmental interest in recreation in the United States. Typically individuals project the recreational culture of their own social circle, or social class, on the larger society. Members of each class or circle either believe that others share their recreational interests or that it would be good for them if they did. The absurdity is now apparent. Each social group uses recreation, in part, to work through different problems.

Outdoor recreation planners and officials in the United States come from a narrow band within the middle class. The policy making, operating, and research personnel are almost entirely white, of English or Western European descent, disproportionately from rural backgrounds and devoted to a physically active life style. They have tended to project an image of outdoor recreation—created in their own milieu—upon the whole of the society. Thus, prominence is given to activities in the woods, such as hunting and fishing, or water-related activities, such as boating and swimming (Bureau of Outdoor Recreation, 1967).

Samuel Z. Klausner

The wealthy among inner-city residents create their own, nongovernmentally dependent, recreational facilities. The demands of the inner-city impoverished population for allocation of funds and facilities will be increasingly visible as they learn to exercise the vote and other means of political influence. At present their pressure is most directly felt at the municipal level. Some municipalities are projecting the demands of these groups to Washington and attracting federal funds to urban recreational projects.

Recreational requirements of the impoverished sector of inner-city populations are not easily communicated to decision makers. One reason is the inability of this population to formulate and articulate its preferences. A second reason has to do with the clogging of the channels—through which such information should flow—because of the lack of research or of other mechanisms for gathering information. And, finally, the natural limitations to appreciation by one class of the message of another affects the reception of the message. Research is one way to open the flow of information at all three points—by articulating demand, opening communications channels, and interpreting the demand to the policy maker.

166

☆☆☆☆☆☆☆☆☆☆☆☆☆☆☆☆☆☆☆☆☆

CHAPTER VIII

Social Policy for the Environment

🌳🌳🌳🌳🌳🌳🌳🌳🌳🌳🌳🌳🌳🌳

O ur vision now shifts abruptly from theory and research to policy. What are the requirements for the development of knowledge about man and environment? What is the best way to transmit this knowledge? How may this knowledge be applied to the improvement of society and its environment? Respectively, these are issues of research, education, and resource and social management policy. A rounded exposition of these three policy problems would require another book. The following discussion is limited to some marginal comments on pitfalls in the articulation of knowledge and its application in forming policies. After a cautionary word about hasty actions, some technical problems are raised concerning the articulation of disciplinary knowledge, the links between abstract concepts and concrete facts, and the wedding of these facts to personal and social values in planning social action.

This discussion provides some criteria for outlining an organizational structure for the production and application of knowledge. It is composed of research institutes, demonstration institutes, and operating agencies—each with its own relation to the educational system. To complement our previous emphasis on research, the epilogue closes with an illustration of applied socio-environmental planning.

Activities of man induce environmental, physical, and chemical changes which threaten the quality of human life and, sometimes, even threaten biological survival. We have surveyed possibilities of a sociological analysis of these activities implicating physical environmental elements, a disciplinary issue. Indisputably, public concern with the cognate social problem has goaded us to consider this technical sociological problem. Public support is offered in diagnosing the social problems which are enmeshed with the environmental problems and in designing social policy to meet this dual challenge.

In moving from practical problems of the environment to abstract research concepts, we traverse a murky corridor. Should automobile-generated air pollution be attacked, say, in terms of drivers' personalities, through an analysis of how dispositions toward dominance/subordination may control the propensity to use excessively powered engines? Should the researcher begin his efforts to understand the community's failure to penalize drivers for spewing toxic gases into the air with an analysis of the cultural status of property norms? The return through the corridor from theoretical abstractions to practical applications is treacherous. Yet, connecting the practical and the abstract enhances the value of this book as a contribution to our creature comfort as well as to the life of cognitive spirit. The Talmudic adage asserts that where there is no flour there is no enlightenment.

The citizen who wants ameliorative action now may be impatient with the tentativeness of the scholar. The mass media alternate warnings of environmental crisis and ecological catastrophe with detached documentation of the countdown to doomsday. Urgency is justified in alerting the population to nature's hidden wallop. Nevertheless, the deadline for biological obliteration is still some years away. In all but scattered—though paradigmatic—cases the point of no return from cataclysm may be measured in decades. There is time to think and to plan. Mankind may stumble out of danger as stupidly as he is stumbling into it. More likely, the traditional evolutionary controls of tooth and claw will eventually set the course of salvation. Few of us want to relinquish our destiny to a process of natural selection in which the insects may be the final victors. Most of us prefer to elect the style of our survival through the exercise of rationally grounded and morally directed choice—a course of action resting on cognitively right knowledge applied to morally right social policy. For society to achieve this freedom, the scholar and the policy maker must resist being intellectually stampeded by urgent cries of crisis. True, precious moments are being lost in the battle to reverse environmental deterioration. Yet, in the judgment of history, that loss may be insignificant compared to the disaster of whelping a sterile mule of a social policy by mismating physical and societal conceptualizations.

The term *ecology* has been distended into a slogan. Traditionally, it labels the concern of biologists with the interdependence of species of plants and between plants and their nutrients and the concern of zoologists with the interdependence of animal species—between prey and predator, host and parasite. A biological schema binds all these objects together.

The term is currently used to refer to a complex of schemata for interpreting the interdependence of geological, plant, animal, and human events. Furthermore, the older use of ecology as a scientific term refers in a value-neutral way to the functional connectedness of parts of the system. Current usage carries a warning that the system is becoming imbalanced and may be entering its death throes—an ominous eschatology. Such a slogan term, though, is a morally useful reminder that holding constant experimental

169

conditions while varying a limited phenomenon is a figment of the laboratory. When man builds dams or applies insecticides, nature holds nothing constant. As a slogan, ecology calls for a united effort by social and physical scientists and engineers.

The technical problems of coordinating scientific disciplines, with an eye to the practical solution of problems of man and environment, are formidable. A moderate sized literature on the integration of the social sciences has accumulated over the last half century (see, for example, Ogburn and Goldenweiser, 1927; Smelser, 1967). This literature calls for a breaching of disciplinary walls. Roy Grinker organized and participated in seven annual conferences of social scientists aimed at developing a "unified theory of human behavior." After the seventh conference, he wrote as follows (1956, p. 366):

> The members of the conference were committed with great zeal and seriousness of purpose toward a program of developing a unified theory of human behavior. Yet all of us implicitly knew that this could in reality not be attained by us in our time and that we would be satisfied with a little progress toward the ultimate goal. It was amazing that through the years the group continued to be overtly optimistic, each member continually striving to understand aspects of human behavior discussed by the others.

Such notes of little progress or even of "failure" are threaded through this literature on the integration of theory. Talcott Parsons (1951) obtained cooperation of members of several departments in drafting a general statement of the theory of action, but its influence beyond sociological circles has been minimal.

Some attribute this failure to the perspectival nature of social science concepts. If all the specialized concepts were brought into a single whole, it is said, somehow we would reclaim the concreteness of the real society from which each discipline originally abstracted its concepts. This hope is not well founded. Sciences need not recombine like the parts of a mechanical device—as if one discipline were expert in engines, another in the automotive electrical system, and another in body work, and together they would produce a complete car. This seduction succeeds, in part, because in the natural sciences a physical and a chemical analysis may be thought of as dealing with processes at different levels of generality. This same spatiotemporal framework is applied at each level. Often analyses at the microscopic level reveal mediating mechanisms that explain macroscopic events. Among the social sciences, however, and between the social and natural sciences, different frames of reference are in use. The relation between the psychological motive to act in a particular way and the existence of a particular structure of roles requiring that same manifest behavior is highly complex and certainly not direct. The psychologist assessing motives may measure stimuli against responses under some particular reinforcement regime. The sociologist describing a role structure may use a Marxian conflict model in which role prescriptions are generated by objective interests rooted in relations to the system of production. Were psychologists and sociologists all to agree to work within a single frame of reference, such as that proposed by Parsons in his *Toward a General Theory of Action* (1951), this difficulty would be diminished.

The terms of the social sciences are not additive. A researcher may combine a series of measures on intelligence, social class, and life style in a regression analysis to predict, say, consumer preferences. In actuality, the equation is built around three measures of concrete behavior such as test scores, income measures, and reading habits. To assert that he has combined psychological, sociological, and cultural factors respectively is false. Assumedly item responses refer to the construct of intelligence, income measures to the construct of social class, and reading habits to the construct of life style. Basically, these constructs are defined in three separate theoretical nets. The regression equation merely tells of a relation among the concrete behaviors and is moot regarding the relation of these measures to the three inferred entities. Further, any combination of these constructs does not exhaustively reproduce reality. Even when we have considered the economic, sociological, personality, and cultural perspectives, we may still not have treated religious, artistic, and communicative perspectives, among others.

The belief that analytic power is increased by combinations

of social sciences may reflect our social ideology as well as our intellectual desperation. In a country that was conceived as a set of united states and that fosters religious ecumenism, one tends to generalize the thesis of strength from unity. Concepts are not bound by the politics of social relations. All these limitations attest to the magnitude of the interdisciplinary task. They do not detract from its necessity. Discovering links between the social sciences may contribute profoundly to our understanding of human events.

Paradoxically, the assumption of disciplinary brotherhood may be one root of the failure to achieve integration. The concerns shared by members of the various disciplines may obscure a latent —and sometimes manifest—conflict of interests. Each social science discipline, in purveying its particular understanding of human behavior, competes to apply its own concepts and methods to the solution of social problems. Jurisdictional battles between academic departments are an index of this conflict. The political history of the social sciences has been a record of disciplinary hegemonies in various problem areas. Economists have made research in natural resources and the environmental sciences their bailiwick by defining problems in market terms. The area of healing has fallen to psychologists and psychiatrists, who define the task as the enhancement of self-image or the training for competent performance. Mass persuasion tends to be a preserve of the sociologists and psychologists who define the task in terms of the shaping of behavioral dispositions or attitudes. Had other social sciences gained hegemony in any of these areas, the problems might have been differently defined. Anthropologists might have defined healing in terms of cultural equilibria, and, with an orientation to the collectivity rather than the individual, they might have promoted educational and perhaps legislative programs. Had sociologists come to dominate the natural resources field, the central problems might have been defined in terms of the bureaucratic processes in resource management, production, and distribution and the power relations of the various bureaucratic constituencies. Perhaps the politics rather than the economics of technology would be in the forefront. Given the strength of Protestant individualism in our orientation toward healing and the preference for market mechanisms over conquest in the competition for resources, the existing hegemonies in these areas are not surprising. Jurisdictional conflicts surface when members of one discipline invite a colleague of another discipline into their setting. Without realizing the difference in conceptual focus entailed, the anticipated contribution of the visitor may be truncated.

Each discipline is maintained by a relatively separate community of scholars recruited from different sectors of the community. Disciplines are part of their cognitive culture. The concepts and methods of a discipline as cultural elements are responsive to the class and religious strata of the society in which they emerge and to the personalities of individuals who develop them. The character of disciplinary cultures is also responsive to the social characteristics of their clientele and the social structure of the settings in which research is accomplished. These underlying social differences provide nonintellectual fuel for the disciplinary conflicts.

Mindful of these problems, we can approach disciplinary integration through the transfer of methods from one field to another, the reconceptualizations of problems, and the tempering of the socially circumscribed disciplinary recruitment patterns. Interdisciplinary *articulation* might be a better goal term than *integration*. An organic solidarity based on the interdependence of specialties seems to be what is at issue. Interdisciplinary forums and research teams may be conceived as arenas for the articulation of the sciences.

Articulated social science knowledge or social and physical science knowledge is still abstract knowledge. How may it be applied? The step from social science to social policy introduces all the difficulties of the step from physical science to engineering technology, and then some. In both cases, as mentioned above, the knowledge is developed under certain conditions, other things being equal. This limitation is less in the physical than in the social sciences. The Newtonian model of the law of falling bodies works in a practical situation if one but allows for additional factors, such as the friction between the body and the medium through which it is falling. The operative principles do not differ in the realms of theory and of practice. The builder computes the theoretical load which a beam will sustain and enters a tolerance factor in his design. Only a quantitative difference, not one of principle, is anticipated when the law of moments is applied.

Sociological propositions resist translation into individual and social technologies. Social science and social policy follow different models. First, social policy deals not with abstract systems but with real people in real groups. Second, social science develops functional if-then statements as if the elements were related in a deterministic or, at least, stochastic or statistical fashion. Concrete social action proceeds in the light of individual freedom, consciousness, and personal responsibility. Third, social science knowledge, like physical science knowledge, is cognitive, contemplating its objects at a distance. Social action involves engagement which, in turn, implies decisions and choices based on rules. The rules for choosing among the means and ends of human action are described in social science but are evolved in the process of action and are formulated theoretically in religion and philosophy. The value and factual elements mesh in social policy. These three issues are considered here in turn.

Applying a scientific proposition usually means pretending to the reification of its terms and then manipulating the value of one of its variables in anticipation of change in the value of another variable. The referent or operational indicator of a concept may be taken as identical with the concept rather than as a token for the phenomenon to which the concept refers. We assume that if we classify people by the indicator attribute, they are sorted out in the way intended by the concept. The relation between a social science concept and its operational indicator is, however, nontransitive. For example, suppose social class is defined as a clustering of population groups into hierarchical ranks with differential access to social power. Research might treat income as a proxy for assigning individuals to these ranks. Alternatively, individuals might be assigned to social classes according to the power of their occupational group, according to their relation to the means of production, or according to subjective ratings expressed by significant members of the community.

174

On Man in His Environment

A multiplicity of indicators are being used for classifying people with respect to the same theoretical concept.

The question may be reversed, and we may begin with an observation. From an observed income level, one may infer differential access to power and also differences in styles of life, political attitudes, attitudes toward education or religion, or potential demand for some consumer goods. Similarly, a multiplicity of concepts may be associated with each one of the class indicators mentioned above. Based on a proposition that different social classes orient differently toward recreation, should the policy planner establish recreation facilities according to the income distribution of the community, according to the occupational characteristics of nearby residents, or according to the distributions obtained from subjective ratings of significant members of the community? Researchers try to reduce the uncertainty in the correspondence between the classification intended by a concept and that obtained from an operational indicator by using patterns of indicators, constructing types based on clusters of indicators. This practice attenuates but does not resolve the dilemma.

The reconciliation of the deterministic or stochastic character of scientific knowledge with freedom and responsibility posited for practical action requires little more than a clarification. Determinism is merely a postulate of a theoretical model which the scientist finds useful for generalizing about patterns in a multitude of acts. The real actor proceeds with great concern as to whether his chosen course of behavior conforms with or deviates from his internal standards or the standards of others in his group. The notion of responsibility resides in his consciousness of this last consideration.

Finally, we turn to the status of values in theory and in practice. Value-determined choices are dealt with both in social research and in social policy, but they are treated differently in each instance. In research, values may be inferred from observed regularities in behavior or from the statements of the actors. Their scientific status is that of explanatory terms. Like other conceptual elements, the meaning of the term referring to the actor's values derives from

175

its location in a nexus of cognitive concepts. In the realm of application, however, choice is part of a concrete action sequence. It is a directional factor in a course of action. Its meaning is given in terms of the goals toward which it propels the actor or in terms of the past experience invoked to account for it.

The positions set forth above delimit appropriate institutional contexts for the development and application of socioenvironmental knowledge. To articulate different frames of reference and resolve conflicts of interest a single interdisciplinary setting could be counter-productive. At this stage in the development of socioenvironmental studies, each discipline is in baby shoes and needs initial independence to work out the logical conclusions of its frame of reference with respect to this field. Creative interaction can follow later. Before there can be interdisciplinary knowledge, there must be disciplinary knowledge. A retreat from the specialized development of disciplinary knowledge is regressive with respect to science. The scientist strives to make cognitive the very process by which knowledge is developed. The application of knowledge cannot take place without the intrusion of values and ideology. The cognitive process can only be blunted or distorted by this intrusion. Thus, research and application must remain as different stages of overall socioenvironmental planning. A blurring of the line between science and its application is regressive with respect both to the development and to the application of that knowledge.

It is proposed, therefore, that development of knowledge about man in his environment is served best by a complex of disciplinary research, demonstration, and implementation institutes. The term *institute* is used in a loose sense to refer to a working group which persists for a number of years in pursuing a limited family of problems. Such working groups may be part of a larger university structure or of a research center. Some of the disciplinary institutes can specialize in social research. These institutes should be linked to the instructional capabilities of university disciplinary departments. The students and faculty can be an intellectual manpower resource and offer a channel for the transmission of specialized socioenvironmental knowledge. The conceptualizations presented in this book offer one possible orientation for institute research. A separate set of institutes, let us call them demonstration institutes, can be centers for interdisciplinary team efforts, can generate and test applications, and can provide project demonstration. Demonstration institutes should be linked to professional training programs or schools. A final set of institutes can be mission oriented parts of agencies responsible for implementing programs. They can maintain their connections with professional schools as a resource for personnel and offer curricular support to primary and secondary school programs. The research and demonstration institutes should be linked chainwise to the implementing agencies. The entire set may be coordinated and funded in part by an environmental council.

Why recommend organizational settings for the development of socioenvironmental knowledge? Why not simply encourage promising individual scholars? Individual support programs are more acceptable in university settings because they bolster the conception of a collegium of independent scholars. The creation of institutes within universities may encounter administrative resistance in that they constitute foci of power which do not emerge from or accept the discipline of traditional departmental authority. However, a single grant to a lone scholar is likely to be applied to that scholar's general interests and often, when the work is completed or the scholar moves, no cultural residual remains beyond his journal publications. The results of individual support are likely to be a scatter of discrete efforts rather than a cumulatively growing program of studies. Such a cumulative program can consist of a series of studies pursuing a family of problems by means of a family of methods. This program is most likely to result from a long term commitment of individuals to an area. It is also likely to result from the development of a culture of ideas and methods which—transcending the institutional affiliation of a particular individual—may grow continuously. Institutes do not compel teamwork but do make it possible, concentrating individuals of common interest in a single setting. Partly because of their physical arrangements and work-time structures, the amount of informal interaction among colleagues at institutes is greater than is ordinarily available in departments

177

oriented to varied instructional schedules. Creative brainstorming may alternate with disciplined scrutiny of the intellectual product.

The intellectual and social case for separate disciplinary, rather than interdisciplinary, research institutes is given above in the argument about the special perspectival character of each discipline and the notion that the disciplines grow through increased specialization of function. There are some further practical arguments for this approach. Researchers are likely to increase understanding of environmental problems by using the well-tried concepts of their disciplinary traditions. New concepts should evolve in response to specific new problems. The alternative—defining socioenvironment as a new interdisciplinary field—implies a new frame of reference and new concepts. To create a new body of knowledge that does not rest on a supporting network of established concepts is to assume an overwhelming task in which the scholar must fail— unless he be a Plato, Kant, Marx, or Freud. Continuity with the tradition is most likely in socioenvironmental research which remains amidst a discipline's more usual undertakings. Thus, expansion of existing disciplinary research facilities is preferable to the creation of new ones. In addition, new facilities require a basic exercise in organizational prowess. Environmental researchers should be spared responsibility for administrative innovation while being asked to innovate intellectually. Further, interdisciplinary efforts tend to produce knowledge at a low level of abstraction. In this sense such a move is regressive.

An interdisciplinary institute would not be likely to persist long before some frame of reference would be imposed on it. This might be a process of natural selection of the schema most adaptable intellectually to the problem at hand. More likely, it would be the schema of the disciplinarians who dominate the social structure of the institution. An interdisciplinary institute would also have weaker links with current departmental structures than would a disciplinary institute. Its connection to the transmission of knowledge would suffer. Cut off from the institutional reward structures of both the profession and the school the institute would have serious problems recruiting personnel. Finally, separate disciplinary settings help keep conceptual options open. The definition of the problem is one of the major problems of the field. It would not be wise, at this stage, to commit the field to the problem definitions arrived at in a single conceptual frame, whether it be psychological, sociological, economic, or cultural.

A few possible types of research that can be pursued in each institute may be mentioned without suggesting a priority or order of significance. A psychological institute may explore questions of psychological ecology, the personal meanings of space, the relation of spatial arrangements and interpersonal motivation, the symbolic meanings of natural features for personality, and the sensory adaptation in extreme environments. For such work the psychologist may employ experimental and clinical methods. A sociological institute may study resource management organizations, the relations between the social organization of work and the consumption and processing of materials, the norms of recreation groups, and the special character of norms relating the individual to the collective. The methodologies for such studies may be participant-observation and surveys. An anthropological institute may study the relation of societal organization to the consumption of resources, the impact of religious values on the exploitation of nature, and the cultural aspects of technological change in the developing world. Besides in-house library research, this institute can sponsor extended field trips. An economic institute may work on problems of consumer demand for resources and conduct cost/effectiveness analyses of various management procedures and resource uses. Economists may explore market and nonmarket mechanisms and how they interact with political mechanisms and organizational exigencies in developing environmental policy. Secondary analyses of aggregate economic and population data would probably receive more attention than the gathering of new data. In political science and history, relevant research programs may be developed to study the allocation of power in relation to environmental legislation or the interplay between structures of authority and land use patterns. Historically based longitudinal studies focused on macrosystems would be important for the work of all the institutes.

Senior staff of these institutes should have faculty status and retain teaching responsibilities. Teaching alerts researchers to major theoretical issues of their field. The senior staff can mediate the relation of research to instruction in the disciplinary departments. The junior staff may include graduate students who work for salary, are assigned to an institute as research apprentices, or receive individual research grants and use the institutes as bases for their work.

Within departmental curricula, no special majors in socioenvironmental studies should be evolved. Students should be prepared as sociologists, psychologists, anthropologists, or economists. Specialization in socioenvironmental studies should follow the earning of a graduate degree. This approach is prudent for the student, who will find positions available to those with impeccable disciplinary credentials. While specific socioenvironmental positions may develop under the impact of major funding, students should not narrow their career options in such a way that a shift in public concern would render them obsolete. Further, an interdisciplinarian must first be a disciplinarian or risk dilettantism. The principal curricular reason, however, is that the analysis of social action oriented to the physical environment should not be treated as a special study but should be a regular theoretical foundation for all the social sciences. Special courses in each department may examine various frames of reference for environmental studies and critically survey the growing literature. A student preparing for an administrative post in environmental management may develop a combined major comprising a set of such courses.

In accord with current trends, the disciplinary research and teaching activity may be expected to generate professional associations and journals (or promote the growth of those already existing) in the socioenvironmental areas. These would tend to be problem oriented and to offer a natural interdisciplinary forum. Members of the various institutes—as well as others concerned with the area— can meet, share ideas, and criticize approaches. To some extent, these forums can be formalized as committees specifically working on the integration of theoretical knowledge developed in the several disciplines. Associations and their forums can also provide a mechanism through which members of one discipline can be detached for temporary specialized work in the institute of another discipline. At a later stage in the development of the field, when the work of each discipline is firmly grounded, it will be useful to consider disciplinary sharing on an extensive basis.

Similar developments in environmental research and teaching may be anticipated in the physical and biological sciences. Although regular consulting arrangements must be maintained between the physical and social science groups, it is not recommended that institutional measures be taken to press these faculties to coordinate their theoretical perspectives. Disparate frames of reference and objects of research are at issue. Social scientists analyze human action. Physical scientists study nature. Of course, relevant physical science thought must be part of the education of social scientists. How else can they understand the basic physical dimension of the problem and the impacts of human activities on the physical environment? Physical scientists are, for their part, curious about the social impacts of technical development. Coordination of the physical and social sciences can take place in the demonstration institutes.

Applications of knowledge can be designed and tested in demonstration institutes. Such institutes can be organized around concrete problems. Currently, the tendency is to organize them with reference to the activities of mission oriented agencies. This organization implies a stress on abating environmental pollution and on managing environmental resources. Pollution oriented programs may be classified by the medium—air or water—which receives residuals, and the resource oriented activities may be classified according to whether resources are used for recreation or are consumed in production. The advantage of remaining within this framework, at least initially, is that it is compatible with current technologies and can receive the support of established political and economic constituencies. This support can ease liaison with the implementing agencies. Alternatively, demonstration institutes may organize their work with reference to problems associated with particular patterns of human settlement—the dense urban and the sparse rural forms or the problems of living in arid zones, jungle forest, or mountains.

Another possibility is to follow forms of economic organization—industrial, agricultural, or commercial.

A demonstration institute should be multidisciplinary. The staff should work toward coordinating the behavioral science concepts derived from the disciplinary institutes with engineering knowledge and with the knowledge of planners—city, regional, and industrial. This work should be informed by the above description of problems of articulating and applying various cognitive schemata and, in application, wedding the factual and value elements. In the articulation of knowledge, the forums of the professional association mentioned above have a contribution to make to the demonstration institutes. Values of individuals, expressive of their philosophies of life, are usually crystalized in formal religious settings. Values which enter program development should be made explicit. The tools of technical philosophy and of theology have traditionally been used for the critique of values. Close links with the field of philosophy, with the humanities in general, and with religious institutions and theological seminaries are crucial in this phase of the program. Whether value choices are, as our society sometimes assumes, adequately expressed through economic market mechanisms or through the political process can be examined. Programs may be implemented by the demonstration institute on an experimental basis. A division of operations research can develop practical simulations of programs prior to field testing. An evaluation unit can assess program outcomes and assist in program amendment for retest. The demonstration institutes should also have a division of law to study legislative aspects of programs and judicial aspects of the protection of rights.

The demonstration institute should maintain close ties with those university schools and departments organized around the application of knowledge to socioenvironmental problems. These are generally the professional schools and departments of mines, agriculture, forestry, natural resources, architecture, city and regional planning, law, business, education, theology, and medicine. Environmental policy makers and managers can be trained in these departments. The leaders of demonstration institutes and teachers in primary and secondary school programs should be drawn from these faculties or have studied in them. Professional preparation in these faculties should include apprenticeships on demonstration projects.

Upon successful completion of field tests, programs can be recommended to mission oriented agencies for implementation. Initially, the mission agencies should not be reorganized to accommodate these programs. Full benefit of the support of the regular operating staff and procedures should be available. In the longer run, programs may require organizational adjustments. Since most agencies in the field are oriented to the physical environment, their earliest adjustment should be to the exigencies of social policy implementation. Initially, these requirements, too, should be met through the personnel and facilities of established agencies. Implementing organizations should, by and large, be operating public agencies, staffed by engineers and social scientists with an operational interest and specialists in administration and community relations. The organization of resource management agencies is itself a research focus for the research and demonstration institutes.

Community values and the political climate are significant for the success of programs. Implementation requires artful management. The packaged program of a demonstration institute should not be applied unmindfully in a local situation. The implementing agency should involve various community interests in developing the program. The political art is applicable in determining when to press, when to tread softly or to issue an order, and when to invite public discussion.

Like the demonstration institutes, implementing agencies should also be linked to the professional schools, but, unlike the research institutes, they should draw little from disciplinary departments. Most importantly, operating agencies should contribute to primary, secondary, and undergraduate education on socioenvironmental problems. The basic, professional educational system aims to prepare citizens for living in the community. The programs of mission oriented agencies directly influence the lives of citizens. Local boards of education may have special offices of environmental education, which, maintaining liaison with operating agencies, would be responsible for curriculum and for drawing agency resources into the educational process. The development of study syllabi may draw on the experience of agency personnel, industrial leaders, and community moral leaders as well as on the subject matter specialists and classroom teachers. Such programs can inform children of ways their individual and social activities influence the quality of the environment, instill in them an appreciation for the man-environment balance, and teach them to think rationally about local programs for socioenvironmental maintenance and enhancement. Because of the many facets of knowledge involved, this is an opportunity for developing an integrative program. The role of art, nature study, mathematics, geography, and social studies in socioenvironmental-centered curricula is obvious. Socioenvironmental studies at the elementary level are an occasion for developing a sense of social responsibility.

This entire network of institutes and their relation to instructional facilities could be served by an environmental council. The council should concern itself with the environmental relevance of social programs as well as with the social relevance of engineering programs. It should be an overarching agency with responsibility for coordinating and providing basic funding for research, demonstration, and implementation as well as curriculum advice to the associated educational programs. Sources of funding may differ at each level. The disciplinary institutes may be funded by both private foundations and government through research and training grants. Contract work for mission oriented agencies and for private industry may supplement the grants, providing the problem presented requires for its solution a reconceptualization or the development of a new methodology. The demonstration institutes may be funded largely by government through special grants. They too could accept contract work. A typical contract may involve the development and demonstration of a socioenvironmental plan for a locality. The operating agencies should appear on the regular operating budget lines of the federal, state, and local governments, as the case may be. The mandate to the council should be broad enough to allow it to integrate the requirements of government agencies now dealing with special sectors of the environment.

The council should be constituted as a federally chartered nonprofit corporation. Its charter should be designed so that the council maintains touch with the legislative process and with operating agencies, and, at the same time, the charter should preserve freedom of the council in defining problems and setting funding priorities. The directing body of the council should represent operating agencies, research groups (including universities), industrial organizations engaged in the exploitation of resources, citizen groups concerned with environmental quality, and government agencies responsible for education at the primary and secondary levels. Through establishing an ex officio status, this directing body should enjoy the advice of political interest groups and religious groups. A small permanent staff is needed to monitor and review programs, policies, and organizational structures as well as to provide support services for the work of the directing body.

More detail on this structure of research, demonstration, and implementation and of the coordinating environmental council would carry us afield. The body of this book has established one framework for the intellectual concerns of a sociologically oriented research institute. Little has been said about social planning as it may occur in a demonstration institute. As a closing note, I illustrate one way of beginning to think about program development in the light of social scientific knowledge. The problem of noise abatement is the case in point. Assume, following basic research on the problem of noise in society, that the demonstration institute is asked by municipal authorities to develop a program for noise abatement. The research, perhaps similar to that sketched earlier in this book, has explored noise as one aspect of a social event. Social relations may exist between noise makers and noise receivers. Noise may be used as a weapon in the struggle among social groups, or it may occur as an unintended adjunct to a productive activity. Often its effect is felt through changing patterns of land use—principally, by inducing the self-eviction of one class or ethnic community from a residential area and thus opening that land and housing to a suc-

185

cessor community or by imposing a condition which helps shift land from residential to commercial or industrial use.

Let us assume psychological research has shown that the personality responds to noise much as it does to violence, that noise is productive of tension when it occurs in an action system other than that in which the subject is involved. It may generate a mild euphoria if it is associated with social action in which the subject is participating. These tension processes underlie the observed social responses to noise. Let us assume, also, that engineering studies have measured the objective acoustical environment in the city and offered the planner a noise contour map of the area. Engineers also have provided information about the technological steps required for silencing productive machinery and transportation vehicles. Economic studies have attested to the costs of hearing loss from high intensity noise as well as to that part of the cost of changing land use—to individuals and to the community—which may be assessed to noise. Costs directly incurred through acquisition of technical noise abatement devices, building structure improvements to retard noise penetrations, and the effect on the market of adding such costs to the price of an item have also been computed. Legal research has produced several model noise abatement codes, and political science research has described interests that support or oppose several types of noise abatement legislation and the problems of enforcing codes. With this informational input, the demonstration institute is asked to design and test a noise abatement program. The criteria for judging a program are not simply elimination of noise but a balancing of social, economic, and cultural costs and benefits associated with various noise levels. In developing policy for the program, the demonstration institute consults with operating agencies which ultimately have the responsibility for its implementation. These agencies may include the police, the courts, and health and welfare groups, among others. One part of a scenario for beginning to think about this problem follows. A full description of an approach to such a demonstration program would require another book.

Social interest in noise abatement already exists to some extent. The degradation of our auditory environment has been well documented (for example, Federal Council for Science and Technology, 1968). Home, office, street, and play areas are feeling the impact of screeching, pounding, and clattering machines. The futility of attempts to escape the din will become increasingly obvious in the years to come. Urbanization and the concentration of population imply more exposure than is true now to the ordinary sounds of living, as well as a greater concentration of machines which are part of that living. Not all advances in production technology increase noise. Technological interest in reducing the number of moving parts of a machine or in changing from mechanical to electronic power, although motivated by concern with efficiency, is a built-in noise abatement program. On the other hand, the trend toward increasing the amount of energy released at a given point produces jet engine noise exceeding that of steam engines. Individuals and groups not involved in the activity producing the noise are the source of political pressure for abatement. Sounds are a normal accompaniment to the noise maker's activities. He has little interest in expenditures to curtail his noise unless it is truly painful. Where does a practical program begin?

On the surface, it would seem that silencing the grinding and clashing of metal against metal should be the first step in a noise abatement program. Thus, technologically oriented moves would be the leading edge of the program. Initial investment would be in muffling the offending machines or, in effect, inducing producers and users to muffle them. Doubtless, noisy products of a new technology should be fought by a newer technology. Technology, however, is impelled by social demands—the demands for reducing the friction of distance, coordinating the activities of large populations, and packing more activities in smaller time frames. Human beings produce noise when they use technology in their pursuit of social aims. The failure of institutions to stay abreast of technology is at the core of the problem, but the disparity between technology and society is more than social lag (Ogburn, 1950; Merrill, 1968; Nef, 1964; Mumford, 1934).

Intervention in the problem of machine-produced noise may

take place at any stage in the development or use of the machine. Each stage has its own social setting. Ameliorative effort must engage the social as well as the technical aspect of the settings selected for intervention. It is often suggested that provision for noise abatement be made in the original design of the product. Doubtless this must be done, but the logic of social policy need not follow the chronology of product development. It may not be most useful to intervene directly at the product design stage. In fact, attempts to intervene at this stage have proved futile. The social setting at the stage of product use influences the interest in design of quieter products.

The market is the relevant social setting in product development and design. The producing firm and the consumer are the two principal actors; this market comprises their interaction, expressed primarily in monetary terms. Silenced equipment tends to cost more. Time and again—whether the product is an air conditioner, a blender, or a jet airplane—consumers have refused this additional cost by choosing a lower priced though noisier competitor. This choice is not surprising. Producers of sound are generally not annoyed by it. The pilots of airplanes and the operators of power lawn mowers may even be rather pleased by the noise they control. The victims are not engaged in the activities. They are the people over whose houses airplanes fly. They are neighbors of power-propelled gardeners.

A noise receiver attenuates noise which interferes with his goals. When receiver and producer are the same person, as in the case of a lone radio listener, he pays more for a radio without static. If his car is a private home in which he listens to music, he pays for quiet engine performance. The simultaneous enjoyment of music and of automotive power may be incompatible. Here individuals evolve their personal noise abatement program to balance engine noise and music. The stimulus for this noise abatement program arises at the point at which the noise is made and is heard. The analogy may be carried to the case in which the noise producer and the noise maker are discrete individuals or discrete groups.

This pair of actors constitutes the social setting at the point of noise production.

Noise maker and noise receiver are both behaviorally oriented to the noise. The physical phenomenon of noise mediates their social relationship. The actual or potential social conflict between these actors offers a felicitous situation for initial research and policy intervention. Initially this situation, too, may be approached technologically. The physical access of noise may be controlled. The characteristics of highways, for instance, could be changed to reduce traffic noise and so modify the tensions between operators and residents along the highway. Highways could be designed with fewer stops, with more underpasses, and without sudden climbs in populated areas. Legislative action could focus directly on the locating of noise sources relative to potential noise receivers. Through appropriate land use planning, residential properties and airports could be located at a distance fron one another. Rescheduling, a kind of time use planning, could move some noise to times when people are least likely to be disturbed. In these ways, noise sources could be isolated from noise receivers. Where such isolation is not reasonable, the source of the noise and the potential receiver may be insulated from one another. Housing may be soundproofed and noise muffled. The availability of technology for isolation and for insulation has not been too effective in producing practical relief. The homeowner is reluctant to accept the cost of insulating his home, and public authorities have resisted the cost of buffer zones around airports. These attempts have been aimed directly at reducing the physical access of noise. Technology, however, is an instrument of social action. To influence people's use of technology, it is necessary first to influence people.

Take, for instance, the above research finding that social orientations toward noise may be elements in social conflict. The programmatic problem then is one of conflict management. Noise receivers may be frustrated by the absence of any mechanism to influence the noise producer to lower the noise. To develop a mechanism and resolve the conflict, increasing social access between noise producers and noise receivers may be required. Increasing social access to reduce the physical access of noise may seem paradoxical. However, social conflicts are generally not resolved without some engagement between the parties. Of course, society may prefer to suffer the conflict or to pay the price in loss of community flexibility that results from isolating the conflicting parties from one another.

Social access may be increased along the symbolic communicative, political, economic, and juridical dimensions of the relationship. The noise producer and the noise receiver may be placed within the same social action system—just as the economist places them in the same market. When individuals in one market have no defense against costs imposed on them by individuals in another, there is a lack of social-economic access. One solution recommended by economists to this problem of externalities is to redefine the boundaries of the system. By making both noise producer and noise receiver part of the same economic system, the costs are internalized in that system. The party producing the disturbance accepts the cost of the loss suffered by the noise receiver.

Although the economic is but one dimension of social relationships, it is usually considered a crucial form of social leverage. Direct economic sanctions are rarely available to the victims of noise. Those affected, for example, by airport noise can bring little economic pressure to bear on aircraft operators. They may, however, be able to mobilize other kinds of economic sanctions, perhaps through the government. The government may engage in direct economic regulation, subsidize the reduction of noise by producers by assuming part of the cost for developing and manufacturing silenced equipment, and provide economic incentives enabling a firm to internalize some of the social costs. These incentives may include tax rebates, the financing of research and development on noise control, or the purchase of land around a noisy area. Any of these methods help the noise producer and noise receiver to adjust the economic elements of their relationship.

Open channels of communication permit the noise receiver to express his annoyance to the noise maker. In this way the noise maker may assess the impact of his act on others. The noise receiver

may obtain some appreciation of the problem of the noise producer
if he is made aware of the context in which the noise arises. Public
noise monitoring stations can help here. Information on respective
rights and remedies available to the individuals and groups involved
can help the conflict to surface so that it may be channeled con-
structively. The noise receiver must know how to register his complaints and must be able to do so. The noise producer should learn
to evaluate complaints. Citizenship education seems to be the choice
means to meet this need. On a technical level, designers should be
aware of the acoustical environment desired and the building codes
which control it. Information about the noise producing properties
of equipment is, surprisingly, not always available to the designer.
Such information may be collected and exchanged through a technological library.

Political access between noise producer and noise receiver
can enable them to negotiate the conflict from their respective positions of power. A discrepancy between noise maker and noise receiver in political power may affect conflict resolution. An aroused
citizenry may press its demands on a relatively powerless small
businessman. Or a large corporation may produce noise affecting
a few citizens quite helpless in the face of corporate power. Some
equalizing mechanism could be provided by government regulatory
agencies which attempt to balance the rights and remedies of individuals against the rights and remedies of corporate groups or of
society as a whole. Most of the current problems of environmental
pollution cut across major political boundaries and, in consequence,
must be met on a regional or national or international basis. Because of the local character of noise, it is one environmental problem which should be met at the municipal level. Thus, initially,
municipal political arrangements are involved.

Juridical social access is needed to guarantee the openness
of communication and the just implementation of political and
economic relations. The courts may weigh the harm to the plaintiff
against the social service and reasonableness of the defendant's conduct. Four legal theories have been used to deal with the problem
of noise. The theory of trespass has been applied, for instance, in

controlling air rights over property. The theory of taking or eminent domain has been invoked when the right to the use of one's land is the issue. The theory of nuisance has been applied. Here the plaintiff must establish that his normal activities are disturbed. Constitutional damaging has also been the basis for action in which, for instance, the decline in value of property is demonstrated.

Increasing the social access between the noise producer and the noise receiver by opening communication channels, establishing mechanisms to allow them to negotiate politically and economically, and providing juridical mechanisms to guarantee the other types of access extend the scope of joint social activities of noise producers and noise receivers. The technological isolation of the noise source or the insulation of the producer or of the receiver are adjustments which may emerge from these social negotiations. As a result of the new pressures, it may become worthwhile for the noise producer to incur the costs of noise abatement. The economic or political costs which the noise receiver may impose on him may exceed those of abatement. The noise producer will be prepared to pay more for a silenced machine. This demand, exerted by the noise producer in his role as consumer, makes it worthwhile for a firm to invest in alterations of machine design. As a result, silenced machines are more likely to be produced and sold. Thus, technological innovation becomes possible as a result of a shift in social organization.

The above scenario describes how a socioenvironmental shift might result from the creation of conditions for free operations of market and political processes. The assumption here is that justice is best served and community values are optimally realized through free competition. When this Adam Smith element is made explicit in the above program, some people will want to reevaluate their commitment to it. This is a point at which one's social philosophy will affect the action chosen. Recent social history provides evidence that free political and economic competition may not optimize the community-value realization. Another limitation is that the above scenario considers only one line of possible social organizational development. Increasing the social access of citizens to one another will certainly have an impact on the integration of the community. Without obtaining a good deal of further social and cultural data about the community involved, it would be difficult to specify all the ramifications. Under certain conditions, the program can contribute to an improvement in community morale and to a cooperative spirit among the citizens. It may also open the gates to deeper community conflicts and exacerbate struggles within the community which have been kept beneath the surface by the very mechanisms which have socially isolated noise makers from noise receivers. In most situations, however, a program following a scenario of this type would not fundamentally shift the structure of local society. It is limited to what would be, in economic terms, the removal of some imperfections in the socioeconomic market. If the noise itself is the occasion for a distinct social conflict rather than a weapon in a broader conflict, social action for noise abatement has only limited social change implications. Group interests which crystalize around an intrinsic noise problem do not tend to coincide with major social cleavages. The grouping around a noise problem would tend to cut across lines of race, class, and religion, and across urban/rural alignments. If, on the contrary, noise is a weapon in a deeper conflict, the abatement program may simply open the wound.

This book has intentionally avoided the proverbial happy ending of the Hollywood movie. The French film model in which we traverse a vignette of life revealing new complexities as we move ahead seems more realistic. The cautionary words about interdisciplinary work and the application of knowledge are not meant to discourage the attempt but to increase the probability of success by dispelling some illusions. Work toward socioenvironmental change must be carried forward with mature persistence, restrained enthusiasm, and humility before the magnitude of the task and the paucity of our understanding.

> "And the Lord God took the man, and settled him in the Garden of Eden to cultivate it and to protect it."
>
> (Genesis 2:15)

Bibliography

ABRAHAM, K. "A Constitutional Basis of Locomotor Anxiety." In *Selected Papers*. London: Hogarth Press, 1927.

ABRAMS, R. H. "Residential Propinquity as a Factor in Marriage Selection." *American Sociological Review*, 1943, 8, 288–294.

ACKERMAN, E. A. "Geography and Demography." In P. M. Hauser and O. D. Duncan (Eds.), *The Study of Population*. Chicago: University of Chicago Press, 1959.

ACKERMAN, E. A., "Population and Natural Resources." In P. M. Hauser and O. D. Duncan (Eds.), *The Study of Population*. Chicago: University of Chicago Press, 1959.

ALLEN, H. C. *Bush and Backwoods*. East Lansing, Mich.: Michigan State University Press, 1959.

ALTMAN, I. "Ecological Aspects of Interpersonal Relationships." Paper

195

presented at the 135th meeting of the American Association for the Advancement of Science, Dallas, December 1968.

ANDERSON, K. M. "Ethnographic Analogy and Archeological Interpretation." *Science,* 1969, *163* (3863), 133–138.

ANDRZEJEWSKI, S. *Military Organization and Society.* New York: Harper and Row, 1954.

ANTONITIS, J. J. "Group-Operant Behavior: Reinforcing Effects of Pure Tones and Other Sounds on the Bar Pressing of Pre-School Children in a Real-Life Situation." *Journal of Genetic Psychology,* 1965, *107,* 75–83.

AQUINAS, ST. THOMAS. *On the Governance of Rulers.* Translated by Gerald B. Phelan. New York: Sheed and Ward, 1938.

ARBUTHNOT, J. *An Essay Concerning the Effects of Air on Human Bodies.* London: Printed for J. and R. Tonson and S. Draper on the Strand, 1751.

ARGYLE, M. AND DEAN, J. "Eye Contact; Distance and Affiliation." *Sociometry,* 1965, *28,* 289–304.

BAKER, G. W. AND CHAPMAN, D. W. (Eds.) *Man and Society in Disaster.* New York: Basic Books, 1962.

BAKER, G. W. AND RUHRER, J. H. (Eds.) *Human Problems in the Utilization of Fallout Shelters. Disaster Study Number 12.* Washington, D.C.: National Academy of Sciences, National Research Council, 1960.

BALINT, M. *Thrills and Regressions.* New York: International University Press, 1959.

BARBER, B. *Science and the Social Order.* New York: Free Press, 1952.

BARBER, B. "Resistance by Scientists to Scientific Discovery." *Science,* 1961, *134* (3479), 596–602.

BATES, M. "Human Ecology." In A. Kroeber (Ed.), *Anthropology Today.* Chicago: University of Chicago Press, 1953.

BAUER, R. A. (Ed.) *Social Indicators.* Cambridge, Mass.: M.I.T. Press, 1966.

BECKER, H. S. "Marihuana Use and Social Control." In H. S. Becker (Ed.), *Outsiders: Studies in the Sociology of Deviance.* New York: Free Press, 1963.

BEN-DAVID, J. "Scientific Productivity and Academic Organization in Nineteenth Century Medicine." *American Sociological Review,* 1960, *25* (6), 828–843.

BENEDICT, R. *Patterns of Culture.* Boston: Houghton-Mifflin Company, 1934.

BENNETT, J. W. "Interaction of Culture and Environment in the Smaller Societies." *American Anthropologist,* 1944, *46,* 461–478.

BENSON, L. *Turner and Beard—American Historical Writing Reconsidered.* New York: Free Press, 1960.

BERENDT, R. D. *Noise in Buildings.* U. S. Department of Commerce. National Bureau of Standards. Institute for Basic Standards. Memorandum No. 4. Washington, D.C.: Government Printing Office, 1968.

BERMAN, I. M. "Noise in the Home." Thesis submitted to the Moore School of Electrical Engineering, University of Pennsylvania, 1961.

BIASE, D. V. AND ZUCKERMAN, M. "Sex Differences in Stress Response to Total and Partial Sensory Deprivation." *Psychosomatic Medicine,* 1967, *29* (4), 380–390.

BITTER, C. AND HORCH, C. *Social-Psychological Aspects of Noise Nuisance in Blocks and Dwellings.* Research Institute for Public Health Engineering, T.N.O. of the Organization for Health Research. Report No. 25. Delft, The Netherlands, 1958.

BLACKETT, P. M. S. "Science, Technology and World Advancement." *Nature,* 1962, *193* (4814), 416–420.

BODIN, J. *Method for the Easy Comprehension of History.* Translated by B. Reynolds. New York: Columbia University Press, 1945 (Orig. 1566).

BOGARDUS, E. S. *Social Distance.* Yellow Springs, Ohio: Antioch Press, 1959.

BOLT, BERANEK AND NEWMAN, INC. *Literature Survey for the FHA Contract on Urban Noise.* U. S. Department of Housing and Urban Development, Federal Housing Administration. Report 1460 (FH-954). Washington, D.C.: Government Printing Office, 1967, 65–115.

BOLT, BERANEK AND NEWMAN, INC. *Noise Environment of Urban and Suburban Areas.* U. S. Department of Housing and Urban Development, Federal Housing Administration. Washington, D.C.: Government Printing Office, 1967.

BRAGDON, C. R. "Noise—A Syndrome of Modern Society." *Scientist and Citizen,* 1968, *10* (2), 29–37.

BRESLER, J. B. (Ed.) *Human Ecology: Collected Readings*. Reading, Mass.: Addison-Wesley, 1966.

BREWER, M. F. AND BORDNER, B. "Organizational Alternatives for Recreational Resources Management: An Analysis of State Agencies." *Natural Resources Journal*, 1966, *6* (4), 560–579.

BROCKMAN, C. F. *Recreational Use of Wild Lands*. New York: McGraw-Hill Book Co., Inc., 1959.

BROOKFIELD, H. C. "Questions on the Human Frontiers of Geography." *Economic Geography*, 1964, *40*, 283–303.

BRUNER, J. S., GOODNOW, J. J. AND AUSTIN, G. A. *A Study of Thinking*. New York: John Wiley and Sons, 1956.

BURCH, W. R., JR. "The Play World of Camping: Research into the Social Meaning of Outdoor Recreation." *American Journal of Sociology*, 1965, *70*, 604–612.

BURCH, W. R., JR. "Wilderness—The Life Cycle and Forest Recreational Choice." *Journal of Forestry*, 1966, *64* (9), 606–610.

BUREAU OF OUTDOOR RECREATION. National Conference on Policy Issues in Outdoor Recreation in Logan, Utah (September 6–8, 1966). Washington, D.C.: Bureau of Outdoor Recreation, 1967.

BURKE, K. *The Philosophy of Literary Form; Studies in Symbolic Action*. Baton Rouge, La.: Louisiana State University Press, 1941.

BURNS, N. M., CHAMBERS, R. M. AND HENDLER, E. (Eds.) *Unusual Environments and Human Behavior*. New York: Free Press, 1963.

CAILLOIS, R. *Man, Play and Games*. Translated by M. Barash. New York: Free Press, 1961 (Orig. 1958).

CALDWELL, L. K. "Environment: A New Focus for Public Policy?" *Public Administration Review*, 1963, *23*, 132–139.

CALHOUN, J. B. "Population Density and Social Pathology." *Scientific American*, 1962, *206* (2), 139–148.

CAPLOW, T. *The Sociology of Work*. Minneapolis: University of Minnesota Press, 1954.

CAPLOW, T. *Principles of Organization*. New York: Harcourt, Brace and World, 1964.

CASSIRER, E. *The Phenomenology of Knowledge*. Vol. III of *The Philosophy of Symbolic Forms*. Translated by R. Manheim. New Haven, Conn.: Yale University Press, 1957.

CESARIO, F. J., SR. "Operations Research in Outdoor Recreation." *Journal of Leisure Research*, 1969, *1* (1), 33–51.

CHOTLOS, J. W. AND GOLDSTEIN, G. "Psychophysiological Responses to

Meaningful Sounds." *Journal of Nervous and Mental Disease,* 1967, *145* (4), 314–325.

CLARK, W. *Reaction to Aircraft Noise.* Armed Services Technical Information Agency. Technical Report 61–610 (AD278622). Arlington, Va., 1961, 12–15.

CLAUSEN, J. A. AND KOHN, M. L. "The Ecological Approach in Social Psychiatry." *American Journal of Sociology,* 1954, *60,* 140–151.

CLAWSON, M. "Methods of Measuring Demand for and Value of Outdoor Recreation." Reprint No. 10. Washington, D.C.: Resources for the Future, 1959.

CLEPPER, H. (Ed.) *Careers in Conservation.* New York: Ronald Press, 1963.

CLEPPER, H. *Origins of American Conservation.* New York: Ronald Press, 1966.

COHEN, A. "Physiological and Psychological Effects of Noise on Man." Paper presented at a meeting of the Boston Society of Civil Engineers, Boston, December 2, 1964, 86–87.

COHEN, A. et al. *Effects of Noise on Task Performance.* Public Health Service. Division of Occupational Health. Occupational Health Research and Training Facility. Cincinnati, Ohio, 1966.

COHEN, A. "Noise and Psychological State." Paper presented at the National Conference on Noise as a Public Health Hazard, Washington, D.C., June 13–14, 1968, 3–19.

COMMITTEE ON THE PROBLEM OF NOISE. *Noise: Final Report.* London: Her Majesty's Stationery Office, July 1963, 5–217.

CONVERSE, P. E. "Time Budgets." In D. L. Sills (Ed.) *International Encyclopedia of the Social Sciences.* Vol. XVI. New York: Macmillan Company, 1968.

CROZIER, M. *The Bureaucratic Phenomenon.* Chicago: University of Chicago Press, 1964.

DAHRENDORF, R. *Class and Class Conflict in Industrial Society.* Stanford, Calif.: Stanford University Press, 1959.

DAVENPORT, S. J. AND MORGIS, G. G. *Air Pollution: A Bibliography.* U. S. Department of the Interior. Bureau of Mines. Bulletin 537. Washington, D.C.: Government Printing Office, 1954.

DAVIS, K. AND BLAKE, J. "Social Structure and Fertility: An Analytic Framework." *Economic Development and Cultural Change,* 1956, *4* (3), 211–235.

DAVIS, R. K. "The Value of Outdoor Recreation: An Economic Study of the Maine Woods." Unpublished preliminary draft for Resources for the Future, Inc., Washington, D.C., 1967.

DAY, L. H. AND DAY, A. T. *Too Many Americans*. Boston: Houghton-Mifflin, 1964.

DEMOLINS, E. *Les Grandes Routes des Peuples*. Vol. I: *Les Routes de L'Antiquité*. Vol. II: *Les Routes du Monde Moderne*. Paris: Firmin-Didot et cie, 1901–1903.

DERRUAU, M. *Précis de Géographie Humaine*. Reviewed in *Economic Geography* by P. L. Wagner. 1962, *38*, 373–374.

DEXTER, E. G. *Weather Influences*. New York: Macmillan Company, 1904.

DOWNS, J. F. "Domestication: An Examination of the Changing Social Relationships between Man and Animals." *Kroeber Anthropological Society Papers*, 1960, *22*, 18–67.

DUBOS, R. J. *Man Adapting*. New Haven, Conn.: Yale University Press, 1965.

DUMAZEDIER, J. *Toward a Society of Leisure*. Translated by S. E. McClure. New York: Free Press, 1967 (Orig. 1962).

DUNCAN, O. D. "Human Ecology and Population Studies." In P. M. Hauser and O. D. Duncan (Eds.) *The Study of Population*. Chicago: University of Chicago Press, 1959.

DUNCAN, O. D. AND SCHNORE, L. F. "Cultural Behavioral and Ecological Perspectives in the Study of Social Organization." *American Journal of Sociology*, 1959, *65*, 132–153.

DUNCAN, O. D. AND SPENGLER, J. J. (Eds.) *Population Theory and Policy: Selected Readings*. New York: Free Press, 1956.

DURKHEIM, E. *The Division of Labor in Society*. Translated by G. Simpson. New York: Free Press, 1933 (Orig. 1893).

DURKHEIM, E. "Suicide and Cosmic Factors." In *Suicide*. Translated by J. Spaulding and G. Simpson. New York: Free Press, 1951 (Orig. 1897).

DURKHEIM, E. *The Elementary Forms of the Religious Life*. Translated by J. W. Swain. New York: Free Press, 1954 (Orig. 1912).

EDGERTON, R. "Cultural vs. Ecological Factors in the Expression of Values, Attitudes, and Personality Characteristics." *American Anthropologist*, 1965, *67*, 442–447.

EISELEY, L. C. AND SPECK, F. "The Significance of Hunting Territory Systems of the Algonkian in Social Theory." *American Anthropologist*, 1939, *41*, 269–280.

ETZIONI, A. *A Comparative Analysis of Complex Organizations.* New York: Free Press, 1961.

EVELYN, J. *Fumifugium.* London: The National Society for Clean Air, 1961 (Orig. 1661).

FARR, L. E. "Medical Consequences of Environmental Home Noises." *Journal of the American Medical Association,* 1967, *202* (3), 99–102.

FEDERAL COUNCIL FOR SCIENCE AND TECHNOLOGY. Committee on Environmental Quality. *Noise-Sound Without Value.* September 1968.

FERRISS, A. L., et al. *National Recreation Survey. Outdoor Recreation Resources Review Commission Study Report 19.* Washington, D.C.: Government Printing Office, 1962.

FERRY, W. H. "Ping, Pang, Pow." *The Center Magazine,* 1968, *1* (7), 93–95.

FESTINGER, L., RIECKEN, H. W. AND SCHACHTER, S. *When Prophecy Fails.* Minneapolis: University of Minnesota Press, 1956.

FESTINGER, L., SCHACHTER, S. AND BACK, K. *Social Pressures in Informal Groups: A Study of Human Factors in Housing.* Stanford, Calif.: Stanford University Press, 1950.

FINLAYSON, H. H. *The Red Centre: Man and Beast in the Heart of Australia.* Sydney, Australia: Angus and Robertson, Limited, 1943.

FIREY, W. I. *Land Use in Central Boston.* Cambridge, Mass.: Harvard University Press, 1947.

FIREY, W. I. *Man, Mind and Land: A Theory of Resource Use.* New York: Free Press, 1960.

Forest Recreation, A Bibliography. Washington, D.C.: U. S. Forest Service Library, 1938.

FRANK, L. K. *Nature and Human Nature.* New Brunswick, N.J.: Rutgers University Press, 1951.

FREUD, S. "Some Psychological Consequences of the Anatomical Distinction Between the Sexes." *International Journal of Psychoanalysis,* 1927, *8.*

FRIEDRICH, C. J. (Ed.) *Alfred Weber's Theory of the Location of Industries.* Chicago: University of Chicago Press, 1929.

FROMM, E. "Sex and Character." *Psychiatry,* 1943, *6.*

GALBRAITH, J. K. *The Affluent Society.* London: Hamish H. Hamilton, 1958.

GARNSEY, M. E. AND HIBBS, J. R. (Eds.) *Social Sciences and the Environment*. Boulder, Col.: University of Colorado Press, 1967.

GASTER, T. H. (Ed.) *The New Golden Bough: A New Abridgement of the Classic Work by Sir James Frazer*. New York: Criterion Books, 1959.

GEERTZ, C. J. *Agricultural Involution: The Process of Ecological Change in Indonesia*. Berkeley, Calif.: University of California Press for the Association of Asian Studies, 1963.

GEORGE, H. B. *The Relations of Geography and History*. Oxford: Clarendon Press, 1901.

GERSHINOWITZ, H. *Report to Environmental Studies Board*. Annual Meeting of The National Research Council, Washington, D.C., March 10, 1969.

GETTYS, W. E. "Human Ecology and Social Theory." *Social Forces*, 1940, *18*, 469–476.

GILLISPIE, C. C. "Science in the French Revolution." *Behavioral Science*, 1959, *4*, 67–73.

GILPIN, A. *Control of Air Pollution*. London: Butterworth and Co., 1963.

GLACKEN, C. J. "Count Buffon on Cultural Changes of the Physical Environment." *Annals of the Association of American Geographers*, 1960, *50* (1), 1–21.

GLASS, D. AND SINGER, J. E. "Tests Show Noise Causing Tension." Report of study in *The New York Times*, September 11, 1968.

GLOCK, C. Y. AND SELZNICK, G. "The Wilderness Vacationist." In Outdoor Recreation Resources Review Commission. Study Report 3. *Wilderness and Recreation: A Report on Resources, Values and Problems*. Washington, D.C.: Government Printing Office, 1962, 126–202.

GOFFMAN, E. *Behavior in Public Places: Notes on the Social Organization of Gatherings*. New York: Free Press, 1963.

GOLDENWEISER, A. A. "Culture and Environment." *American Journal of Sociology*, 1916, *21* (5), 628–633.

GOODE, W. J. "Outdoor Recreation and the Family to the Year 2000." Outdoor Recreation Resources Review Commission. Study Report 22. *Trends in American Living and Outdoor Recreation*. Washington, D.C.: Government Printing Office, 1962, 101–113.

GRAHAM, F. K., CLIFTON, R. K. AND HATTON, H. M. "Habituation of Heart Rate Response to Repeated Auditory Stimulation During the First Five Years of Life." *Child Development,* 1968, *39,* 35–52.

GRINKER, R. *Toward A Unified Theory of Human Behavior.* New York: Basic Books, 1956.

GRODZINS, M. "The Many American Governments and Outdoor Recreation." Outdoor Recreation Resources Review Commission. Study Report 22. *Trends in American Living and Outdoor Recreation.* Washington, D.C.: Government Printing Office, 1962, 61–80.

GROSS, B. M. *The State of the Nation.* London: Tavistock Publications, Social Science Paperbacks, 1966.

GROSS, E. E., JR. AND PETERSON, A. *Handbook of Noise Measurement.* West Concord, Mass.: General Radio Co., 1963.

GULICK, L. H. *A Philosophy of Play.* New York: Charles Scribner's Sons, 1920.

GURIN, G. AND MUELLER, E. "Participation in Outdoor Recreation, Factors Affecting Demand Among American Adults." Outdoor Recreation Resources Review Commission. Study Report 20. Ann Arbor, Mich.: University of Michigan Survey Research Center, 1962.

GUYOT, A. *The Earth and Man.* Translated by C. C. Felton. Boston: Gould and Lincoln, 1860.

HAGEN, E. E. *On the Theory of Social Change.* Homewood, Ill.: Dorsey Press, 1962.

HALLOWELL, A. I. "The Size of Algonkian Hunting Territories: A Function of Ecological Adjustment." *American Anthropologist,* 1949, *51,* 35–45.

HARDY, G. *La Géographie Psychologique.* Paris: Librairie Gallimard, 1939.

HAUSER, P. M. "Demographic and Ecological Changes as Factors in Outdoor Recreation." Outdoor Recreation Resources Review Commission. Study Report 22. *Trends in American Living and Outdoor Recreation.* Washington, D.C.: Government Printing Office, 1962, 27–60.

HAUSER, P. M. AND DUNCAN, O. D. (Eds.) *The Study of Population.* Chicago: University of Chicago Press, 1959.

HAWLEY, A. H. *Human Ecology: A Theory of Community Structure.* New York: Ronald Press Co., 1950.

HELM, J. "The Ecological Approach in Anthropology." *American Journal of Sociology,* 1962, *67,* 630–639.

HERFINDAHL, O. C. "What is Conservation?" *In Three Studies in Mineral Economics.* Washington, D.C.: Resources for the Future, 1961.

HERFINDAHL, O. C. AND KNEESE, A. V. *Quality of the Environment: An Economic Approach to Some Problems in Using Land, Water, and Air.* Baltimore: Johns Hopkins Press, for Resources for the Future, 1965.

HILGARD, E. *Theories of Learning.* 2nd Edition. New York: Appleton-Century-Crofts, 1956.

HOFSTADTER, R. *Social Darwinism in American Thought.* Boston: Beacon Press, 1955 (Orig. Philadelphia: University of Pennsylvania Press, 1944).

HUDDLESTON, H. F. "Vertical Sinusoidal Vibration as a Psychological Stress." *Nature,* 1966, *211,* 324–325.

HUIZINGA, J. *Homo Ludens.* Boston: Beacon Press, 1955 (Orig. 1938).

HUNTER, F. *Community Power Structure.* Garden City, N.Y.: Doubleday and Co., 1953.

HUNTINGTON, E. *Palestine and Its Transformation.* Boston: Houghton-Mifflin Co., 1911.

HUNTINGTON, E. *Civilization and Climate.* New Haven, Conn.: Yale University Press, 1915.

HUNTINGTON, E. *The Pulse of Progress.* New York: Charles Scribner's Sons, 1926.

HUNTINGTON, E. AND CUSHING, S. W. *Principles of Human Geography.* New York: John Wiley and Sons, 1921.

IBN KHALDUN. *The Muqaddimah.* Translated by Franz Rosenthal. Vols. I–III. New York: Pantheon Books, 1958 (Orig. 1377).

INTERNATIONAL CONFERENCE ON HEALTH EDUCATION. "Man in His Environment." *International Journal of Health Education.* Geneva, Switzerland, 1962, *4.*

ISARD, W. *Location and Space-Economy.* Cambridge, Mass.: M.I.T. Press, 1956.

JAMES, W. *The Principles of Psychology.* Two volumes. New York: Dover Publications, 1950 (Orig. 1890).

JARRETT, H. (Ed.) *Perspectives on Conservation.* Baltimore: Johns Hopkins Press for Resources for the Future, 1958.

JOINT HOUSE-SENATE COLLOQUIUM. *Congressional White Paper on a National Policy for the Environment.* Serial T. Washington, D.C.: Government Printing Office, 1968.

JORAVSKY, D. "Soviet Scientists and the Great Break." In R. Pipes (Ed.) *The Russian Intelligentsia.* New York: Columbia University Press, 1961.

KADUSHIN, C. "Power, Influence and Social Circles: A New Methodology for Studying Opinion Makers." *American Sociological Review,* 1968, *33* (5), 685–699.

KAHN, A. E. "The Tyranny of Small Decisions: Market Failures, Imperfections, and the Limits of Economics." *Kyklos,* 1966, *19,* 28–42.

KAPLAN, B. A. "Environment and Human Plasticity." *American Anthropologist,* 1954, *56,* 780–800.

KAPLAN, M. *Leisure in America: A Social Inquiry.* New York: John Wiley and Sons, 1960.

KAPLAN, M. AND LAZARSFELD, P. "The Mass Media and Man's Orientation to Nature." Outdoor Recreation Resources Review Commission. Study Report 22. *Trends in American Living and Outdoor Recreation.* Washington, D.C.: Government Printing Office, 1962, 187–214.

KAPLAN, N. (Ed.) *Science and Society.* Chicago: Rand McNally and Co., 1965.

KATES, R. W. "Hazard and Choice Perception in Flood Plain Management." Department of Geography Research Paper No. 78. Chicago: University of Chicago Press, 1962.

KATONA, G. "Rational Behavior and Economic Behavior." *Psychological Review,* 1953, *60* (5), 307–318.

KATONA, G. *The Powerful Consumer: Psychological Studies of the American Economy.* New York: McGraw-Hill, 1960.

KATONA, G. *The Mass Consumption Society.* New York: McGraw-Hill, 1964.

KAUFMAN, H. *The Forest Ranger: A Study in Administrative Behavior.* Baltimore: Johns Hopkins Press, 1960.

KING, A. "Science and Technology in the New Europe." *Daedalus,* 1964, *93* (1), 434–458.

KIRCHHOFF, A. *Man and Earth.* London: George Routledge and Sons, Limited, 1914.

KIRWAN, L. P. "Geography as a Social Study." *Geographical Journal,* 1965, *131,* 373–375.

KLAUSNER, S. Z. "An Empirical Study of Ethical Neutrality Among Behavioral Scientists." *Sociological Analysis,* 1966, *27* (4), 223–238.

KLAUSNER, S. Z. "Rationalism and Empiricism in Studies of Behavior in Stressful Situations." *Behavioral Science,* 1966, *11* (5), 329–341.

KLAUSNER, S. Z. "Links and Missing Links Between the Sciences of Man." In S. Z. Klausner (Ed.) *The Study of Total Societies.* New York: Doubleday-Anchor, 1967.

KLAUSNER, S. Z. "Choice of Metaphor in Behavior Research." *Methodology and Science,* April, 1968a, 69–91.

KLAUSNER, S. Z. "The Intermingling of Pain and Pleasure: The Stress Seeking Personality in Its Social Context." In S. Z. Klausner (Ed.) *Why Man Takes Chances: Studies in Stress Seeking.* New York: Doubleday and Co., 1968.

KLAUSNER, S. Z. AND KINCAID, H. V. "Social Problems of Sheltering Flood Evacuees." New York: Columbia University, Bureau of Applied Social Research, 1956.

KNEESE, A. V. "Economic and Related Problems in Contemporary Water Resources Management." *Natural Resources Journal,* 1965, *5* (2), 236–258.

KNEESE, A. V. AND AYRES, R. O. "Environmental Pollution." In *Federal Programs for the Development of Human Resources.* Washington, D.C.: Government Printing Office, 1968.

KNEESE, A. V. AND HERFINDAHL, O. G. *Quality of the Environment.* Washington, D.C.: Resources for the Future, Inc., 1965.

KOLLER, A. *Theory of Environment.* Part I. Menasha, Wis.: Banta Publishing Company, 1918.

KOMAROVSKY, M. (Ed.) *Common Frontiers of the Social Sciences.* New York: Free Press, 1957.

KRADER, L. "Ecology of Central Asian Pastoralism." *Southwestern Journal of Anthropology,* 1955, *11* (4), 301–326.

KROPOTKIN, P. *Mutual Aid: A Factor of Evolution.* Boston: Extending Horizons, 1955 (Orig. 1890–1896).

KRUSKAL, J. B. "Multidimensional Scaling by Optimizing Goodness of Fit to a Nonmetric Hypothesis." *Psychometrika,* 1964, *29,* 1–27.

On Man in His Environment

KRUTILLA, J. V. "An Economic Approach to Coping with Flood Damage." *Water Resources Research,* 1966a, *2* (2), 183–190.

KRUTILLA, J. V. "The International Columbia River Treaty: An Economic Evaluation." In A. V. Kneese and S. C. Smith (Eds.) *Water Research.* Baltimore: Johns Hopkins Press for Research for the Future, 1966b.

KRUTILLA, J. V. "Is Public Intervention in Water Resources Development Conducive to Economic Efficiency?" *Natural Resources Journal,* 1966c, *6* (1), 60–75.

KRUTILLA, J. V. AND ECKSTEIN, O. *Multiple Purpose River Development.* Baltimore: Johns Hopkins Press, 1958.

KRYTER, K. D. AND PEARSONS, K. S. "Some Effects of Spectral Content and Duration on Perceived Noise Level." *Journal of the Acoustical Society of America,* 1963, *35,* 866–883.

KUHN, T. S. *The Structure of Scientific Revolutions.* Chicago: University of Chicago Press, 1962.

LANCASTER, K. J. "A New Approach to Consumer Theory." *The Journal of Political Economy,* 1966, *74,* 132–157.

LANCASTER, K. J. "Change and Innovation in the Technology of Consumption." *The American Economic Review,* 1966, *56,* 14–23.

LANSING, J. AND KISH, L. "Family Life Cycle as an Independent Variable." *American Sociological Review,* 1957, *22,* 512–519.

LAZARSFELD, P. F. "The Art of Asking Why." In D. Katz *et al.* (Eds.) *Public Opinion and Propaganda.* New York: Dryden Press, 1954 (Orig. 1934).

LAZARSFELD, P. F., SEWELL, W. H. AND WILENSKY, H. L. *The Uses of Sociology.* New York: Basic Books, 1967.

LEBO, C. P. AND OLIPHANT, K. P. "Music as a Source of Acoustic Trauma." *Laryngoscope,* 1968, *78* (7), 1211–1218.

LEEDS, A., SMITH, D. B. AND VAYDA, A. P. "The Place of Pigs in Melanesian Subsistence." In V. Garfield (Ed.) *Proceedings of the 1961 Annual Meeting of the American Ethnology Society.* Seattle: University of Washington Press, 1961.

LEFFINGWELL, A. *Illegitimacy and the Influence of Seasons upon Conduct.* London: Swan Sonnenschein and Company, 1892.

LEWIN, B. D. "Claustrophobia." *Psychoanalytic Quarterly,* 1935, *4.*

LEWIN, K. *A Dynamic Theory of Personality.* Translated by D. K. Adams and K. E. Zener. New York: McGraw-Hill Company, 1959.

LIEBERMAN, L. R. AND WALTERS, W. M., JR. "Effects of Repeated Listening as Connotative Meanings of Serious Music." *Perceptual and Motor Skills,* 1968, *26,* 891–895.

LORENZ, K. *On Aggression.* Translated by M. K. Wilson. New York: Harcourt, Brace and World, 1966.

LOWENTHAL, D. AND PRINCE, H. C. "The English Landscape." *The Geographical Review,* 1964, *54,* 309–346.

LOWENTHAL, D. AND PRINCE, H. C. "English Landscape Tastes." *The Geographical Review,* 1965, *55,* 186–222.

LOWENTHAL, L. *Literature and the Image of Man.* Boston: Beacon Press, 1957.

MAASS, A. "Conservation: Political and Social Aspects." In D. Sills (Ed.) *International Encyclopedia of the Social Sciences.* Vol. III. New York: Macmillan Company, 1968.

MC CLELLAND, D. C. *The Achieving Society.* Princeton, N.J.: Van Nostrand, 1961.

MACK, R. P. "Trends in American Consumption and the Aspiration to Consume." *American Economic Review,* 1956, *46* (2), 55–68.

MACKINDER, H. J. *Democratic Ideals and Reality: A Study in the Politics of Reconstruction.* New York: H. Holt and Company, 1942 (Orig. 1919).

MALINOWSKI, B. *Magic, Science and Religion.* New York: Doubleday-Anchor, 1954.

MALTHUS, T. R. An Essay on Population. New York: E. P. Dutton, 1960 (Orig. 1798).

MANNHEIM, K. *Ideology and Utopia: An Introduction to the Sociology of Knowledge.* Translated by L. Wirth and E. Shils. New York: Harcourt, Brace and World, 1936 (Orig. 1929).

"Man's Response to the Physical Environment." *Journal of Social Issues,* 1966, *22,* 1–36.

MARCH, J. G. AND SIMON, H. A. *Organizations.* New York: John Wiley and Sons, 1958.

MARSH, G. P. *Man and Nature; or, Physical Geography as Modified by Human Action.* New York: Charles Scribner, 1864.

MARX, K. AND ENGELS, F. *The German Ideology.* New York: International Publishers, 1947 (Orig. 1846).

MAY, H. L. AND PETGEN, D. *Leisure and Its Use.* New York: A. S. Barnes and Company, 1928.

On Man in His Environment

MAYER, A. C. *Land and Society in Malabar*. London: Oxford University Press, 1952.

MEAD, G. H. *Mind, Self and Society*. Chicago: University of Chicago Press, 1934.

MEAD, M. "Outdoor Recreation in the Context of Emerging American Cultural Values: Background Considerations." Outdoor Recreation Resources Review Commission. Study Report 22. *Trends in American Living and Outdoor Recreation*. Washington, D.C.: Government Printing Office, 1962, 1–24.

MECH, E. V. "Performance on a Verbal Addition Task Related to Experimental 'Set' and Verbal Noise." *Journal of Experimental Education*, 1953, *22*, 1–17.

MEGGARS, B. J. "Environmental Limitation on the Development of Culture." *American Anthropologist*, 1954, *56* (5), 801–824.

MEIER, R. L. "Resource Planning." In D. Sills (Ed.) *International Encyclopedia of the Social Sciences*. Vol. XII. New York: Macmillan Company, 1968.

MENZEL, H. AND KATZ, E. "Social Relations and Innovation in the Medical Profession: The Epidemiology of a New Drug." *Public Opinion Quarterly*, 1955–56, *19* (4), 337–352.

MERRILL, R. S. "Technology: The Study of Technology." In D. Sills (Ed.) *International Encyclopedia of the Social Sciences*. Vol. XV. New York: Macmillan Company, 1968.

MERRIMAN, L. C., JR. AND AMMONS, R. B. *The Wilderness User in Three Montana Areas*. St. Paul, Minn.: School of Forestry, University of Minnesota, 1965.

MERTON, R. K. *Social Theory and Social Structure*. Enlarged Edition. New York: Free Press, 1968.

MERTON, R. K., BROOM, L. AND COTTRELL, L. S. JR. (Eds.) *Sociology Today: Problems and Prospects*. New York: Basic Books, 1959.

MEYERSOHN, R. "The Sociology of Leisure in the United States: Introduction and Bibliography, 1945–1965." *Journal of Leisure Research*, 1969, *1* (1), 53–68.

MILLER, N. P. AND ROBINSON, D. M. *The Leisure Age: Its Challenge to Recreation*. Belmont, Calif.: Wadsworth Publishing Company, 1963.

MONTESQUIEU, C. L. "Essai sur les Causes qui Peuvent Affecter Les Esprits et les Caractères." In *Oeuvres Completes*. New York: Macmillan Company and Editions du Seuil, 1964.

MOORE, H. L. *Generating Economic Cycles.* New York: Macmillan Company, 1923.

MOORE, W. E. "Sociology and Demography." In P. M. Hauser and O. D. Duncan (Eds.) *The Study of Population.* Chicago: University of Chicago Press, 1959.

MORGAN, C. T. AND STELLAR, E. *Physiological Psychology.* New York: McGraw-Hill Book Company, Inc., 1950.

MORRIS, C. W. *Signs, Language and Behavior.* Englewood Cliffs, N.J.: Prentice-Hall, 1946.

MOSES, L. "Location and the Theory of Production." *The Quarterly Journal of Economics,* 1958, *72,* 259–272.

MOSTELLER, F. AND NOGEE, P. "An Experimental Measurement of Utility." *The Journal of Political Economy,* 1951, *59* (5), 371–404.

MUMFORD, L. *Technics and Civilization.* New York: Harcourt, Brace and World, 1934.

MURPHREE, C. E. "Resource Use and Income Implications of Outdoor Recreation." Bulletin 690. Gainesville, Fla.: University of Florida Agricultural Experiment Stations, March, 1965.

MURRA, J. V. "Rite and Crop in the Inca State." In S. Diamond (Ed.) *Culture in History, Essays in Honor of Paul Radin.* New York: Columbia University Press for Brandeis University, 1960.

NATIONAL ACADEMY OF SCIENCES. Ad Hoc Panel on Technology Assessment of Subsonic Aircraft Noise. *Report.* Washington, D.C.: National Academy of Sciences, 1968a.

NATIONAL ACADEMY OF SCIENCES. Committee on SST-Sonic Boom. *Report on Human Response to the Sonic Boom.* Washington, D.C.: National Academy of Sciences, 1968b.

NATIONAL BUREAU OF ECONOMIC RESEARCH. *The Quality and Economic Significance of Anticipations Data.* Princeton, N.J.: Princeton University Press, 1960.

NEF, J. U. *The Conquest of the Material World.* Chicago: University of Chicago Press, 1964.

NEUMEYER, M. H. AND NEUMEYER, E. S. *Leisure and Recreation: A Study of Leisure and Recreation in Their Sociological Aspects.* New York: Ronald Press, 1958.

NEUTRA, R. J. *Survival Through Design.* New York: Oxford University Press, 1954.

OFFICE OF NOISE ABATEMENT. U. S. Department of Transportation.

On Man in His Environment

Summary Status Report, Federal Aircraft Noise Abatement Program. Washington, D.C.: Government Printing Office, 1968.

OGBURN, W. F. *Social Change with Respect to Culture and Original Nature.* New York: Viking Press, 1950.

OGBURN, W. F. "Population, Private Ownership, Technology, and the Standard of Living." *American Journal of Sociology,* 1951, *56* (4), 314–319.

OGBURN, W. F. AND GOLDENWEISER, A. (Eds.) *The Social Sciences and Their Interrelation.* Boston: Houghton Mifflin Company, 1927.

OLSON, M., JR. "Economics, Sociology and the Best of All Possible Worlds." *The Public Interest,* 1968, *12,* 96–118.

PANEL ON SOCIAL INDICATORS. U. S. Department of Health, Education and Welfare. *Toward a Social Report.* Washington, D.C.: Government Printing Office, 1969.

PARRACK, H. O. "Community Reaction to Noise." In C. M. Harris (Ed.) *Handbook of Noise Control.* New York: McGraw-Hill Company, Inc., 1957.

PARSONS, T. *The Social System.* New York: Free Press, 1951.

PARSONS, T. *The Structure of Social Action.* New York: Free Press, 1949.

PARSONS, T., BALES, R. F. AND SHILS, E. A. "Phase Movement in Relation to Motivation, Symbol Formation and Role Structure." In *Working Papers in the Theory of Action.* New York: Free Press, 1953.

PARSONS, T. AND SHILS, E. A. "Values, Motives and Systems of Action." In T. Parsons and E. A. Shils (Eds.) *Toward a General Theory of Action.* Cambridge, Mass.: Harvard University Press, 1951.

PARSONS, T. AND SMELSER, N. J. *Economy and Society.* New York: Free Press, 1956.

PERLOFF, H. S. AND WINGO, L., JR. "Urban Growth and the Planning of Outdoor Recreation." Outdoor Recreation Resources Review Commission. Study Report 22. *Trends in American Living and Outdoor Recreation.* Washington, D.C.: Government Printing Office, 1962.

PETERLE, T. J. "Characteristics of Some Ohio Hunters." *Journal of Wildlife Management,* 1967, *31* (2), 375–389.

PETERSEN, W. *Population.* New York: Macmillan Company, 1961.

PIAGET, J. AND INHELDER, B. *The Child's Conception of Space.* London: Routledge, 1956. (Orig. 1948).

211

PRICE, D. K. *The Scientific Estate*. Cambridge, Mass.: Belknap Press of Harvard University Press, 1965.

QUINE, W. V. O. *Word and Object*. New York: John Wiley and Sons, 1960.

RATZEL, F. *Anthropo-Geographie*. Vols. I and II. Stuttgart: Engelhorn, 1921–22 (Orig. 1882).

REICHENBACH, H. *The Rise of Scientific Philosophy*. Berkeley, Calif.: University of California Press, 1951.

REID, L. M. *Outdoor Recreation: A Nationwide Study of User Desires*. East Lansing, Mich.: Department of Resource Development, Michigan State University, 1963.

REISMAN, D. *Abundance for What?* Garden City, N.Y.: Doubleday and Company, 1964.

RIECKEN, H. AND HOMANS, G. "Psychological Aspects of Social Structure." In G. Lindzey (Ed.) *Handbook of Social Psychology*. Vol. II. Reading, Mass.: Addison-Wesley Publishing Company, Inc., 1954.

RITTER, K. *Geographical Studies*. Translated by W. L. Gage. Boston: Gould and Lincoln, 1861.

ROBBINS, F. G. *The Sociology of Play, Recreation and Leisure Time*. Dubuque, Iowa: William C. Brown Company, 1955.

ROGERS, E. M. *Diffusion of Innovations*. New York: Free Press, 1962.

ROSSI, A. M. AND SOLOMON, P. "Effects of Sensory Deprivation on Introverts and Extroverts: A Failure to Find Reputed Difference." *Journal of Psychiatric Research*, 1966, *4* (2), 115–125.

RUSSETT, B. M., ALKER, H. R., DEUTSCH, K. W. AND LASSWELL, H. D. *World Handbook of Political and Social Indicators*. New Haven, Conn.: Yale University Press, 1964.

SAARINEN, T. F. "Perception of Drought Hazard on the Great Plains." Research Paper 106. Department of Geography. University of Chicago, 1966.

SAYCE, R. U. "The Ecological Study of Culture." *Scientia*, 1938, *63*, 279–285.

SCHACHTER, S. "The Interaction of Cognitive and Physiological Determinants of Emotional State." In L. Berkowitz (Ed.) *Advances in Experimental Social Psychology*. Vol. I. New York: Academic Press, 1964.

SCOTT, A. "Conservation: Economic Aspects." In D. Sills (Ed.) *Inter-

national Encyclopedia of the Social Sciences. Vol. III. New York: Macmillan Company, 1968.

SEARLES, H. F. *The Nonhuman Environment in Normal Development and in Schizophrenia.* New York: International Universities Press, 1960.

SEARS, P. B. "Changing Man's Habitat: Physical and Biological Phenomena." In W. L. Thomas, Jr. (Ed.) *Current Anthropology.* Supplement to *Anthropology Today.* Chicago: University of Chicago Press, 1956.

SECKLER, D. "On the Uses and Abuses of Economic Science in Evaluating Public Outdoor Recreation." *Land Economics,* 1966, *42* (4), 485–494.

SELIGMAN, E. R. A. *The Economic Interpretation of History.* New York: Columbia University Press, 1902.

SELIGMAN, E. R. A. AND JOHNSON, A. (Eds.) *Encyclopedia of the Social Sciences.* Fifteen volumes. New York: Macmillan Company, 1934.

SELZNICK, P. *TVA and the Grass Roots: A Study in the Sociology of Formal Organization.* Berkeley, Calif.: University of California Press, 1949.

SELZNICK, P. *The Organizational Weapon.* New York: Free Press, 1960.

SEMPLE, E. C. *Influences of Geographic Environment.* New York: Henry Holt and Company, 1911.

SHAFER, E. L., JR., HAMILTON, J. E., JR. AND SCHMIDT, E. A. "Natural Landscape Preferences: A Predictive Model." *Journal of Leisure Research,* 1969, *1* (1), 1–20.

SHRYOCK, R. H. *American Indifference to Science During the 19th Century.* Archives Internationales D'Historire des Sciences, No. 28, 1948–49, 3–18.

SILLS, D. (Ed.) *International Encyclopedia of the Social Sciences.* Seventeen volumes. New York: Macmillan Company and Free Press, 1968.

SILLS, D. *The Volunteers.* New York: Free Press, 1957.

SIMMEL, G. *Conflict and the Web of Group Affiliations.* Translated by K. H. Wolff and R. Bendix. New York: Free Press, 1955.

SKINNER, B. F. *The Behavior of Organisms.* New York: Appleton-Century-Crofts, 1938.

SMELSER, N. J. "Sociology and the Other Social Sciences." In P. F. Lazarsfeld, W. H. Sewell and H. L. Wilensky (Eds.) *The Uses of Sociology*. New York: Basic Books, 1967.

SMELSER, N. J. *Social Change in the Industrial Revolution*. Chicago: University of Chicago Press, 1959.

SONNENFELD, J. "Equivalence and Distortion of the Perceptual Environment." *Environment and Behavior*, 1969, *1* (1), 83–99.

SOROKIN, P. *Contemporary Sociological Theories*. New York: Harper and Brothers, 1928.

SOROKIN, P. *Sociocultural Causality, Space, Time: A Study of Referential Principles of Sociology and Social Science*. Durham, N.C.: Duke University Press, 1943.

SOROKIN, P. AND BERGER, G. A. *Time-Budgets of Human Behavior*. Harvard Sociological Studies. Vol. 2. Cambridge, Mass.: Harvard University Press, 1939.

SORRE, M. *L'Homme Sur la Terre*. Reviewed by M. W. Mikesell in *Geographical Review*, 1963, *53*, 470–471.

SPECK, F. "The Family Hunting Band as the Basis of Algonkian Social Organization." *American Anthropologist*, 1915, *17*, 289–305.

SPECK, F. "Mistassini Hunting Territories in the Labrador Peninsula." *American Anthropologist*, 1923, *25*, 452–471.

SPECK, F. "Montagnais-Naskapi Bands and Early Eskimo Distribution in the Labrador Peninsula." *American Anthropologist*, 1931, *33*, 557–600.

STANFORD RESEARCH INSTITUTE. *Noise in Mass-Transit Systems. Stanford Research Institute Journal*, 1967, *16*, 2–7.

STERN, A. C. (Ed.) *Air Pollution*. New York: Academic Press, 1968.

STERN, B. J. "Restraints upon the Utilization of Inventions." In *Historical Sociology*. New York: Citadel Press, 1959.

STEVENS, S. S. "The Psychophysics of Sensory Function." In W. A. Rosenblith (Ed.) *Sensory Communication*. New York: John Wiley and Sons, 1961.

STILLMAN, C. W. "The Issues in the Storm King Controversy." *Black Rock Forest Papers No. 27*. Cornwall, N.Y.: Harvard Black Rock Forest, 1966.

STILLMAN, C. W. "The Price of Open Space." *Black Rock Forest Papers No. 28*. Cornwall, N.Y.: Harvard Black Rock Forest, 1966.

STORER, N. W. "The Coming Changes in American Science." *Science,* 1963, *142* (3591), 464–467.

STOUFFER, S. A. *et al. Measurement and Prediction.* Princeton, N.J.: Princeton University Press, 1950.

SYDENSTRICKER, E. *Health and Environment.* New York: McGraw-Hill, 1933.

SULLIVAN, H. S. *The Interpersonal Theory of Psychiatry.* New York: W. W. Norton and Company, 1953.

THOMAS, F. *Environmental Basis of Society.* New York: Century Company, 1925.

THOMPSON, L. "The Relations of Men, Animals and Plants in an Island Community (Fiji)." *American Anthropologist,* 1949, *51* (2), 253–267.

TIME MAGAZINE. "Otology: Going Deaf from Rock'n'Roll." August 9, 1968, *92* (6), 47.

"Urban Noise Control." *Columbia Journal of Law and Social Problems,* 1968, *4* (1), 104–119.

U. S. Department of the Interior. *Report of the Special Study Group on Noise and Sonic Boom in Relation to Man.* Washington, D.C.: (Unpublished), 1968.

VAN LOON, H. B. "Population, Space and Human Culture." *Law and Contemporary Problems,* 1960, *25,* 397–405.

"Variation and Adaptability of Culture: A Symposium." *American Anthropologist,* 1965, *67* (2), 400–447.

VAYDA, A. P. "Expansion and Warfare Among Swidden Agriculturists." *American Anthropologist,* 1961, *63* (2), 346–358.

VAYDA, A. P. "A Re-Examination of Northwest Coast Economic Systems." *Transactions of the New York Academy of Sciences.* New York: Academy of Sciences, 1961, *23* (7).

VITZ, P. C. "Affect as a Function of Stimulus Variation." *Journal of Experimental Psychology,* 1966, *71,* 74–79.

VOGT, E. *Modern Homesteaders: The Life of a Twentieth-Century Frontier Community.* Cambridge, Mass.: Belknap Press of Harvard University Press, 1955.

WAGAR, J. A. "The Carrying Capacity of Wildlands for Recreation." *Forest Science.* Monograph 7. Washington, D.C.: Society of American Foresters, 1964.

WAKSTEIN, C. "The Noise Problem in the United States." Fifth International Congress for Noise Abatement, London, 1968.

215

WARD, R. D. *Climate, Considered Especially in Relation to Man.* New York: G. P. Putnam's Sons, 1918.

WEBER, M. *The Theory of Social and Economic Organization.* Translated by A. M. Henderson and T. Parsons. New York: Free Press, 1947.

WEBER, M. "The Meaning of 'Ethical Neutrality' in Sociology and Economics." In *The Methodology of the Social Sciences.* Translated and Edited by E. A. Shils and H. A. Finch. New York: Free Press, 1949 (Orig. 1917).

WEBER, M. *The Religion of China.* Translated by H. H. Gerth. New York: Free Press, 1951.

WEDEL, W. R. "Some Aspects of Human Ecology in the Central Plains." *American Anthropologist,* 1953, *55* (4), 499–514.

WEINBERG, A. M. "Impact of Large-Scale Science on the United States." *Science,* 1961, *134* (3473), 161–164.

WENGER, W. D., JR. AND GREGERSON, H. M. "The Effect of Non-response on Representativeness Wilderness-Trail Register Information." U. S. Department of Agriculture Forest Service, 1964.

WESTERN RESOURCES CONFERENCE, 1959. In F. S. Pollack (Ed.) *Resources Development: Frontiers for Research.* Boulder, Col.: University of Colorado Press, 1960.

WHITBECK, R. H. "The Influence of Geographical Environment upon Religious Beliefs." *The Geographical Review,* 1918, *5,* 316–324.

WHITE, G. F. "Formation and Role of Public Attitudes." In H. Jarrett (Ed.) *Environmental Quality in a Growing Economy.* Baltimore: Johns Hopkins Press for Resources for the Future, 1966.

WHITE, L., JR. "The Historical Roots of Our Ecological Crisis." *Science,* 1967, *155,* 1203–1307.

WISSLER, C. *Man and Culture.* New York: Thomas Y. Crowell Company, 1923.

WITTFOGEL, K. A. *Oriental Despotism: A Comparative Study of Total Power.* New Haven, Conn.: Yale University Press, 1957

WOODRUFF, C. E. *Effects of Tropical Light on White Men.* New York: Rebman Company, 1905.

WRIGHT, H. F. AND BARKER, R. G. *Methods in Psychological Ecology: A Progress Report.* University of Kansas, 1952. Later incorporated into R. F. Baker and H. F. Wright, *Midwest and Its Children.* Evanston, Ill.: Row Peterson, 1955.

WRIGHT, J. K. "Miss Semple's influences of Geographic Environment." *Geographical Review,* 1962, *52,* 346–361.

ZIMMERMAN, C. C. AND FRAMPTON, N. E. *Family and Society: A Study of the Sociology of Reconstruction.* Princeton, N.J.: Van Nostrand, 1935.

ZIMMERMAN, E. W. "Natural Resources." In E. R. A. Seligman (Ed.) *Encyclopedia of the Social Sciences.* Vol. XI. New York: Macmillan Company, 1963 (Orig. 1933).

Subject Index

A

Adaptation, 25, 27ff, 43, 66, 80, 179
Air pollution, 80, 108ff, 181
American Sociological Association, 2
Anthropogeography, 6
Anthropological analyses of environment, 28, 49, 62, 179; and culture, 23, 27f, 50, 64f, 80; and domestication, 67; and semantics, 66; and social values, 32, 73, 182

B

Boundary processes, man-environment, 39f
Bureau of the Census, Current Population Survey, 132, 160

C

Committee on Disaster Studies of the National Academy of Sciences—National Research Council, 1
Conservation, 61
Criminology, 7
Crowding, 27f, 47

D

Demography, 17ff
Deterministic perspective on man-nature, 4ff
Disaster research, 1, 69
Disposition properties, 24

E

Ecology, human, 25ff, 46, 50f, as a slogan, 169f
Economic: analyses of environment, 7f, 22f, 33f, 50f, 98f, 179; cycle, 7f; efficiency, 94f, 97; institutions, 68; externalities, 96ff, 190; utility, 33, 57, 94f, 100, 107; utility and social meaning of, 95
Education, environmental, 176, 180, 184
Engineering and society, 15, 86, 183
Ethology, 27, 47
Evolutionary theory, 7, 9, 25, 31, 45
Exceptionalism of man, doctrine of, 8ff, 25

F

Federal Civil Defense Administration, 2

H

History of man-nature theories, 3
Human geography, 6

I

Institutes for research, demonstration, and implementation, 176

L

Law, environmental, 182, 191f; and juridical institutions for resource management, 104, 191
Location theory, 32ff

M

Management, environmental, 3, 57f
Management institutions, 91ff, 179
Meaning analysis, modes of; affective, 57f; cognitive, 56f; evaluative, 58f
Models for socioenvironmental analysis; biologistic, 24ff; physicalist, 19ff; rationalistic, 32ff; voluntaristic, 16, 34, 41ff, 52

219

Subject Index

N

National Opinion Research Center, 121

Natural environment, 2, 91, 140; natural resources, 2, 4, 15, 22, 27, 91f; resource process, 50, 59, 67; resource system, 50, 107

Noise, 65, 114ff; abatement, 115, 185ff; acoustical privacy and, 124; aircraft, 121, 123, 126; attitudes toward, 118f, 123, 129; Committee on the Problem of Noise, 119; high intensity, 127f, 130; Office of Noise Abatement, 125; psychophysics of, 128, 130; sonic boom, 119, 130

P

Police as management institution, 104

Political institutions, 68f, 103, 191

Population, principle of, 18

Psychological analyses of environment: and ecology, 60, 179; and imagery of nature, 61f; and perception, 34, 58, 86f; and personality, 39, 51f; and reinforcement, 10, 99; and self-identification, 59f, 112; and space, 46; and stress seeking, 161f; and symbolic meaning of environment, 54ff

R

Recreation; definition of, 141f; demographic variables of, 133, 135; as drama, 147f; equipment, 132; facility, 140; facilities and vacation system, 162f; groups, 143ff; and National Recreation Survey, 132ff; outdoor, demand for, 134, 138ff; outdoor, demographic studies of, 132f; outdoor, studies of specific populations of, 135ff; and play, 146f; and vacations, 148ff; and vacations, in relation to social institutions, 156f; and vacations, typology of forms, 154; work and, 102

Religion, Residuals

Religion, 42f, 92, 143, 146, 147; and magic, 77, 82f

Residuals, 80, 92

S

Social Darwinism, 29

Sociological analyses of environment; and bureaucracy, 101f; and community organization, 25ff; and functional problems of social system, 67f; and rural sociology, 2; and social action, 37ff, 53f; and social institutions, 43f, 67; and social norms, 118, 129; and social organization, 31, 46, 47, 80, 107; and sociological significance of the environment, 37; and symbolic interactionism, 11; and theory of action, 2

Sociology of knowledge, 11ff, 42, 86; and anthropology of technology, 80; and application of knowledge to policy, 173f; and implementation of knowledge, 183; and interdisciplinary research, 170ff; and science and other social institutions, 89; scientific and mythic paradigms compared, 83f; and social bases for disciplinary conflict, 173; and social ecology of technological innovations, 81; and sociology of science, 82ff; and sociology of technology, 76ff; and technological innovations and social institutions, 79, 187; and technology, 20f

Stanford Research Institute, 124

System, man-environment, 39ff

T

Theories that failed, 4ff, 42

Transformation concepts, 108

Transportation, 26, 33, 49

W

Water pollution, 109, 181

Work, definition of, 142ff

Name Index

Name Index

222

Name Index

Name Index